Reading Comprehension

*Books and Strategies for the
Elementary Curriculum*

Kathryn I. Matthew
Kimberly Kimbell-Lopez

The Scarecrow Press, Inc.
Lanham, Maryland, and Oxford
2003

SCARECROW PRESS, INC.

Published in the United States of America
by Scarecrow Press, Inc.
A wholly owned subsidary of
The Rowman & Littlefield Publishing Group, Inc.
4501 Forbes Boulevard, Suite 200, Lanham, MD 20706
www.scarecrowpress.com

PO Box 317
Oxford
OX2 9RU, UK

British Library Cataloguing in Publication Information Available

Library of Congress Cataloging-in-Publication Data

Matthew, Kathryn I.
  Reading comprehension : books and strategies for the elementary
curriculum / Kathryn I. Matthew, Kimberly Kimbell-Lopez.
    p. cm.
  Includes bibliographical references and indexes.
  ISBN 0-8108-4752-3 (alk. paper)
  1. Reading comprehension—Study and teaching (Elementary)—United
States. 2. Reading (Elementary)—United States—Curricula. 3. Content
area reading—United States. 4. Children—Books and reading—United
States. I. Kimbell-Lopez, Kimberly. II. Title.
LB1573.7 .M29 2003
372.47—dc21   2003000838

⊖™ The paper used in this publication meets the minimum requirements of
American National Standard for Information Sciences—Permanence of
Paper for Printed Library Materials, ANSI/NISO Z39.48-1992.
Manufactured in the United States of America.

Contents

Introduction

Children's literature provides a rich source of material to use through-out the curriculum. Consulting a variety of information sources provides students with an in-depth coverage of the classroom content and makes it more interesting and comprehensible (Tomlinson and Lynch-Brown, 1996). Working together, librarians and teachers can collect resources that meet the needs of individual students and enhance the classroom curriculum. Children exposed to diverse, quality literature in school develop a basis for judging excellence and develop reading preferences that last a lifetime (Burke, 1990).

In contrast to fiction books, nonfiction books require different reading and comprehension strategies. Comprehension strategies enable students to interact with the text, which aids retention of the material and helps create a classroom community of learners with common understandings (Oyler and Barry, 1996). Using comprehension strategies as they read helps students to understand and to remember the material. Additionally, learning comprehension strategies in the elementary school helps students as they progress through the grade levels where the focus of their studies is learning content area curriculum.

The purpose of this book is to provide teachers and librarians with a collection of reading comprehension strategies that help students learn and remember content area curriculum. Comprehension strategies enable students to reflect on and respond to their reading. Providing them with different ways to respond has the potential to guide their literature transactions (Smagorinsky and Coppock, 1995) and to foster their understanding and retention of the content. As teachers and librarians select different strategies to teach, they carefully consider their students' abilities and make a determination as to which strategy is the most appropriate for the content they are teaching. Salmon, Goldfarb, Greenblatt, and Strauss (1996) stress the importance of librarians working with teachers to assure that students learn study skills and transfer their knowledge of study skills to inquiry projects. Further, they contend that the direct teaching of study skills can be done by either the teacher or the librarian. Teachers and librarians planning and teaching as a team and recognizing each other's expertise assure that students develop an in-depth understanding of content (Stripling, 1995). Students need opportunities to use each strategy with different books and in different content areas. With multiple opportunities to use a particular strategy, students become familiar with the strategy and are more likely to use the strategy on their own to help them understand and remember content material they encounter throughout their school years.

Reading Comprehension: Books and Strategies for the Elementary Curriculum contains three content area sections: science, social studies, and mathematics. Each section begins with a brief introduction, the national content standards for that subject area, and where to locate additional information on incorporating the standards into the curriculum. The content standards serve as guideposts for teachers as they develop curriculum for their classrooms. Section 1, Science, includes chapters on gardens, insects and bugs, the solar system, weather, habitats and biomes, and animals. Section 2, Social Studies, includes chapters on American history, the United States, landforms, the world, cultures, and biographies. Section 3, Mathematics, includes chapters on numbers and operations, time, money, and problem solving.

Each chapter begins with a brief introduction to the topic. Within each chapter are descriptions and instructions for three comprehension strategies. For each strategy there are examples of how the strategy was used with at least two books at different reading levels. Following the examples is a section containing additional books and resources. This section of the chapter has annotations for other books on the same topic that can be used with the comprehension strategy. These annotations are arranged by suggested grade levels with books for younger students listed first. Following some of the book annotations are software programs and Internet sites that can be used to enhance the curriculum. Teachers and librarians are encouraged to adapt the strategies to a variety of books and different content areas. Additionally, these strategies should be modified to fit the reading levels and needs of students in the classrooms.

References

Burke, Ellen M. *Literature for the Young Child*, 2nd ed. Needham Heights, Mass.: Allyn and Bacon, 1990.

Oyler, Celia, and Anne Barry. "Intertextual Connections in Read-Alouds of Information Books." *Language Arts* 73, no. 5 (Sept. 1996): 324–329.

Salmon, Shelia, Elizabeth K. Goldfarb, Melinda Greenblatt, and Anita Phillips Strauss. *Power Up Your Library: Creating the New Elementary School Library Program*. Englewood, Colo.: Libraries Unlimited, 1996.

Smagorinsky, Peter, and John Coppock. "The Reader, the Text, the Context: An Exploration of a Choreographed Response to Literature." *Journal of Reading Behavior* 27, no. 3 (Sept. 1995): 271–298.

Stripling, Barbara K. "Learning-Centered Libraries: Implications for Research." *School Library Media Quarterly* 23, no. 3 (Spring 1995). http://www.ala.org/aasl/SLMR/slmr_resources/select_stripling1.html (5 Dec. 2002).

Tomlinson, Carl M., and Carol Lynch-Brown. *Essentials of Children's Literature*, 2nd ed. Needham Heights, Mass.: Allyn and Bacon, 1996.

Section 1
SCIENCE

Science opens up worlds of wonder to students as they learn to explore and ask questions about their environment. Teachers and librarians guide students as they formulate questions and conduct research and experiments to find answers to their questions. Science trade books not only help students find answers, but also motivate students to become actively involved in their learning and to extend their understanding.

Children's literature can be used in the classroom to support curriculum consistent with the *National Science Education Standards* (NSES, 1995). These standards consist of eight categories:

1. unifying concepts and processes in science,
2. science as inquiry,
3. physical science,
4. life science,
5. earth and space science,
6. science and technology,
7. science in personal and social perspectives, and
8. history and nature of science.

An online version of the standards including detailed information for implementing them at different grade levels can be accessed at http://stills.nap.edu/readingroom/books/nses/. The standards provide guideposts for educators as they engage students in active, hands-on science inquiry. Science education encompasses learning science principles and concepts, acquiring scientific reasoning and procedural skills, and understanding the nature of science as a human endeavor (Alberts, 2000).

When selecting science trade books for use in the classroom it is important to examine them to assure that the content is accurate (Rice, 2002). Authors such as Gail Gibbons, Seymour Simon, Jean Craighead George, and Dorothy Hinshaw Patent are noted for writing children's trade books that contain accurate science content (Lowe and Matthew, 2000). When gathering science trade books, Ebbers (2002) suggests that these nonfiction genres be included: reference, explanation, field guides, how-to, narrative/expository, biography, and journal. Reading several books on the same topic furnishes students with opportunities to note consistencies and discrepancies between the books and engages the students in using higher order thinking skills as they ponder their discoveries.

Chapters in this section include comprehension strategies and annotations on a variety of nonfiction and fiction books on gardens, insects and bugs, the solar system, weather, habitats and biomes, and animals. Lists of outstanding science trade books can be found on the National Science Teachers Association web site at www.nsta.org/ostbc.

References

Alberts, Bruce. Preface to *Inquiry and the National Science Education Standards: A Guide for Teaching and Learning.* Washington, D.C.: National Academy Press, 2000.

Ebbers, Margaretha. "Science Text Sets: Using Various Genres to Promote Literacy and Inquiry." *Language Arts* 80, no. 1 (Sept. 2002): 40–50.

Lowe, Joy L., and Kathryn I. Matthew. "Puppets and Prose: Using Puppets and Children's Literature in the Science Classroom." *Science and Children* 37, no. 8 (May 2000): 41–45.

National Science Education Standards. Washington, D.C.: National Academy Press, 1995. http://stills.nap.edu/readingroom/books/nses/ (20 Nov. 2002). Eight categories on p. 5 reprinted with permission from NSES, 1995, by the National Academy of Sciences. Courtesy of the National Academies Press, Washington, D.C.

Rice, Diana C. "Using Trade Books in Teaching Elementary Science: Facts and Fallacies." *The Reading Teacher* 55, no. 6 (March 2002): 552–565.

· 1 ·
Gardens

Introducing gardens provides students the opportunity to explore how to plant a seed, tend the seed as it grows, and harvest what was grown. Since most children love to play in the dirt, it is not too difficult to move them into the types of hands-on activities involved with gardening. In addition, a study of gardens and related topics can build on their natural curiosity about nature. Students can learn about what plants need to continue growth and tools that are useful in tending to the garden. The type of planting can range from using a cup for growing a bean seed, to container gardens, to larger plots of land. As students explore the world of gardening, they can keep a journal documenting how the garden progressed by recording descriptions and measurements related to growth. Strand two of the *National Science Education Standards* (NSES, 1995) highlights the characteristics of organisms, life cycles of organisms, and organisms and their environment, and the fourth strand includes a look at the properties of earth materials. Semantic maps, circle maps, and semantic feature analysis charts are useful strategies that can be used during the exploration of gardens.

Semantic Maps

Three of the most commonly used applications of the semantic mapping strategy are: a) for general vocabulary development, b) for pre- and postreading, and c) as a study skill technique (Heimlich and Pittelman, 1986). Semantic mapping is especially useful as a means for activating prior knowledge (Johnson and Pearson, 1984). Background knowledge that students possess needs to be activated through discussion or by other means, just as related concepts students do not possess need to be developed before further reading begins (Burns, Roe, and Ross, 1999). Following the prereading discussion and reading of the book, this strategy can be expanded through a postreading activity to summarize and integrate ideas. (See figure 1.3.) The semantic map can also be used as a postreading strategy without the map being created prior to reading the story. (See figure 1.4.) When utilized strictly as a postreading activity, then the categories may correspond to the book alone. Other categories could still be added after reading other books pertaining to the topic.

Steps

1. Write the central concept on the board, overhead, or butcher paper then brainstorm with the class ideas about the concept. Record ideas randomly on butcher paper while asking students to elicit and extend their responses. This stage of the process is illustrated in figure 1.1 where the initial brainstorming of ideas is represented using the web format.
2. When students have no new ideas to contribute, then work together to classify and categorize the information that was recorded. Figure 1.2 illustrates how the initial information was reorganized according to categories that included needs of a plant, types of plants, and parts of a plant.
3. Add new information that was learned through the reading of the text. This step can be done using a different color to differentiate between what was known and what will be added. Figure 1.3 illustrates how new information is added after reading the book.
4. Determine if the map needs any revisions to information that was already recorded, then encourage the students to reread the text to verify whether or not information needs to be changed.

Examples

Gibbons, Gail. *From Seed to Plant*. 1991. Unp. New York: Holiday House. (pbk. 0-8234-1025-0).
Grades: K–3. Gibbons' text is full of colorful illustrations and labeled diagrams that help the reader follow the process a seed moves through as it becomes a plant.

Semantic Map Part One

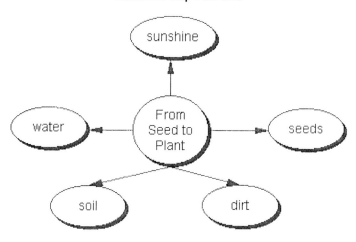

Figure 1.1. Prior to reading the story, students brainstorm what they know already about plants.

Semantic Map Part Two

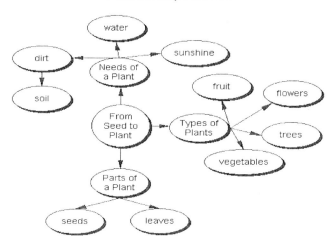

Figure 1.2. After the initial brainstorming session, work with students to identify major categories that were identified, then rearrange the semantic map using those categories.

Semantic Map Part Three

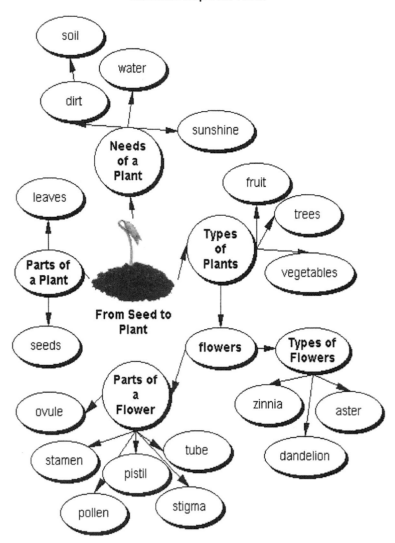

Figure 1.3. After reading, students add new ideas and concepts learned from the book.

Gibbons, Gail. *The Pumpkin Book*. 1999. Unp. New York: Scholastic. (pbk. 0-439-14785-9).
Grades: K–3. The life cycle of a pumpkin is illustrated in vivid pictures and diagrams. The book includes a brief historical element, steps on carving a pumpkin, and tips on how to dry your own pumpkin seeds.

Semantic Map

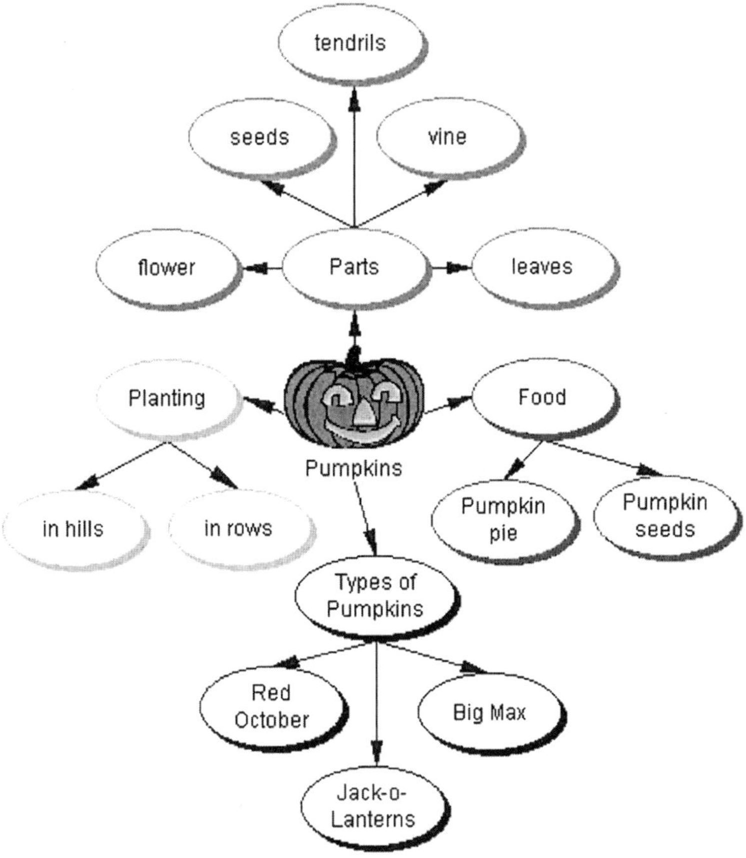

tendrils

seeds · vine

flower · Parts · leaves

Planting · Pumpkins · Food

in hills · in rows · Pumpkin pie · Pumpkin seeds

Types of Pumpkins

Red October · Big Max

Jack-o-Lanterns

Figure 1.4. After reading the story, the teacher can identify the basic categories and ask students to brainstorm ideas for each one. A second option is to identify the categories once the class has finished brainstorming, and then rearrange the subcategories accordingly.

Additional Books and Resources

Bunting, Eve. *Flower Garden*. Illustrated by Kathryn Hewitt. 1994.
   Unp. Orlando, Fla.: Harcourt Brace. (hc. 0-15-228776-0).
Grades: P–3. Bunting's book follows a young girl and her father as
they buy what they need to plant a flower garden for her mother. The
book includes a two-page illustration with one page of large-print text.
The simple vocabulary and sentence structure of the text makes it easy
for young readers to follow along or listen while the teacher reads the
story.

Ehlert, Lois. *Planting a Rainbow*. 1988. Unp. Orlando, Fla.: Harcourt
   Brace. (pbk. 0-15-262610-7).
Grades: P–4. This text introduces children to the concept of flower gardens by looking at what can be done during each season. The book also
looks at different types of flowers based on color. For example, there
are red flowers, such as tulips, carnations, and roses, and there are orange flowers, such as zinnias, poppies, and tiger lilies along with tulips
again.

——. *Eating the Alphabet: Fruits and Vegetables from A to Z*. 1989.
   Unp. New York: Scholastic. (pbk. 0-590-05302-7).
Grades: K–3. Starting with apricots, artichokes, and avocados and
ending with xigua, yams, and zucchini, Ehlert's alphabet includes colorful and vivid illustrations depicting a variety of fruits and vegetables.
A glossary of fruits and vegetables also provides a simple picture, pronunciation, and other selected information about each of the fruits and
vegetables shown throughout the book.

Lobel, Anita. *Allison's Zinnia*. 1989. Unp. New York: Mulberry
   Books. (pbk. 0-688-14737-2).
Grades: K–3. Lobel's book introduces children to a wealth of beautiful
flowers from A to Z by illustrating one flower per letter using watercolor and gouache paints. Simple alliterative sentences, such as "Allison acquired an Amaryllis for Beryl," follow a girl-verb-flower format
that eventually links the reader back to the beginning of the book.

de Bourgoing, Pascale, and Gallimard Jeunesse. *Vegetables in the
   Garden*. Illustrated by Gilbert Houbre. 1989. Unp. New York:
   Scholastic. (hc. 0-590-33946-X).
Grades: K–3.This First Discovery Book talks about the fact that vege-
tables are plants, and that their roots, stems, seeds, leaves, or flowers
are eaten as food. It discusses root systems and the parts of the plant

that are eaten, and identifies plants that are commonly thought to be vegetables but are actually fruits.

Kalman, Bobbie, and Kathryn Smithyman. *The Life Cycle of a Tree.* Illustrated by Barbara Bedell. 2002. 32p. New York: Crabtree Publishing. (hc. 0-7787-0659-1; pbk. 0-7787-0689-3).

Grades: 2–5. Photographs and text are used to illustrate the life cycle of a tree, describe facts about trees, discuss the function of trees in the forest, and address how trees benefit animals, people, and the environment. Other topics included in the book are seedling to sapling, making seeds, seeds on the move, and amazing trees.

Bial, Raymond. *A Handful of Dirt.* 2000. 32p. New York: Walker. (hc. 0-8027-8698-7).

Grades: 4–8. This author shares how soil is one of the essential building blocks of life on Earth. He identifies the organic and inorganic ingredients that make up soil and makes the reader appreciate that our soil is a common but precious resource to us all.

The University of Illinois Extension web site provides additional information about pumpkins that could be used when adding information to the semantic map. Some of the links included at this site are a history of pumpkins, varieties, nutritional value, recipes, facts about pumpkins, and information on growing pumpkins. This web site is located at http://www.urbanext.uiuc.edu/pumpkins/.

The web site for World Class Giant Pumpkins has links to statistics about giant pumpkins, seed sources, books, videos, problems when planting pumpkins, festivals, recipes, and other links. This web site is located at http://www.backyardgardener.com/wcgp/index.html.

Dirt software is published by Scholastic and is available through Tom Snyder Productions. Designed for grades two through four, this software discusses the composition of dirt, how dirt helps people, how it supports vegetation, the ecosystem that lives under dirt, how contaminated dirt can harm us, and what makes dirt move. *Dirt* is part of the Sidewalk Science series, and is correlated to the National Science Standards.

The Dragonfly Tree provides links to many different topics for young investigators. Originally begun as a joint venture of the School of Interdisciplinary Studies at Miami University in Oxford, Ohio, and the National Science Teachers Association (NSTA) Project, the Dragonfly web site is now maintained through Miami University (http://www.units.muohio.edu/dragonfly/).

Circle Maps

Circle maps are a great way to illustrate life cycles, since the circular format shows the connections so clearly from one stage to the next. The circle map also illustrates how the cycle is actually never-ending. For example, the cycle can illustrate how a seed becomes a plant then produces the seeds that begin the cycle anew. Similar to a circular story map used to identify story elements in a narrative text, this type of map illustrates how the cycle can start and end at the same place with a series of events occurring in between. Steve Moline (1995) calls this type of map a cyclical flow diagram and states it is best suited to describing continuous processes such as the carbon cycle, the water cycle, or life cycles. When making the diagram, students can place arrows to establish the direction in which the process moves, and use smaller arrows to link labels with the pictures (Moline, 1995). Along with the illustrations, students can include a parallel text that explains each stage in the process. (See figures 1.5 and 1.6.)

Steps

1. Draw a large circle on butcher paper or the chalkboard and divide the circle into parts.
2. The number of parts shown in the circle should correspond to the number of stages shown on the circle map.
3. After reading, discuss the text together as a group and decide what stages should be represented.
4. Students can work together in small groups or large groups for this part of the circle map.
5. Once the stages have been identified, students can make their version of the life cycle using paper plates, manila paper, or butcher paper. Whatever material is used, it is helpful to divide the paper into the sections necessary to complete the stages before students begin working.
6. Have the students share their completed circle maps with their classmates.

Examples

Titherington, Jeanne. *Pumpkin, Pumpkin.* 1986. Unp. New York: Scholastic. (pbk. 0-590-42871-3).
Grades: K–3. The simple format of the book depicts the life cycle of a plant as it moves from seed to pumpkin. The pictures, text structure, and simple vocabulary used in the book provide enough support structures for young readers wishing to retell the story.

Circle Map

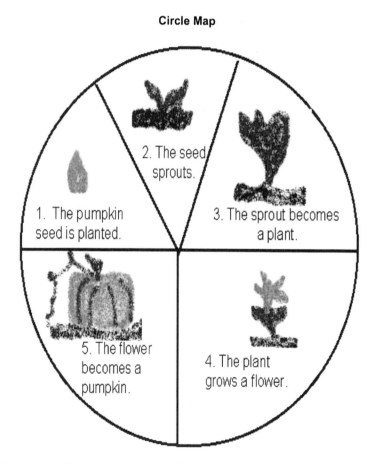

Figure 1.5. The pictures used on this circle map were made using *Microsoft Paint.*

Johnson, Neil. *A Field of Sunflowers*. 1997. Unp. New York: Scholastic. (pbk. 0-590-96549-2).

Grades: 3–8. The vocabulary (e.g. germinate, cotyledon, phototropism, stalk fibers, florets, pollination, etc.) introduced in this book makes it more appropriate for older readers. Johnson follows a farmer's deviation to the planting of sunflowers instead of the regular crops he would plant in his fields. Full-color photographs document the growth of the sunflower field from the plowing of the field to planting of the seeds along with the gradual growth that occurs until the plants mature. Johnson's whimsical ending (The End?) followed by a question mark encourages children to reflect on the cyclical nature of life.

Circle Map

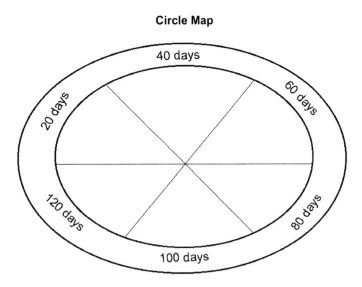

Figure 1.6. The life cycle of a sunflower takes about 120 days until it is fully grown. This cycle can be represented using a series of days. Students can measure growth and record descriptive information for the sunflower.

Additional Books and Resources

Medearis, Angela Shelf. *Seeds Grow!* Illustrated by Jill Dubin. 1999. Unp. New York: Scholastic. (pbk. 0-590-37974-7).

Grades: P–1. This Hello Reader has easy-to-read vocabulary that young readers will be able to follow as they watch the seed grow into a plant.

Ehlert, Lois. *Growing Vegetable Soup*. 1987. Unp. San Diego, Calif.: Harcourt. (hc. 0-15-232575-1; pbk. 0-15-232580-8).

Grades: P–3. With colorful illustrations, Ehlert captures a father and child sharing the planting, watering, and tending of their garden. At the back of the book, a recipe for making vegetable soup is listed.

Marzollo, Jean. *I'm a Seed*. 1996. Unp. New York: Scholastic. (pbk. 0-590-26586-5).

Grades: K–1. Beneath the ground are a marigold seed and a mystery seed. The growth and development of the seeds are illustrated throughout the book. Students follow along as the first shoots appear, then leaves, followed by the blossoms, until finally the mystery seed is revealed to be a round, orange pumpkin.

Carle, Eric. *The Tiny Seed*. 1987. Unp. New York: Aladdin. (hc. 0-88708-015-4; pbk. 0-689-84244-9).

Grades: K–3. Carle shares the journey of a flower seed as it moves through the air until it finally falls to the ground. He shows the resting place of the seed during the winter months, then how it starts to grow when spring arrives. The cycle of life is illustrated as the plant that the seed has become releases its own seeds into the wind to start the process all over again.

Legg, Gerald. *From Seed to Sunflower*. Illustrated by Carolyn Scrace. 1998. 29p. New York: Franklin Watts. (pbk. 0-531-15334-7).

Grades: K–5. This book follows the process of a seed as it grows into a sunflower plant. Topics covered include germination, roots and shoots, buds, pollination, ripe seeds, and withering.

Rylant, Cynthia. *This Year's Garden*. 1984. Unp. New York: Aladdin Books. (pbk. 0-689-71122-0).

Grades: 1–5. Rylant looks at the cycle of a garden from the perspective of a family as it moves through the year. She shares the family's conversations as they move through each season: winter is for planning, spring is for planting, summer is for waiting for the vegetables to be ready to eat, and fall is for harvesting.

Semantic Feature Analysis Charts

Semantic Feature Analysis (SFA) is intended to provide a systematic procedure for exploring and reinforcing vocabulary concepts through the use of categorization (Tierney and Readence, 2000). Like semantic mapping, semantic feature analysis is an instructional strategy for vocabulary development that takes advantage of the way the brain organizes information (Pittelman, Heimlich, Berglund, and French, 1991). In addition, SFA is helpful in relating concepts in a postreading situation in content-area classrooms (Tierney and Readence, 2000). An extension to the SFA is to use the chart to write analogies. For example, in figure 1.6 the following analogy could be written: Carrots are to below the ground as corn is to above the ground. Students can use the chart to write incomplete analogies, and their classmates work to complete the analogy correctly (e.g. *Potatoes* are to _____ as *cucumbers* are to *on the ground*.). (See figures 1.7, 1.8.)

Steps

1. List a group of words with known properties or concepts down the left side of a matrix.
2. Together with your students, brainstorm a group of features possessed by items on the list. A feature only needs to apply to at least one item on the list in order for it to be included. These features should then be written across the top of the list. For example, in figure 1.7, the names of vegetables that were grown in the book *Tops and Bottoms* by Janet Stevens are listed down the left side of the semantic feature analysis chart, and ways they grow (i.e. below the ground, on the ground, above the ground) are listed across the top columns.
3. The matrix is then filled in using a plus or check to indicate the feature is present in the term listed on the left, or a minus sign to indicate it is absent.
4. If students decide that some degree of the feature is present, then a numerical system of coding (i.e. using 0 for none, 1 for some, 2 for much, and 3 for all) (Burns et al., 1999) could be used.

Examples

Stevens, Janet. *Tops and Bottoms.* 1995. Unp. New York: Harcourt Brace. (hc. 0-15-292851-00).
Grades: K–3. Lazy Bear may have the land, but Hungry Rabbit has the smarts to figure out how to feed his own family by outwitting Bear in a *Tops and Bottoms* scheme to beat all others. When Bear agrees to let

Rabbit plant on his land, Bear is then asked to decide if he wants tops, bottoms, or middles of the vegetables that will be harvested. Each time Bear makes a choice and thinks he will get the better end of the deal. Each time, Lazy Bear is outwitted by Rabbit. During the first growing cycle, Bear chooses tops, so Rabbit plants carrots, radishes, and beets. After harvest, Bear is left with only the leafy tops. For the second growing cycle, Bear chooses bottoms, so Rabbit plants lettuce, broccoli, and celery. After harvest, Bear is left with roots of the plants. For the third growing cycle, Bear chooses tops and bottoms, so Rabbit plants corn. Bear is left with the roots and the stalk instead of the actual corn. At the end of the story, Bear finally learns that he will have to do his part if he expects to get anything from his garden.

Semantic Feature Analysis

	Below the Ground	On the Ground	Above the Ground
Celery	-	√	-
Corn	-	-	√
Carrots	√	-	-
Lettuce	-	√	-
Broccoli	-	√	-
Radishes	√	-	-
Beets	√	-	-

Figure 1.7. In the book *Tops and Bottoms*, Rabbit plants the vegetables listed in this chart. Students determine whether the vegetables would be grown below the ground, on the ground, or above the ground.

Bullock, Ivan, and Diane James. *Gardening: I Can Do It!* 1998. 32p. Chicago, Ill.: World Book and Two-Can. (pbk. 0-7166-2602-0). Grades: 4–8. This book provides a general overview of gardening that covers a wide range of gardening-related tasks that includes getting started, tips and tools, planting bulbs, planting in pots, free plants, and much more. Combine this activity with an Internet search to locate plants that would fit some of the categories listed in the SFA matrix.

Semantic Feature Analysis

	Indoor Plant	Out-door Plant	Flower	Tree	Fruit	Veg.
Apple	No	Yes	No	Yes	Yes	No
Tomato	Yes	Yes	Yes	No	Yes	No
Pear	No	Yes	Yes	Yes	Yes	No
Dandelion	No	Yes	Yes	No	No	No
Cucumber	No	Yes	Yes	No	No	Yes
Plum	No	Yes	Yes	Yes	Yes	No

Figure 1.8. Older students can identify more features to compare using the SFA chart.

Additional Books and Resources

Florian, Douglas. *Vegetable Garden.* 1991. Unp. Orlando, Fla: Harcourt Brace. (pbk. 0-15-201018-1).
Grades: P–1. The format of the book includes a two-page picture spread illustrating tools used to plant the garden or plants that grow in the garden. The text includes two to three words in a large print that is easily viewed by young readers.

Gibbons, Gail. *The Berry Book.* 2002. Unp. New York: Holiday House. (hc. 0-8234-1697-6).
Grades: 1–4. Gibbons covers the gamut from edible to nonedible berries that can be found on every continent except Antarctica. She talks about how berries are cultivated and harvested, gives directions for growing particular berries, and lists recipes for blueberry pie, blackberry jam, and raspberry ice cream. At the end of the book, Gibbons also includes a page on facts about berries.

——. *Apples.* 2000. Unp. New York: Holiday House (hc. 0-8234-1497-3).
Grades: K–3. This book has a potpourri of information about apples that ranges from pollination, picking, and growing information to the parts of an apple, different varieties, and instructions on caring for the apple tree.

——. *Farming.* 1988. Unp. New York: Holiday House. (hc. 0-8234-0682-2; pbk. 0-8234-0797-7).
Grades: K–5. Gibbons vividly illustrates life on a farm through a comparison of indoor versus outdoor chores as the farm moves through

each season. Gibbons' artwork includes a look at the people and the animals that are connected with the working of a farm.

Heller, Ruth. *The Reason for a Flower.* 1983. Unp. New York: Penguin Putnam Books. (pbk. 0-698-11559-7).
Grades: 1–5. Heller introduces the vocabulary of botany with the vocabulary words *flowers, nectar, pollen, anther, stamen, stigma, style, weeds, seeds,* and more. Along with her full-color illustrations, she describes in vivid detail each of the different concepts.

McCormick, Rosie. *Arty Facts: Plants and Art Activities.* 2002. 48p. New York: Crabtree Publishing Company. (hc. 0-7787-1110-2).
Grades: 2–8. *Arty Facts* follows a two-page format for each topic in the book where one page is basic information for children to learn more about the concept and the second page focuses on an art activity that could be completed. For example, one topic in the book is woody skin. McCormick shares with the reader that trees have skin, what it is composed of, what plants need to survive, and what is made from the bark. On the second page, materials are listed that are needed to complete a bark-rubbing project along with simple directions and an illustration of the final product. There are twenty-four different topics addressed in the book, some of which include sprouting seeds, tropical beauties, gum and sap, opening petals, fancy fossils, paper and pulp, exploding spores, wings and pods, and medicinal plants.

KidsGardening.Com offers teacher resources and theme-based information that will assist in setting up a classroom garden. Teachers can explore ways to promote literacy, hone math skills, identify native plants, and nurture the young scientist (www.kidsgardening.com).

References

Burns, Paul C., Betty D. Roe, and Elinor P. Ross. *Teaching Reading in Today's Elementary School*, 7th ed. Boston, Mass.: Houghton Mifflin, 1999.

Heimlich, Joan E., and Susan D. Pittelman. *Semantic Mapping: Classroom Applications*. Newark, Del.: International Reading Association, 1986.

Johnson, Dale D., and P. David Pearson. *Teaching Reading Vocabulary*, 2nd ed. New York: Holt, Rinehart and Winston, 1984.

Moline, Steve. *I See What You Mean: Children at Work with Visual Information*. York, Maine: Stenhouse, 1995.

National Science Education Standards. Washington, D.C.: National Academies Press. Washington, D.C.: National Academies Press, 1995. http://stills.nap.edu/readingroom/books/nses/ (20 Nov. 2002). Reprinted with permission from NSES, 1995, by the National Academy of Sciences. Courtesy of the National Academies Press, Washington, D.C.

Pittelman, Susan D., Joan E. Heimlich, Roberta L. Berglund, and Michael P. French. *Semantic Feature Analysis: Classroom Applications*. Newark, Del.: International Reading Association, 1991.

Ruddell, Robert B. *Teaching Children to Read and Write: Becoming an Influential Teacher*, 2nd ed. Needham Heights, Mass.: Allyn and Bacon, 1999.

Tierney, Robert J., and John E. Readence. *Reading Strategies and Practices: A Compendium*, 5th ed. Needham Heights, Mass.: Allyn and Bacon, 2000.

· 2 ·
Insects and Bugs

There are "twice as many insects as there are all other kinds of animals combined" (Hickman, 1999, p. 4). Without a doubt, there are insects all around us. Although you may not always see them, insects can be found under the ground, on the ground, in the air, in the water, on plants, and even in your home. The vast world of insects encompasses dragonflies, flies, cockroaches, termites, crickets, grasshoppers, lice, beetles, fleas, butterflies, ants, bees, wasps...to name just a few! A look at insect records finds that they range from the heaviest insect, the Goliath beetle that weighs 3.5 ounces, to the smallest insect, Mymarid wasps that are 0.0067 inches long (Maynard, 2001). Other amazing insects include the Desert Locust that can jump the longest distance at 19.5 inches, and the Australian termite that builds the largest nest, which can be up to 23 feet high and 100 feet in diameter.

Features that set insects apart include the three body parts: a head, a middle part called a thorax, and an abdomen. Insects also have a pair of antennae that are used for touching, smelling, and telling the temperature. Bugs, included within the major category of insects, actually mean something different to insect scientists known as entomologists (Maynard, 2001). Within the thirty or so main groups of insects, there is one group known as *Hemiptera* or "true bugs." True bugs are different from the larger category of insects in that they do not have teeth and mouths that chew. Instead, they have a beak in the shape of a straw with a needlelike point (Maynard, 2001). Aphids, stinkbugs, and bedbugs are considered to be "true bugs." Also important to note here is that spiders are not considered to be insects. Therefore, when exploring insects, be sure to not make the mistake of calling a spider an insect.

The second strand of the *National Science Education Standards* (NSES, 1995) encompasses the characteristics of organisms and their

23

environments. Graphic organizers in this chapter that can be used during the insects and bugs investigation include labeled diagrams, fishbones or bug skeletons, and vocabulary puzzles or concept of definition word maps.

Labeled Diagrams

Labeled diagrams, labeled pictures, picture glossaries—all are the same concept in that the text and words work together to illustrate or describe a topic. Moline (1995, p. 25) states that the labeled diagram is more powerful than a simple vocabulary list, because "a diagram can show the relationships between the parts and the structure of the whole." "When a cluster of terms is related chiefly by the location of the things to which they refer, a picture with the terms as labels can be highly effective" (McKenna and Robinson, 1997, p. 123). The labeled diagram can be used to show such structural features as the relative and actual sizes, the relative positions, and the overall structure itself (e.g. parts of an insect, as in figures 2.1 and 2.2). Moline stresses the importance of having students create and draw the diagrams versus simply completing an existing diagram given as a worksheet. "A large part of the understanding that students gain from these texts lies in reconstructing the pictorial elements of the diagram" (Moline, 1995, p. 26).

Steps

1. Provide students with print and electronic resources that have pictures of various insects. Select one of the insects to draw and label together as a class.
2. Talk together about important parts that should be included to represent the insect. List this information on the chalkboard, overhead, or butcher paper to keep as a reference while drawing the diagram.
3. For the next step, one option is to draw the insect together as a class. A second option is to assign small groups or partners various parts of the insect to construct.
4. Once all of the parts have been completed, then come back together as a class to put the insect together. Use index cards or sticky labels to identify important features of the insect.
5. Discuss together the information that was placed on the labeled diagram and why it was important to include as part of the dia-

gram. Once the class activity has been completed as a model, then students can select their own insect to draw and label.

Examples

Maynard, Chris. *Bugs: A Close-Up View of the Insect World.* 2001. 96p. New York: Dorling Kindersley. (hc. 0-7894-7969-9; pbk. 0-7894-7970-2).

Grades: 1–4. This informative book tells the reader exactly what is meant by insects and bugs. The photographs, captions, and accompanying text describe the world of insects in a clear, concise manner that will be enjoyable to students. Topics discussed in the book are where insects live, how they move around, a look at shapes and colors, insect wars, and insects on trial. Reference sections students can use to obtain additional information are insect classifications, key insect orders, insect records, web sites, and a bug glossary.

Labeled Diagram

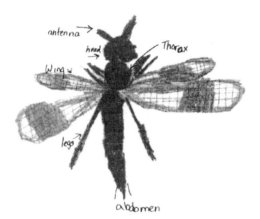

Figure 2.1. This labeled diagram illustrates the main body parts of the dragonfly. The three main parts (head, abdomen, and thorax) are shown as well as the wings, legs, and antennae. Notice the attention to the network of veins that has been drawn on the wings.

Chinery, Michael. *Butterfly.* Photographs by Barrie Watts. Illustrated by Helen Senior. 1991. 32p. Mahway, N.J.: Troll Associates. (pbk. 0-8167-2101-7).

Grades: 3–8. Part of the Life Story series, this text focuses solely on the life cycle of the butterfly. Detailed explanations of how the butterfly starts life and the changes it undergoes from caterpillar to butterfly are covered.

Labeled Diagram

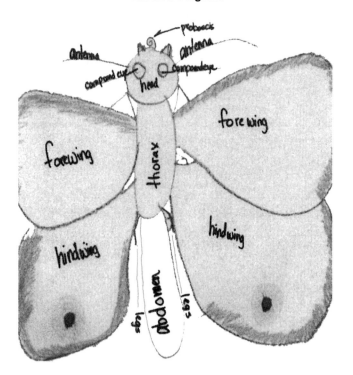

Figure 2.2. After reading the book, a student created this labeled diagram showing major parts of the butterfly.

Additional Books and Resources

Carle, Eric. *The Very Hungry Caterpillar.* 1987. Unp. New York: Philomel. (hc. 0-399-20853-4).
Grades: P–2. Eric Carle uses his collage art technique to tell the life cycle of a butterfly as it moves from caterpillar to butterfly.

——. *The Very Lonely Firefly*. 1995. Unp. New York: Philomel. (hc. 0-399-22774-1).

Grades: P–2. The lonely firefly flashes its light looking for other fireflies but finds only other sources of light instead (e.g. a light bulb, a candle, a flashlight, etc.). His search finally ends when he finds a group of fireflies also flashing their lights.

——. *The Very Quiet Cricket*. 1997. Unp. New York: Philomel. (hc. 0-399-22684-2).

Grades: P–2. This is a story of a cricket searching for his voice, which is the sound he makes when rubbing his wings together.

Marzollo, Jean. *I'm a Caterpillar*. Illustrated by Judith Moffatt. 1997. Unp. New York: Scholastic. (pbk. 0-590-84779-1).

Grades: P–2. This Hello Reader Level 1 book uses simple vocabulary with full-page illustrations. The text follows a caterpillar through his food journey until he forms a pupa and transforms into a butterfly. The full cycle is completed when the full-grown caterpillar finds a mate and lays more eggs, which hatch into caterpillars. The complete life cycle is shown on a one-page illustration at the end of the book.

Pallotta, Jerry. *The Icky Bug Alphabet Book*. Illustrated by Ralph Masiello. 1986. Unp. Watertown, Mass.: Charlesbridge Publishing. (hc. 0-88106-456-4; pbk. 0-88106-450-5).

Grades: 1–4. This text follows a simple alphabet book concept with the lowercase and uppercase letter, a picture of the insect that starts with that letter, and a short description of the insect. There are also pictures of spiders included in Pallotta's book, so it would be important to note that spiders are not insects.

Parker, Steve, and Polly Parker. *Arty Facts: Insects, Bugs, and Art Activities*. 2003. 48p. New York: Crabtree Publishing. (hc. 0-7787-1109-9; pbk. 0-7787-1137-4).

Grades: 2–8. Combine an insect and bug investigation with fun art activities using the materials and resources included in this book. The book covers ladybugs, bees, dragonflies, caterpillars, butterflies, houseflies, and more. The photographs provide children with a close-up view of what the insects actually look like. Interesting information about each example is also included. Each insect has an accompanying art activity page that gives step-by-step directions along with materials that will be needed to complete the project.

Greenbacker, Liz. *Bugs: Stingers, Suckers, Sweeties, and Swingers*. 1993. 64p. New York: Franklin Watts. (hc. 0-531-20072-8; pbk. 0-531-15673-7).

Grades: 3–8. Insects are categorized by where they live: in the woods, in the fields, in the garden, and in the house. The author discusses the many different types of bugs, and how bugs protect, assist, harm, and provide food for each other and for humans. The text includes information about bees, mosquitoes, ticks, flies, ladybugs, and more. The common name, class, order, number of species, habitat, life span, and diet are covered for bugs included in the book. Close-up photographs of each bug help children to actually see the features and characteristics that can make insects and bugs so interesting.

The University of Kentucky hosts a website called Katerpillars and Mystery Bugs. The misspelling of "caterpillars" is intentional and in honor of the school mascot, the Wildcats, or "kats." Designed by the University of Kentucky Entomology Department, this web site is geared towards teachers, 4'Hers, young people, and anyone else who wants to pursue an interest in entomology. There are several articles that offer resources and basic information about insects located at http://www.uky.edu/Agriculture/Entomology/ythfacts/entyouth.htm.

The Iowa State University Department of Entomology has an image gallery located at http://www.ent.iastate.edu/imagegallery/. Some of the insects that can be accessed through this web site include beetles, butterflies, moths, caterpillars, cicadas, leafhoppers, flies, mosquitoes, grasshoppers, crickets, and true bugs. A resource linked to their Insect Zoo (http://www.ent.iastate.edu/zoo/enhanced4.html) offers live insects, which provides streaming video of the insect of the month.

AntBoy's BugWorld! was created by parents for their young son. The web site, http://www.heatersworld.com/bugworld/, offers information about ants, bees, butterflies, and roaches as well as other interesting links about insects and bugs.

Enchanted Learning's web site includes information found at http://www.enchantedlearning.com/subjects/insects/printouts.shtml. As a particular insect is selected, the reader is taken to a linked page that includes a wealth of basic information ranging from labeled diagram, to life stages, to the food it requires along with classification information.

Houghton Mifflin's EduPlace has a web site that breaks down the activities by a range of grade levels. A variety of links for language arts, art, and science activities are provided for teachers and students. For example, one activity that could be selected is to make trading cards about bugs that can be swapped with other students in the classroom. Another activity that can be developed is Name That Bug where students get four clues to try to name a particular insect or bug. Visit www.eduplace.com/monthlytheme/october/activities_bugs.html to use this resource.

Fishbone or Bug Skeleton

Called a herringbone by Wood (2001), this type of graphic organizer can look at who, what, when, where, why, and how as it relates to insects and bugs. It can also be used to simply list details about a particular insect or bug that has been selected. Once the fishbone is completed, then students can use it as an outline to guide their written response to an insect that was studied. (See figure 2.3.) The bug skeleton, a variation on the fishbone, can be used to identify the topic or main idea along with details. (See figure 2.4.) The main difference between the two is that the bug skeleton categorizes the types of information that can be found about each insect or bug in a slightly different way than the fishbone by looking at four broad categories: a) common and scientific name, b) short description, c) special features, and d) facts. Students like these organizers because they can be completed quickly and easily and then used as study guides to prepare for tests.

Fishbone

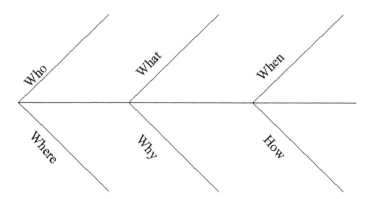

Figure 2.3. This fishbone identifies who, what, when, where, why, and how about a designated insect or bug.

Bug Skeleton

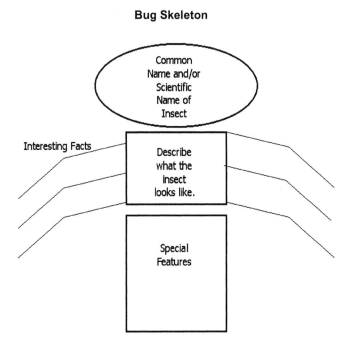

Figure 2.4. The bug skeleton looks at the common and scientific names, short description, special features, and interesting facts.

Steps

1. Model how to complete the fishbone or bug skeleton by completing the format together using the chalkboard, overhead, or computer resource.
2. Once the information is recorded using the organizer, then talk through how to use it as a guide when completing a written response about the topic. Ask questions aloud, such as "What should we write first? What other information should be included?"
3. Students use the completed fishbone or bug skeleton to write a summary paragraph about the topic.
4. Once the class has completed the graphic organizer, then students could work in pairs to do their own insect or bug.

Examples

Himmelman, John. *A Pill Bug's Life.* 1999. Unp. New York: Children's Press. (hc. 0-516-21165-X).
Grades: P–3. The text and illustrations in this book follow a pill bug as it hunts for food, faces its enemies, and survives the winter. (See figure 2.5.)

Fishbone

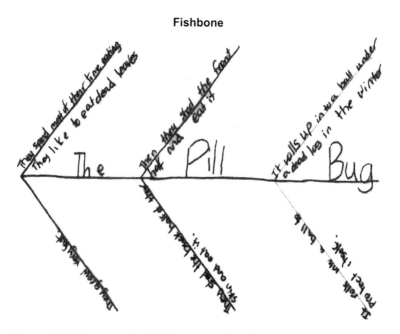

Figure 2.5. Diagram of a fishbone completed about the pill bug. The completed elements highlight basic details about the bug including how it grows, what it eats, and how it survives.

O'Toole, Christopher. *The Dragonfly over the Water.* Photographs by Oxford Scientific Films. 1988. 32p. Milwaukee, Wis.: Gareth Stevens Publishing. (hc. 1-55532-306-5).
Grades: 2–8. A look at dragonflies and where they live, parts of the dragonfly, how they hunt, how they warm up and cool down as well as how they lay eggs and grow up underwater. (See figure 2.6.) Photographs of dragonflies in their natural habitats provide an up close and personal look at this particular insect.

Bug Skeleton

Name of Insect

Dragonfly

Description

Interesting Facts

[handwritten text in description box:] The wings are clear and transparent. They had bright patterns. They have large eyes that help to see. comes get prey, and (to) mates. They have powerful jaws.

[handwritten:] There are about 5,000 different species of dragonflies in the world... Dragonflies are an important part of the ecosystem. Some dragonflies feed on flies...

[handwritten:] Dragonflies lay their eggs in water. Dragonflies are harmless to humans. A dragonfly can fly up to... miles per hour.

[handwritten in special features box:] The dragonfly has all-around vision. They use their legs to reach or grasp food. It has an exoskeleton which is a covering around the outside of the body. They breath through holes called spiracles.

Special Features

Figure 2.6. Diagram of a dragonfly skeleton that outlines the common name of the bug, a short description, special features, and interesting facts. This student also opted to include a small-scale picture of the dragonfly in the top left corner of the bug skeleton.

Additional Books and Resources

Bernhard, Emery. *Ladybug.* Illustrated by Durga Bernhard. 1992. Unp. New York: Holiday House. (hc. 0-8234-0986-4).
Grades: P–3. Rich, colorful illustrations fill the top three-quarters of the pages and beneath the illustrations are a few brief sentences explaining the life cycle of ladybugs and how they benefit farmers. Students familiar with the Mother Goose nursery rhyme about ladybugs enjoy

learning about these colorful creatures. The book concludes with a glossary.

Soutter-Perrot, Adrienne. *Gnat.* Illustrated by Monique Felix. 1993. 32p. Italy: American Education Publishing. (pbk. 1-56189-171-1).

Grades: 2–5. This book covers basic information about a gnat including what it is, what it looks like, where it lives, and what it does. The illustrations and text are fairly simple in structure and vocabulary, which makes it easy for readers to follow. The gnat is also noted as an important food source for many other animals.

Berger, Melvin. *Chirping Crickets.* Illustrated by Megan Lloyd. 1998. 32p. New York: HarperCollins. (hc. 0-06-024961-7; pbk. 0-06-445180-1).

Grades: 2–5. A cricket hears with its knees is just one of the interesting facts in this book about crickets. Who makes the chirping sound you hear at night? It is not the female, since most of them cannot make any sounds. The author describes how the male makes the chirping sound, and how students can simulate that same sound using paper and a nail file. Also discussed are the life stages of crickets as they move from egg to nymph, and the molting process they go through until they are full-grown crickets. Last, the different types of crickets are described including field crickets, ground crickets, tree crickets, and house crickets.

Jackson, Donna M. *The Bug Scientists.* 2002. 48p. Boston, Mass.: Houghton Mifflin. (hc. 0-618-10868-8).

Grades: 3–8. Part of the Scientists in the Field series, this book uses bug scientists to share with students interesting tidbits about insects and bugs. A variety of insects are included in the book such as the monarch butterfly, the ant, and the dung beetle. The book gives basic information about bugs, how they survive, and how they provide valuable information to crime-scene investigators.

Parker, Nancy Winslow, and Joan Richards Wright. *Bugs.* Illustrated by Nancy Winslow Parker. 1988. 40p. New York: William Morrow. (pbk. 0-6880-8296-3).

Grades: 3–8. This book is an interesting meld of large-print, easy-to-read text for young readers along with small-print, more information-rich descriptions for older readers. The illustrations are fairly simple, although there are numerous labeled diagrams included as well. At the back of the book, there is a picture glossary about how bugs grow or go through metamorphosis, an example of a typical bug, and examples of growth stages.

Parker, Steve. *Insects.* 1992. 61p. New York: Dorling Kindersley. (hc. 1-56458-025-3).
Grades: 3–8. Beginning with how to tell if a bug is an insect using the 3 + 3 rule of three body parts and three pairs of legs, this small book starts readers on a journey to explore the insect world. Different ways are described to capture and borrow insects for observations. Students are reminded to return the insects to their homes when they are finished. Labeled, colorful drawings and photographs and clear, succinct text provide students with the information they need to conduct observations. The book concludes with an index. This book is from the Eyewitness Explorers series.

Bugs, software published by Scholastic for grades two through four, is part of the Sidewalk Science series. Students can explore why there are so many bugs, how bugs change, what is a true bug, how bugs communicate, and how bugs live together.
The Children's Butterfly Site by the U.S. Geological Society, http://www.mesc.usgs.gov/resources/education/butterfly/bfly_start.asp, provides information about the butterfly's life cycle as well as other resources and activities.
Alien Empire (http://www.pbs.org/wnet/nature/alienempire/) from PBS Online has a wealth of resources about insects that is divided into three shows with each show including an article and at least one multimedia segment. For example, Show One examines Hardware and Replicators by looking at an article on aerodynamics, an insect scramble puzzle, a video clip focusing on microscopic zoom, a presentation on the bee anatomy, an article on mayflies, a presentation on mayflies, and a video clip about the Vapourer Moth. Other shows at this web site are Show Two, Battlezone and Metropolis, and Show Three, Voyagers and War of the Worlds.

Vocabulary Puzzles and Concept of Definition Word Maps

Vacca and Vacca (2002, p. 373) state that "diverse learners will often encounter an enormous number of unfamiliar words during reading that may pose comprehension problems"; therefore, "strategy instruction should take into account tactics and procedures that will help students build meaning for important concept terms." Two types of vocabulary scaffolding activities discussed in this next section include vocabulary puzzles and concept of definition word maps. The vocabulary puzzle, also called word bubbles (Richardson and Morgan, 2003), has a main overarching category along with three key identifying pieces of information that would be associated with the vocabulary word. (See figure 2.7.)

The concept of definition word map (see figure 2.8) helps students to understand a word or concept (Schwartz and Raphael, 1985). This strategy uses conceptual information "organized around three types of relationships: a) what the concept is, b) what the concept is like, and c) examples and illustrations of the concept" (Vacca and Vacca, 2002, p. 377). Advantages to using the concept of definition word map are that "students expand their understandings of key vocabulary and concepts beyond simple definitions, construct a visual representation of a concept's definition that helps them in remembering, and are encouraged to integrate their background knowledge into a definition" (Buehl, 2001, p. 42).

Steps

1. Select the vocabulary word or words that will be targeted.
2. Identify three examples of information that would be related to this vocabulary word.
3. Fill in at least one piece of the vocabulary puzzle to give students a point of reference when making decisions about where to place pieces of the puzzle.
4. It is better to keep the puzzles to only three or four words at a time. Along with those three or four words will be another three examples each of information that has to be correlated with the word. Too many words tend to cause information overload for students, which makes it difficult to successfully solve the puzzles.

Examples

Young, Caroline. *The Big Bug Search*. Illustrated by Ian Jackson. 1996. 32p. New York: Scholastic. (pbk. 0-590-12076-X).
Grades: 1–5. The large pictures and illustrations in this book would be enjoyable to young children, since they can examine the insect up close as well as see it in its natural habitat. Along with the illustrations that are in the perimeter of the larger habitat picture, there are text descrip-

tions that provide a bit more information for the interested reader. The different habitats covered for these bugs include deserts, islands, the rain forest, the woods, the water, swamps, jungles, and more.

Vocabulary Puzzles

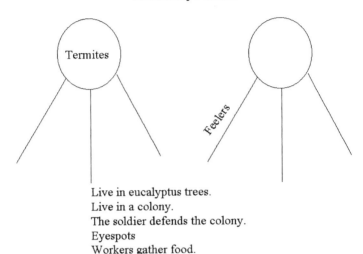

Live in eucalyptus trees.
Live in a colony.
The soldier defends the colony.
Eyespots
Workers gather food.
Emperor Gum Moth

Figure 2.7. This example of a vocabulary puzzle has five pieces of information that need to be placed in the correct puzzle. The answers to the puzzles are that termites live in a colony, the soldier defends the colony, and workers gather food. The overarching category for the second puzzle is the Emperor Gum Moth, which is a more specific kind of moth. The Emperor Gum Moth lives in eucalyptus trees and has eyespots on its wings to scare off enemies.

Steps

1. Select the vocabulary word or words that will be targeted. Display a blank concept of definition word map on the overhead or other visual means of display.
2. Ask students to help complete the word map by brainstorming together information to complete each category.
3. After the word map is completed, then work together to write a definition of the word.

Wexo, John Bennett. *Insects 2.* 1996. 24p. Mankato, Minn.: Creative Education. (hc. 0-88682-776-0).
Grades: 1–5. Part of the popular Zoobooks series by Wildlife Education, this magazine-format book provides students with a variety of visual and textual information about insects. Explanations as to why we need insects, what they eat, how they use their senses, how they communicate, the social nature of some insects, and how they build are covered. A table of contents and an index are included to make specific information easier to locate.

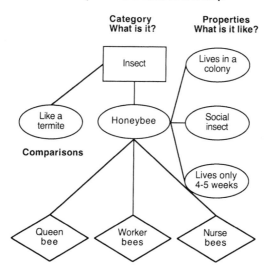

Concept of Definition Word Map

Figure 2.8. This concept of definition word map looks at the honeybee by identifying that it belongs to the insect category, comparing it with a termite, which is another type of social insect, giving three examples of types of jobs the honeybee might have, and giving three examples of what it is like.

Additional Books and Resources

Wallace, Karen. *Born to Be a Butterfly.* 2000. 32p. New York: Dorling Kindersley. (hc. 0-7894-5704-0; pbk. 0-7894-5705-9).

Grades: P–3. A Level 1 Beginning to Read book, this text includes photographs and illustrations of the butterfly as it moves from caterpillar to butterfly. Younger children will be able to follow along in the story using the photographs, while older children will be able to read the simple vocabulary.

Greenaway, Theresa. *The Really Wicked Droning Wasp and Other Things That Bite and Sting.* 1996. Unp. New York: DK Publishing. (hc. 0-7894-1118-0).

Grades: 1–3. The pages of this book are filled with close-ups of wasps, hornets, ticks, caterpillars, scorpions, and other wicked things that crawl, creep, or fly. Older readers tend to hold the book by the edges, so as not to have to touch the creatures on the pages. Large-print text gives a brief introduction to the creatures and then smaller text wraps around them and contains more details. The photographs mesmerize young, fearless readers who delight in the scary creatures.

Maynard, Christopher. *Incredible Mini-Beasts.* 1994. 32p. New York: Covent Garden Books. (pbk. 1-56458-554-9).

Grades: 1–5. This text will be enjoyable for younger and older students alike. The visual format of the book includes large photographs of insects along with accompanying text that extends the information about the insect for readers. The interesting chapter titles (e.g. The Sting Thing, Damsels and Dragons, Old Folks at Home) pique the reader's curiosity to learn more about the different bugs. Questions about bugs are interspersed throughout the book with the answers included at the very end. One of the most interesting sections addresses the different types of mouths that insects have with close-up pictures of each type. You may never look at some bugs the same way again.

Wexo, John Bennett. *Insects.* 1991. 24p. Mankato, Minn.: Creative Education. (hc. 0-88682-776-0).

Grades: 1–5. Part of the popular Zoobooks series by Wildlife Education, this magazine is the first part of a look at insects. Sections in this text cover a look at the body of an insect, the way insects grow, the way they move, and insect wings. The table of contents and index will be helpful in finding more specific information about insects.

Hickman, Pamela. *Starting with Nature: Bug Book.* Illustrated by Heather Collins. 1996. 32p. New York: Kids Can Press. (hc. 1-55074-475-5; pbk. 1-55074-653-7).

Grades: 3–8. This book looks at a variety of bug topics ranging from insects in the water, insects at night, and bug watching in the water to hibernating insects and insect migration. In addition, the author looks at insect homes, insect hunters and endangered insects. The text includes a table of contents and an index for students to easily locate information.

Robertson, Matthew. *Insects and Spiders.* 2000. 64p. Pleasantville, N.Y.: Reader's Digest Children's Books. (hc. 1-57584-710-8). Grades: 4–8. The introduction encourages readers to find their own paths through the book as they search for answers to their questions. It also describes the special features of the book that support students as they read including: inside story, hands on, word builders, that's amazing, and pathfinder. Facts about insects are accompanied by detailed, colorful, labeled illustrations and photographs in this text that is filled with information. The book concludes with a glossary and an index. This book is from the Reader's Digest Pathfinders series.

The Yahooligans' web site provides a listing of other web sites that can be accessed for information about insects. It can be found at http://www.yahooligans.com/science_and_nature/living_things/animals/invertebrates/arthropods/Insects/.

Tales from the Hive is a web site about a cinematographer who filmed inside a hive and followed bees in flight to capture close-ups of honeybee behavior. Topics covered at this site include an anatomy of a hive, the buzz about bees, dances with bees, and how the video was made. Sponsored by PBS, this web site can be found at this location: http://www.pbs.org/wgbh/nova/bees/.

Bugbios.com (http://www.insects.org/) includes stories about insects and the roles they play in our lives. This web site also includes photos and lesson ideas along with thumbnail pictures that can be selected to link to more descriptive information about each insect. For example, if you select the paper wasp, more information is provided about the common name, scientific name, order name, and family name. In addition, a five-to-six-sentence description and larger photograph of the insect are also available.

Scholastic Research Tools includes a Bugs and Insects archives (http://teacher.scholastic.com/researchtools/articlearchives/bugs). There is also a section for children that provides answers to the most asked questions about particular insects. One of the article resources addresses how to tell whether a creature is an insect or a spider (one clue is to count the legs).

References

Buehl, Doug. *Classroom Strategies for Interactive Learning*, 2nd ed. Newark, Del.: International Reading Association, 2001.

Hickman, Pamela. *Starting with Nature: Bug Book*. Buffalo, N.Y.: Kids Can Press, 1999.

Maynard, Chris. *Bugs: A Close-Up View of the Insect World*. New York: Dorling Kindersley, 2001.

McKenna, Michael C., and Richard D. Robinson. *Teaching through Text: A Content Literacy Approach to Content Area Reading*, 2nd ed. White Plains, N.Y.: Longman, 1997.

Moline, Steve. *I See What You Mean: Children at Work with Visual Information*. York, Maine: Stenhouse, 1995.

National Science Education Standards. Washington, D.C.: National Academy Press, 1995. http://stills.nap.edu/readingroom/books/nses/ (20 Nov. 2002).

Richardson, Judy S., and Raymond F. Morgan. *Reading to Learn in the Content Areas*, 5th ed. Belmont, Calif.: Wadsworth, 2003.

Schwartz, Robert, and Taffy Raphael. "Concept of Definition: A Key to Improving Students' Vocabulary." *The Reading Teacher* 39, no. 2 (Nov. 1985): 198–205.

Vacca, Richard T., and Jo Anne L. Vacca. *Content Area Reading: Literacy and Learning across the Curriculum*, 7th ed. Boston, Mass.: Allyn and Bacon, 2002.

Wood, Karen D. *Literacy Strategies across the Subject Areas: Process-Oriented Blackline Masters for the K–12 Classroom*. Needham Heights, Mass.: Allyn and Bacon, 2001.

· 3 ·
The Solar System

On clear, dark nights, students gaze into the sky and wish on twinkling stars. Many are surprised to discover the brightest stars may actually be planets. Sometimes the orbiting International Space Station is visible in the sky. Encouraging children to observe the night sky, to ask questions about what they see, and to seek answers to their questions fosters the natural curiosity of children. These observations of the night sky motivate students to learn more about the vast universe, and they eagerly pursue explorations of the solar system. Students enjoy learning about the constellations and being able to locate them in the sky. Activities such as these help students make connections between what they learn in school and their daily lives. *National Science Education Standard* five relates to the study of earth and space science and the books in this chapter are useful resources for meeting this standard (NSES, 1995). Anticipation guides, inquiry charts, and study guides are comprehension strategies that help students focus their attention and help them make sense of what they read. These strategies not only foster understanding but also become aids to help students remember what they read and learn about our solar system and the universe.

Anticipation Guides

Anticipation guides are used to introduce a reading assignment and activate students' prior knowledge (Readence, Bean, and Baldwin, 1998). Depending on their grade level and reading ability, students read and complete the guide on their own or with assistance. The anticipation guide consists of a series of statements or questions that students

41

react to before reading. The inclusion of controversial statements or
questions motivates students to read to find the answers. The teacher
creates the guides initially, but as students become familiar with using
them, they should be encouraged to create their own. (See figures 3.1
and 3.2.)

Steps

1. Determine the key concepts found in the reading selection.
2. Write statements that will spark discussions about the concepts.
3. Share the statements with the students.
4. Have them respond to the statements.
5. Have students read the selection or read the selection aloud to the
   students.
6. Provide the students opportunities to discuss their responses to the
   statements.

Examples

Branley, Franklyn M. *What the Moon Is Like.* Illustrated by True
     Kelley. 2000. 32p. New York: HarperCollins. (hc. 0-06-027992-3;
     pbk. 0-06-445185-2).
Grades: K–4. Staring up at the Moon on a dark night and wondering
about it is a familiar experience. From this starting point, the author
takes readers on a delightful journey to discover the mysterious Moon
seemingly suspended in the sky. This book is from the Let's-Read-and-
Find-Out Science series.

Anticipation Guide

Statements	Agree	Disagree
There is a man in the Moon.		
A Lunar Roving Vehicle was used to travel on the Moon.		
Just like Earth, the Moon is always changing.		

Figure 3.1. For younger students an anticipation guide may have only
two or three statements.

Simon, Seymour. *Destination: Jupiter.* 1998. Unp. New York: HarperCollins. (hc. 0-688-15620-7; pbk. 0-06-443759-0).
Grades: 1–5. Color photographs of Jupiter and its moons fill the pages of this fascinating book. The accompanying text contains detailed descriptions of Jupiter and several of its sixteen moons. Simon leaves the reader wondering what future spacecraft will discover about the largest planet in the solar system.

Anticipation Guide

Question	Agree	Disagree
1. Jupiter is the smallest planet in the solar system.		✓
2. There is lightning on Jupiter.	✓	
3. Jupiter's Great Red Spot is an enormous storm.	✓	
4. Jupiter's moon Io is covered with brown-tinted ice.		✓
5. Jupiter's moon Ganymede is covered with volcanoes.		✓
6. Craters are holes in the ground with ring-shaped walls around them.	✓	
7. Jupiter has rings.	✓	

Figure 3.2. This is an example of a completed anticipation guide. Before reading, students indicated with a check mark whether they agreed or disagreed with the statements. After reading the book, the students discussed their responses to the anticipation guide and circled the ones they marked incorrectly.

Additional Books and Resources

Branley, Franklyn M. *Neptune: Voyager's Final Target.* 1992. 56p. New York: HarperCollins. (hc. 0-06-022520-3).
Grades: 3–6. It took *Voyager 2* twelve years to reach Neptune. Scientists were astounded that its cameras were still operational and that they sent back stunning photographs of Neptune's surface and four rings.
Stott, Carole. *Moon Landing.* 1999. 48p. New York: DK Publishing. (hc. 0-7894-3968-1).

Grades: 3–6. Detailed, colorful photographs, illustrations, and diagrams accompanied by brief text boxes contain a wealth of information to satisfy eager readers' curiosity about landing on the Moon. Moon data, information on Moon missions, and an index are included.

Ride, Sally, and Tam O'Shaughnessy. *The Mystery of Mars.* 1999. 48p. New York: Crown Publishers. (hc. 0-517-70971-6).

Grades: 4–8. A former astronaut and a science teacher worked together to compile this comprehensive look at the red planet. Comparisons are drawn between Mars and Earth, which help readers make connections between what they already know and what they discover as they read this book. Spectacular photographs, colorful illustrations, and detailed diagrams are interspersed throughout the text. A Mars mission timeline and an index conclude the book.

Spangenburg, Ray, and Kit Moser. *A Look at Jupiter.* 2001. 111p. New York: Franklin Watts. (hc. 0-531-11769-3; pbk. 0-531-16563-9).

Grades: 4–8. The well-written detailed text motivates readers to explore Jupiter. Diagrams, photographs, and charts present additional information that complements the text. The final chapter in the book contains unanswered questions about this giant planet. Vital statistics on missions to Jupiter, a timeline, a glossary, resources for finding out more, and an index are included.

Fradin, Dennis Brindell. *Is There Life on Mars?* 1999. 135p. New York: Margaret K. McElderry Books. (hc. 0-689-82048-8).

Grades: 6 and up. Since the nineteenth century, scientists have wondered about life on Mars. Fradin's own interest in life on Mars began in 1958 with a science fair project. The book explores the past and looks to the future as scientists attempt to answer this intriguing question. A comparison chart of Mars and Earth is included. The book concludes with a listing of additional resources for researching Mars and an index.

Wunsch, Susi Trautmann. *The Adventures of Sojourner: The Mission to Mars That Thrilled the World.* 1998. 63p. New York: Mikaya Press. (hc. 0-9650493-5-3; pbk. 0-9650493-6-1).

Grades: 6 and up. Sojourner was a small rover that explored the surface of Mars and sent back spectacular photographs. The years of hard work that preceded the launch are chronicled. The book includes a comparison chart of Mars and Earth. An index concludes the book.

The NASA Planetary Exploration web site is located at http://www.jpl.nasa.gov. This site has links to information about each of the nine planets and the Sun. Clicking the link for missions provides information on current, future, proposed, and past missions. Images and videos are also located on this site.

Planetary Taxi software includes QuickTime movies and photographs from space missions. Students fly through space in a yellow taxicab engrossed in a game that teaches them about the solar system. This software is appropriate for grades three and up and is available on CD-ROM for both Macintosh and Windows computers from Learn Technologies Interactive.

Inquiry Charts

An Inquiry Chart or I-Chart contains guiding questions that students answer by consulting several information sources (Hoffman, 1992). The chart encourages students to use a systematic process as they research answers to the questions. Using multiple sources requires students to think critically about the text and examine different perspectives as they pursue their research. Large charts drawn on bulletin board paper enable all of the students to see the material and assure that there is room to record all of their responses. For younger students this is usually a teacher-directed whole group activity. Once they become familiar with I-Charts older students can eventually construct their own when they encounter new topics or units of study. Hoffman (1992) suggests three phases including 1) planning, 2) interacting, and 3) integrating and evaluating. (See figures 3.3 and 3.4.)

Steps

1. In the planning phase, the teacher determines the topic, formulates the questions based on the key concepts to be learned, and constructs the I-Chart. These questions are recorded on the top row of the chart.
2. The interacting phase involves activating students' prior knowledge of the topic and recording that information on the chart. At this time, interesting information the students know about the topic and any questions that are raised are entered in the last two columns of the chart. Next, the resources are consulted and the information garnered is recorded on the chart.

3. During the integrating and evaluating phase, summary statements are recorded in the last row of each column. Students then compare the information they gathered with their prior knowledge. As new questions about the topic surface, students continue to research to find answers. These answers are then shared with the whole class.

Examples

Branley, Franklyn M. *The Sun: Our Nearest Star.* Illustrated by Edward Miller. 2002. 25p. New York: HarperCollins. (hc. 0-06-028534-6; pbk. 0-06-445202-6).
Grades: K–2. This simple to understand book explores the Sun by comparing it to things familiar to young children. For example, if the Sun were a beach ball, Earth would be the size of a pea. Vibrant computer-generated art spills across the pages. This book is from the Let's-Read-and-Find-Out Science series.

Gibbons, Gail. *Stargazers.* 1992. Unp. New York: Holiday House. (hc. 0-8234-0983-X).
Grades: 2–4. Basic information about stars including the Sun is accompanied by color illustrations and diagrams. Cross sections of refracting and reflecting telescopes are used to explain the differences between the two. Stargazing history and additional facts about stars are located at the end of the book.

Inquiry Chart

Topic	How far away are stars?	What are stars made of?	Interesting Facts and Figures	New Questions
What We Know				
The Sun: Our Nearest Star				
Stargazers				
Summary				

Figure 3.3. An inquiry chart for younger students might have only two books.

Gallant, Roy A. *Comets, Asteroids, and Meteorites.* 2001. 48p. New
York: Benchmark. (hc. 0-7614-1034-1).
Grades: 2–4. This introductory book includes basic facts and fascinat-
ing pieces of information, such as the comet pills that were sold in 1910
to protect people from the poisonous gas in the tail of Halley's comet.
The book concludes with a glossary, resources for finding out more,
and an index. This book is from the Kaleidoscope series.
Aronson, Billy. *Meteors: The Truth behind Shooting Stars.* 1996. 63p.
New York: Franklin Watts. (hc. 0-531-20242-9).
Grades: 3–5. Questions interspersed throughout the text actively involve readers as they learn about shooting stars. Photographs, illustrations, and diagrams complement the text and provide additional information about shooting stars. The book includes a glossary, books for
further reading, Internet resources, and an index. This book is from the
First Book series.
Bonar, Samantha. *Comets.* 1998. 63p. New York: Franklin Watts. (hc.
0-531-20301-8).
Grades: 3–5. This is a well-written book that provides a great deal of
information on these celestial bodies, such as what they are composed
of, where they come from, and their impact on humans. Color photographs, illustrations, and diagrams enhance the text. The book includes
a glossary, resources for additional research including web sites, and an
index. This book is from the First Book series.
Simon, Seymour. *Comets, Meteors, and Asteroids.* 1994. Unp. New
York: Mulberry Books. (hc. 0-613-07516-1; pbk. 0-688-15843-9).
Grades: 3–5. This book introduces comets, meteors, and asteroids to
students using striking, full-page color photographs and illustrations
accompanied by clear, succinct text. Students learn what comets, meteors, and asteroids are composed of and when they can be seen in the
sky. The material in this book lends itself to having students create a
chart comparing comets, meteors, and asteroids.
Poynter, Margaret. *Killer Asteroids.* 1996. 48p. Springfield, N.J.: Enslow Publishers. (hc. 0-89490-616-X).
Grades: 4–8. The intriguing title of this book immediately captures
students' attention and has them eagerly reading to learn about asteroids. Beginning with the disappearance of the dinosaurs the book then
explores other incidents of damage possibly caused by space debris
such as asteroids. The book includes a glossary, a chart of near-Earth
objects, books for further reading, and an index. This book is from the
Weird and Wacky Science series.

Chapter 3

Inquiry Chart

Topic	What are the differences between comets, meteors, and asteroids?	What are comets, meteors, and asteroids made of?	Why do scientists study comets, meteors, and asteroids?	Interesting Facts and Figures	New Questions
What We Know					
Comets, Asteroids, and Meteorites					
Meteors: The Truth behind Shooting Stars					
Comets					
Comets, Meteors, and Asteroids					
Killer Asteroids					
Summary					

Figure 3.4. Older students can work on inquiry charts using four or more books.

Additional Books and Resources

Asch, Frank. *The Sun Is My Favorite Star.* 2000. Unp. San Diego, Calif.: Gulliver Books. (hc. 0-15-202127-2).
Grades: P–1. Bright, colorful illustrations depict a child participating in everyday activities under a watchful Sun. A repeating refrain makes this a book that youngsters delight in reading again and again. Large print with only a few words on each page assures that beginning readers can read the book on their own.

Branley, Franklyn Masfield. *The International Space Station.* Illustrated by True Kelley. 2000. 32p. New York: HarperCollins. (hc. 0-06-028702-0).
Grades: K–3. Venture into outer space and join the astronauts as they build the space station. Then, head indoors with them to discover what it is like to live on the space station. Detailed diagrams and illustrations help to tell the story and encourage readers to one day travel to outer space. This book is from the Let's-Read-and-Find-Out Science series.

Langille, Jacqueline, and Bobbie Kalman. *The Space Shuttle.* 1998. 32p. New York: Crabtree Publishing. (hc. 0-86505-678-1; pbk. 0-86505-688-9).
Grades: 1–3. Brief chapters filled with color photographs depict life on the space shuttle. Cross sections of the space shuttle and a labeled photograph of the shuttle's toilet capture students' attention as they learn about living and working in space. A glossary and an index are included. From the Bobbie Kalman Eye on the Universe series.

Graham, Ian. *The Best Book of Spaceships.* 1998. 33p. New York: Kingfisher Publications. (hc. 0-7534-5133-6).
Grades: 2–4. Beginning with an introduction to space the book blasts off into a journey into space. Students read about spacecraft, working in space, orbiting satellites, and space probes. Colorful illustrations fill the pages of this exciting book, which includes a glossary and an index.

Bond, Peter. *DK Guide to Space.* 1999. 64p. New York: DK Publishing. (hc. 0-7894-3946-8).
Grades: 3–5. Filled with color photographs taken by the Hubble telescope and NASA's robotic probes, this is a tantalizing visual exploration of space. The planets, the Sun, the Moon, the stars, the space shuttle, and space stations are all included in this survey of space. Short blocks of text encourage students to read the sections most useful to their research. A section on space data contains charts, a chronology, and web sites. The book concludes with an index.

Jones, Thomas D., and June A. English. *Mission Earth: Voyage to the Home Planet.* 1996. 42p. New York: Scholastic. (hc. 0-590-48571-7).

Grades: 4–8. Astronaut Thomas Jones and science writer June English worked together to show students how astronauts are studying Earth from space to determine its ecological health. While in space Jones and his crew photographed Earth and recorded information about their flight. English explains the ecological challenges that make this mission essential to our understanding of Earth's ecological health.

Spangenburg, Ray, and Kit Moser. *A Look at the Sun.* 2001. 111p. New York: Franklin Watts. (hc. 0-531-11764-2; pbk. 0-531-16565-5).

Grades: 4–8. From ancient times to the present, scientists have wondered about the Sun, and this book explores past and present theories and research. The last chapter is an intriguing examination of what will happen when the Sun dies. Photographs, illustrations, and diagrams enhance the text. The book includes a chart of missions to the Sun, a timeline, a glossary, resources for finding out more, and an index.

Fradin, Dennis Brindell. *The Planet Hunters: The Search for Other Worlds.* 1997. 147p. New York: Margaret K. McElderry Books. (hc. 0-689-81323-6).

Grades: 5–8. Will our search for other worlds lead us to the discovery that we are not alone in the universe? Readers ponder that question after they read about the discovery of the planets in our solar system. The book contains interviews and stories about people who discovered and named the planets. Spectacular photographs, black-and-white illustrations, a chart about the numbers used in the book, information on metric measurements, a bibliography, and an index are included.

Starry Night Backyard is an interactive multimedia software program that introduces students to astronomy as they explore the wonders of the night sky. With a click of the mouse students travel to the planets and view the stars. This software is appropriate for ages eight and up and is available on CD-ROM for both Macintosh and Windows computers. Space.com produced this software program.

StarDate Online is a web site maintained by the University of Texas McDonald Observatory. There are links on the site to a news and features section, an image gallery, a solar system guide, a constellation guide, a star guide, a galaxy guide, an astroglossary, and a resources list. The site also contains resources for teachers, which include grade level appropriate classroom activities. Navigating the site is quick and easy. The observatory also publishes *StarDate* magazine.

Study Guides

Study guides focus students' attention as they read content area material. While often used with content area textbooks, study guides are also used with trade books. The statements or questions in study guides include different comprehension levels and take into consideration students' reading levels. Completing study guides requires students to reflect on their reading and reorganize the material to make it personally meaningful. Almasi and McKeown (1996) found that students became engaged learners when they interacted with the text to generate meaningful interpretations. As students become familiar with study guides, they should be encouraged to create their own. (See figures 3.5 and 3.6.)

Steps

1. Locate the key concepts contained in the book.
2. Write statements or questions that will help the students focus on the concepts using a variety of comprehension levels.
3. Go over the study guide with the students and explain to them that as they read they should respond to the questions and statements.
4. To model the use of study guides read a book aloud to the students and stop to complete the guide as the answers are located.
5. Have the students work in small groups to read another book and complete a study guide.
6. Encourage the students to use the study guide when preparing for a test.

Examples

Dussling, Jennifer. *Stars.* Illustrated by Mavis Smith. 1996. 32p. New York: Grosset and Dunlap. (hc. 0-448-41149-0; pbk. 0-448-41148-2). Grades: P–1. The book provides basic information about the stars and is written for beginning readers. Students enjoy reading on their own about the Sun, the composition of stars, the description of what happens during an eclipse, and how early navigators used the stars for

guidance. The colorful illustrations appeal to young readers and provide additional information about stars. This book is from the All
Aboard Reading series.

Study Guide

What is a star?		
If stars are very, very big, why do they look so small?		
Why do we need the Sun?		
What is an eclipse?		

Figure 3.5. Study guides such as this one can be used with younger
students in a whole class setting where the teacher and students complete the guide together.

Simon, Seymour. *Galaxies.* 1991. Unp. New York: A Mulberry Paperback Book. (hc. 0-688-10992-6).

Grades: 3–5. Gazing up at night students see the millions of stars that form the Milky Way. Using picturesque text and full-page color photographs and computer-enhanced pictures of stars, galaxies, comets, meteors, and asteroids, Simon immerses students in learning about them. Students learn about different kinds of galaxies, their locations, and their movements.

Study Guide

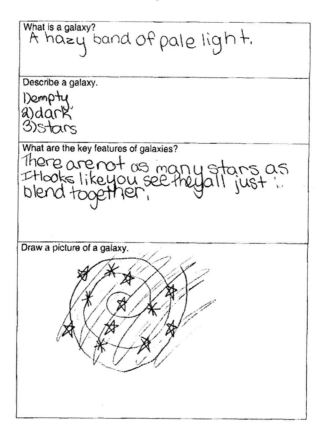

Figure 3.6. This study guide was completed by a fourth-grade student while reading *Galaxies*.

Additional Books and Resources

Brimner, Larry Dane. *Mercury.* 1998. 47p. New York: Children's Press.
(hc. 0-516-20619-2).
Grades: P–2. This is an introductory look at Mercury, the planet closest to
the Sun. Photographs, illustrations, and diagrams combined with easy-to-
read text assure that young astronomers can read and understand this book
on their own. The book includes resources for learning more, a glossary,
and an index. This book is from the A True Book series.

Bredeson, Carmen. *Pluto.* 2001. 63p. New York: Franklin Watts. (hc. 0-
531-11784-7; pbk. 0-531-13988-3).
Grades: 3–5. Students read about the diligent, hard work of Clyde Tom-
baugh that led to the discovery of Pluto. Reproductions, photographs,
charts, and illustrations provide a wealth of information on Pluto. The book
concludes with a glossary, resources for learning more, and an index. This
book is from the Watts Library.

Exploring Space. 1993. 48p. New York: Scholastic. (hc. 0-590-47615-7).
Grades: 3–5. This interactive book has wheels to turn, transparent
pages to flip, pages to fold out, a tiny book to read, and stickers to
place. The glossy, black pages are filled with illustrations. There are
brief descriptions of the stars, the planets, the Moon, and the Sun. Additional resources, sky facts, a glossary, and an index are found at the
back of the book. This book is from the Scholastic Voyages of Discovery series.

Simon, Seymour. *Destination: Space.* 2002. Unp. New York: Harper-
Collins. (hc. 0-688-16289-4).
Grades: 3–5. The Hubble space telescope has been sending spectacular
pictures from space. Simon carefully selected the images included in
the book and provides a descriptive narrative to explain the discoveries
revealed in the pictures and the puzzles that remain.

——. *The Universe.* 1998. Unp. New York: HarperCollins. (hc. 0-688-
15301-1; pbk. 0-06-443752-3).
Grades: 3–5. Bright, fiery illustrations and photographs depict our expanding universe. Simon explains the Big Bang and takes readers on an
exciting exploration of the stars, galaxies, and planets that make up the
universe.

Gallant, Roy A. *The Life Stories of Stars.* 2000. 80p. New York:
Benchmark Books. (hc. 0-7614-1152-6).
Grades: 4–8. Past theories about stars and present research about stars
make fascinating reading. Students meet renowned astronomers and

physicists such as Dr. Annie Jump Cannon who classified more than 350,000 stars. The book includes a glossary, books for further reading, and an index. This book is from The Stories of Science series.

Miller, Ron. *Extrasolar Planets.* 2002. 95p. Brookfield, Conn.: The Millbrook Press. (hc. 0-7613-2354-6).

Grades: 4–8. The book begins with information on the discovery of the nine planets in our solar system. Then, it explores the possibility of planets beyond our solar system. The author's illustrations and photographs from NASA complement the text and contain additional information. The book concludes with a glossary, resources for learning more, and an index. This book is from the Worlds Beyond series.

NASA Kids is a collection of online resources for children from ages five to fourteen. It is located at http://kids.msfc.nasa.gov/. There are links such as Space and Beyond, Rockets and Airplanes, Astronauts Living in Space, and a Club House that includes a Parent Login link. The Teacher's Corner link has resources to supplement the materials for students.

KidsAstronomy.com is an award-winning site just for young stargazers and is located at http://www.kidsastronomy.com/. Designed just for kids this site defines unfamiliar terms such as *parallax* using words and examples that children can understand. There is also a version of the site available for those with low-speed connections. Links take students to information on the solar system, the universe, and space exploration. The Astro Fun Zone link contains a variety of games, puzzles, movies, and jokes. The site also includes a teacher's corner and a dictionary.

SpaceWeather.com posts the current weather conditions in space. Visitors to this site learn about solar flares, geomagnetic storms, asteroids, sunspots, and a variety of other space weather phenomena. There are also galleries of pictures and a collection of essential web links. This site can be accessed at http://www.spaceweather.com/.

References

Almasi, Janice F., and Margaret G. McKeown. "The Nature of Engaged Reading in Classroom Discussions of Literature." *Journal of Literacy Research* 28, no. 1 (March 1996): 107–146.

Hoffman, James V. "Critical Reading/Thinking across the Curriculum: Using I-Charts to Support Learning." *Language Arts* 69, no. 2 (Feb. 1992): 121–127.

National Science Education Standards. Washington, D.C.: National Academy Press, 1995. http://stills.nap.edu/readingroom/books/nses/ (20 Nov. 2002).

Readence, John E., Thomas W. Bean, and R. Scott Baldwin. *Content Area Reading: An Integrated Approach*, 6th ed. Dubuque, Iowa: Kendall/Hunt, 1998.

· 4 ·
Weather

There is perhaps no other topic that so greatly impacts us all than that of weather. We get up in the morning, and what we decide to wear is based on the type of weather that has been forecast. In Seymour Simon's *Weather*, he states:

> It's cloudy today. It's also sunny, rainy, and snowy, hot and cold, calm and windy, dry and damp. Each of these descriptions of the weather is true every day of the year someplace in the world.

There is weather all around us all of the time. The launch date of NASA space shuttles can be delayed or canceled by adverse weather conditions. Severe weather can force people to change daily routines to escape the forces of nature. Hurricanes cause many to flee being in the direct path of high winds and a high storm surge, while tornadoes force many to take shelter in basements to escape destructive winds. Agriculture is impacted regarding when to plant and when to harvest as a direct result of weather conditions during planting seasons. Since we are so dependent on weather conditions in many ways, it is a topic of exploration that is easily pursued and readily available to us all. Using the forecasts available through newspapers, radio, television, and the Internet, students can investigate the weather locally, nationally, and internationally. Working with students to organize this vast array of information becomes even more important when studying the many topics related to weather. The *National Science Education Standards* (NSES, 1995), reflected in this chapter are science as inquiry, earth science, and science and technology. The organizers discussed include concept guides, tree diagrams, and flow diagrams.

Concept Guides

Concept guides extend and reinforce the notions that concepts are hier-
archically ordered in informational material and that some ideas are
subordinate to others (Vacca and Vacca, 2002). This type of organizer
can help students organize details as they relate to main ideas in a passage. The concept guide in figure 4.1 shows students that each of the
weather phenomena listed, tornadoes and hurricanes, has an impact on
whatever is in its path. After reading through a book about hurricanes
and a different book about tornadoes, students identify what impact
each type of weather system has on structures and people.

A variation on the concept guide is the pattern guide, which can be
arranged in a three-tier format with statements in the first addressing
literal level comprehension, in the second addressing interpretive level
comprehension, and in the third addressing applied level comprehension (Vacca and Vacca, 2002). A pattern guide helps students perceive
and use the major text relationships that predominate in the reading
material (Vacca and Vacca, 2002). The statements included in the pattern guide are a mix of ones that would be consistent with patterns in
the story as well as those that would not be consistent with patterns in
the story. The idea is for students to be able to recognize patterns that
predominate over a long piece of text. Figure 4.2 illustrates an example
of the pattern guide that could be used by students to see how information that is read fits together.

Steps

1. Identify the important concepts in the material.
2. Locate information about each concept within the material.
3. Construct the pattern guide listing these concepts. In figure 4.1, the
   concepts are divided into cause and effect. The causes are listed on
   the left side of the pattern guide, and the effects are listed across
   the top columns.
4. Clues can also be provided towards specific portions of text or
   page numbers to help guide students in locating the information.
5. Students can work in small groups or with a partner to locate and
   record the information in the concept guide.
6. Once students have completed the concept guide, then review together the answers they recorded.

7. A class concept guide could be compiled using the information brought together from the individual groups.

8. Display the individual concept guides or class concept guide in the classroom, so students can continue to use the information as a resource.

Examples

Lauber, Patricia. *Hurricanes: Earth's Mightiest Storms.* 1996. 64p. New York: Scholastic. (pbk. 0-590-47407-3).
Grades: 3–8. Lauber provides photographs, maps, and diagrams in this book that describes hurricanes. The destruction that can be caused by hurricanes is addressed through chapters about defining a hurricane, going into the eye of the storm, and assessing winds and damage.
Simon, Seymour. *Tornadoes.* 1999. Unp. New York: Scholastic. (pbk. 0-439-18935-7).
Grades: 3–8. Simon includes photographs of actual tornadoes and the damage caused along with maps and diagrams that detail processes and paths that tornadoes follow. The larger-style, bold-faced text makes the content reader-friendly so that children can easily read about this topic.

Concept Guide

Causes	On Structures	On People	Other
Hurricanes	- destroys buildings --tears off walls and roof --flattens them	- drown people - people lose homes - people go north during hurricanes	high winds - 75 or more mph - flooding
Tornadoes	- takes off roofs - tears down walls - makes trees fall	- people lose their homes, clothing - injures and kills	- wind can pick up animals - 73 to 112 mph winds - F4 - 207-260 mph - F5 - more than 261 mph

Figure 4.1. This pattern guide was developed using Seymour Simon's *Tornadoes* and Patricia Lauber's *Hurricanes*.

Wind and Weather. 1994. 46p. New York: Scholastic. (hc. 0-590-
    47646-7).
Grades: 4–8. This text is part of the Scholastic Voyages of Discovery
series. It includes a variety of information about air, clouds, weather
forms, wind, and climates. Numerous photographs, labeled pictures,
diagrams, and charts are used to illustrate the weather concepts.

Concept Guide

Where is weather measured?	What tools are used?	What does each tool record?
On water		
In a shelter		
In the air		
On land		

Figure 4.2. Students use this concept guide to determine information
about weather tools.

Additional Books and Resources

Anholt, Catherine, and Laurence Anholt. *Chimp and Zee and the
    Big Storm*. 2002. Unp. New York: Putnam. (hc. 0-8037-2700-3).
Grades: P–2. This narrative story is about two chimps, Chimp and Zee,
who go help their father bring in the laundry before a storm. While the
chimps are playing with a sheet, a big wind carries the two monkeys
away. The Anholts' story would be useful in illustrating the concept of
a storm in a visual-friendly format for young children.
Kurtz, Jane. *Rain Romp: Stomping Away a Grouchy Day*. Illustrated
    by Dyanna Wolcott. 2002. Unp. New York: HarperCollins. (hc. 0-
    06-029805-7).

Grades: P–2. This book is a metaphorical contrast between a child's moods and a rainy day and a sunny day. The rhythmic pattern of the text and the colorful illustrations invite students to join in with the reading of the story. Along the way, they can compare and contrast a sunny day and rainy day as to what each looks like and feels like.

Branley, Franklyn M. *Snow Is Falling.* Illustrated by Holly Keller. 2000. 33p. New York: HarperCollins. (hc. 0-06-027991-5).

Grades: 1–4. Originally published in 1963, this text has been updated with illustrations by Holly Keller. The visual nature of the pictures guides readers through a walk in the snow where they learn about snowflakes, how the snow feels, what it looks like, what you can do with it, and how the snow helps hibernating animals. Branley's text also discusses how people build houses out of snow. Included at the back of the book are two snow experiments to investigate, snow web sites, and other books about snow.

Casey, Denise. *Weather Everywhere.* Photographs by Jackie Gilmore. 1995. 36p. New York: Simon and Schuster. (hc. 0-02-717777-7).

Grades: 1–5. Photographs and diagrams illustrate the weather that is all around us. Topics covered include what makes up the atmosphere, the earth's rotation and temperature, and differences in temperature around the world. A three-page glossary at the end of the book further defines weather-related concepts. This book is from the Science Experiments series.

Hooker, Merrilee. *Disaster: Hurricanes.* 1993. 24p. Vero Beach, Fla.: The Rourke Book Company. (hc. 0-86593-243-3).

Grades: 2–6. Concepts covered include how a hurricane begins, how hurricanes work, when and where they strike, and studying hurricanes. Hooker also includes a discussion of how hurricanes are named, as well as what constitutes a hurricane warning. The table of contents, glossary, and index enable the reader to easily locate hurricane-specific information.

Rodgers, Alan, and Angella Streluk. *Temperature.* 2002. 32p. Chicago, Ill.: Reed Educational and Professional Publishing. (hc. 1-58810-689-9).

Grades: 3–6. Questions ranging from how should we read a thermometer to how do we measure soil temperature are answered in this book on temperature. Charts, tables, and diagrams are used to illustrate numerous temperature-related concepts so that children are able to access the information in the text. It includes ideas for measuring the temperature with examples from around the world along with a glossary of weather terminology.

Farndon, John. *Weather.* 2001. 32p. Tarrytown, N.Y.: Marshall Cavendish. (hc. 0-7614-1089-9).
Grades: 3–8. Try out the hands-on explorations in this book to learn
how the Sun impacts our weather, how the winds blow, and how hurricanes and tornadoes form. Then explore clouds, humidity, rain, and
storms. Concise text, color photographs, diagrams, and step-by-step
instructions encourage students to read and experiment as they learn
about weather. The book includes experiments, a glossary, and an index.
Simon, Seymour. *Lightning.* 1997. Unp. New York: Scholastic. (pbk.
0-590-12122-7).
Grades: 3–8. Seymour Simon continues his trademark format by using
full-color photographs to illustrate the power of lightning. The speed
that lightning travels, the brightness of lightning, how it is formed, and
the sequence of events that occurs as lightning travels are discussed.
Gibbons, Gail. *Weather Forecasting.* 1987. Unp. New York: Four
Winds Press. (hc. 0-02-737250-2).
Grades: 4–8. Gibbons uses a seasonal approach to look at variations in
weather and how weather forecasters gather information. The labeled
pictures and diagrams dominate the pages, but the text included adds
information that further extends the concepts.

The Weather Classroom, provided as a service through
Weather.Com (http://www.weather.com/education/?from=footer), has
information and resources for teachers and students. The show is also
available as a Monday–Thursday daily broadcast, and teachers are encouraged to record it to use as a classroom resource for students in
grades five through ten.

Tree Diagrams

The tree diagram can be used to organize information in hierarchies,
according to groups and subgroups (Moline, 1995). Using the tree diagram in such a way enables students to examine relationships between
the groups and subgroups that are determined through the activity. Students can use numbers or arrows to show directionality in a diagram,
they can read a tree and interpret its information as verbal text, and they
can organize a plan of a writing task or a summary of a reading activity,
using a web (Moline, 1995). McKenna and Robinson (1997) encourage

teachers and students to return to past organizers to integrate new words into the existing diagram. Expanding old diagrams in this way causes students to reconsider previous material but does so in a manner that underscores meaning and aids the students in getting the "big picture" of how knowledge in a given content area is organized (McKenna and Robinson, 1997, p. 242).

Steps

1. Identify ten to twelve vocabulary words that are related to the topic being studied.
2. Write the vocabulary words on index cards.
3. Pick out one of the vocabulary words and ask students if any of the other words go with that word. Group those cards together.
4. Continue selecting words and asking students what other words might go with each one.
5. As students work, it should become clear that some of the words could be used as a larger label for groups of words.
6. Gradually rearrange the cards until the relationships between words are identified.
7. Draw the resulting diagram on butcher paper. *Microsoft PowerPoint* or *Inspiration* software can also be used to easily replicate the diagram.
8. Ask students to add more categories to the tree diagram by using the book resources available in the classroom or library. Information could be continuously added during the study of this topic.

Examples

Simon, Seymour. *Weather.* 1993. Unp. New York: William Morrow. (pbk. 0-688-10547-5).
Grades: 3–8. Rich with weather-related vocabulary, this book expands on such concepts as troposphere (see figure 4.3), solar radiation, greenhouse effect, and much more. Full-color photographs along with labeled diagrams and charts help to illustrate air masses and cloud formations. For example, children are helped to understand the concept of dew when they view the picture of two flowers with water droplets clinging to the spider's web that has been spun between them. Simon's visual illustrations join together with text to help readers gain a better understanding of weather.

Tree Diagram

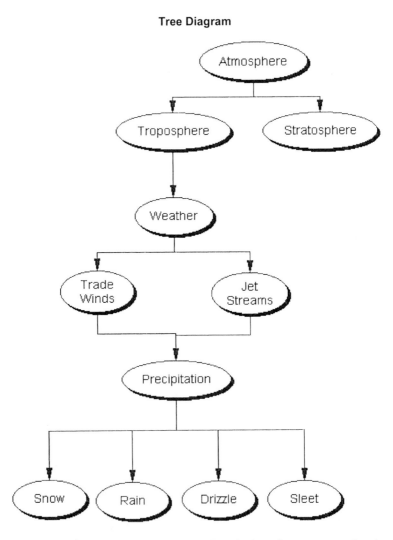

Figure 4.3. This tree diagram is used to look at how our weather is formed in the troposphere.

Rodgers, Alan, and Angella Streluk. *Forecasting the Weather.* 2003.
    32p. Chicago, Ill.: Reed Educational and Professional Publishing.
    (hc. 158810687-1).

Grades: 3–8. This text by Rodgers and Streluk addresses how we get our weather, how it is measured (see figure 4.4), and what weather symbols mean. Using a similar format as their other texts, the authors use charts, tables, and diagrams to organize weather information to help students learn more about how to forecast. Students are introduced to weather stations, weather sayings, professional weather forecasts, and record-breaking weather.

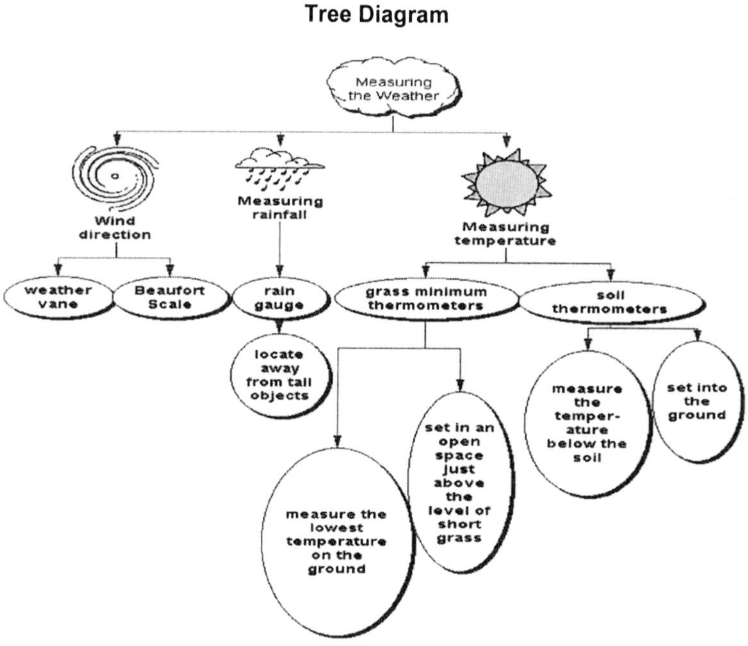

Tree Diagram

Figure 4.4. This tree diagram, drawn using *Inspiration* software, details the concepts and subconcepts of measuring the weather.

Additional Books and Resources

Barrett, Judi. *Cloudy with a Chance of Meatballs.* Illustrated by Ron Barrett. 1984. Unp. New York: Atheneum. (hc. 0-689-30647-4).
Grades: K–3. A tall tale about a huge storm that is told using references to food. In the town of Chewsandswallows, the townspeople had no need to shop for food in stores. Instead, they were supplied all the food

they could want by the sky at breakfast, lunch, and dinner. There would
be soup and juice rain, mashed potatoes and green peas snow, and
hamburger storms. The leftover food was used to feed the dogs and cats
or the fish, turtles, and whales. The weather took a turn for the worse
when there was nothing but Gorgonzola cheese one day, another day
there was only broccoli, and another day only brussels sprouts and pea-
nut butter. The weather became so unstable that the people were forced
to abandon the town. The food illustrations throughout make it a fun
story to begin an investigation of weather.

Berger, Melvin, and Gilda Berger. *Do Tornadoes Really Twist?:
    Questions and Answers about Tornadoes and Hurricanes.* Illus-
    trated by Barbara Higgins Bond. 2000. 48p. New York: Scholastic
    Reference. (hc. 0-439-09584-0; pbk. 0-439-14880-4).

Grades: 3–6. Tornadoes and hurricanes are formidable, destructive
forces of nature. This text is filled with factual information and weird
facts that capture students' imaginations. The question and answer format of the book enables readers to skip around through the text and find
the answers to their questions. One page of each two-page spread has
beautiful, detailed, full-page illustrations and diagrams. An index concludes the book.

Kerrod, Robin. *The Weather.* Illustrated by Ted Evans. 1994. 64p.
    New York: Marshall Cavendish. (hc. 1-85435-630-5).

Grades: 3–8. Comprised of three chapters, the book covers air on the
move, moisture in the air, and seasons and climates. The photographs,
diagrams, charts, and maps help to illustrate weather concepts.

Rodgers, Alan, and Angella Streluk. *Cloud Cover.* 2003. 32p. Chi-
    cago, Ill.: Reed Educational and Professional Publishing. (hc.
    158810686-1).

Grades: 3–8. Rodgers and Streluk look at how the Sun affects the
weather, where clouds come from, and how we measure cloud cover.
Charts, tables, and diagrams are used to illustrate such concepts as
weather symbols, UV exposure levels, and types of clouds. A table of
contents, an index, and a glossary enable the reader to easily access
specific information.

Mogil, H. Michael. *Tornadoes.* 2001. 72p. Stillwater, Minn.: Voyageur
    Press. (pbk. 0-89658-522-0).

Grades: 4–8. Students are always fascinated by weather extremes, and
this text on tornadoes will hold the interest of older readers. The photographs of actual tornadoes along with a discussion of structure and
format help readers to gain a broader understanding of this weather
phenomenon. The many faces of thunderstorms are addressed with

photographs describing what is meant by a "supercell" and the cloud formations that typify it. A map of "Tornado Alley" is included that shows where tornadoes are most often found.

Murphy, Jim. *Blizzard!* 2000. 133p. New York: Scholastic Press. (hc. 0-590-67309-2).

Grades: 5–8. This is a chilling, fascinating account of the 1888 blizzard that hit the Northeast. The focus of the book is on the blizzard's impact on New York City. Personal accounts and newspaper articles present a very personal side to the story and provide glimpses of life in the 1800s. Stark, bleak photographs and illustrations help the reader understand how the snow immobilized the region. The book concludes with an index.

The Weather Underground (www.wunderground.com) is another weather web site that provides information about the heat index, wind chill, humidity, radar maps, the dew point, wind, visibility, and the jet stream. There are a variety of maps that can be accessed through this weather resource, too.

Information about weather for active lives is available through http://www.intellicast.com/. This web site also has a place for the viewer to pick an activity, such as going to the beach, skiing, driving, playing golf, and gardening, then type in a particular city or ZIP Code, and the web site will pull up information for that activity. Students enjoy clicking on their favorite pastimes.

The National Hurricane Center provided through the National Oceanic and Atmospheric Administration (NOAA) includes links for finding out more information about how hurricanes are formed, looking at active tropical systems, and reading about previous deadly hurricanes. This web site (http://www.nhc.noaa.gov/) also includes blank tracking charts that can be printed out and used as a classroom resource. Using these charts to track active hurricanes provides students an authentic learning activity as they practice their map reading skills. These charts can be updated each morning when the students first come to class.

Web Weather for Kids provides information, activities, and resources for thunderclouds, lightning, tornadoes, hurricanes, and blizzards. This site, http://www.ucar.edu/40th/webweather/index.html, also includes information about safety, games, stories, and weather ingredients for students to simulate different types of weather.

Flow Diagrams

A flow diagram links its subjects with lines or arrows to show a process that moves through time (such as a life cycle) or space (such as the water cycle) (Moline, 1995). Using the context of weather, the flow diagram can be used to illustrate or summarize a process using text, arrows, or numbers to show directionality and possible choices. As a summary of interconnected events or causes with several results, a flow diagram can be a clearer and more concise record than several pages of verbal text (Moline, 1995). Flow diagrams can range from simple linear diagrams (see figure 4.5) to cyclical flow diagrams (see figure 4.6).

Steps

1. Select a topic and ask students to brainstorm its origin. Moline (1995) used the topic of where his egg sandwich came from, and asked his students to generate a list of ideas that relate to the origin of the topic (i.e. egg sandwich).
2. Once the ideas are down on paper or chalkboard, then ask students to look at how to sequence the ideas to determine how the topic developed from start to finish.
3. Arrange the ideas in the correct sequence. Arrows, numbers, key vocabulary words, or phrases can be added to join together pieces of information in the flow diagram.
4. Once the diagram is created, then ask students to explain parts of it to the rest of the class going from start to finish.

Examples

Dewitt, Lynda. *What Will the Weather Be?* Illustrated by Carolyn Croll. 1991. 32p. New York: HarperCollins. (hc. 0-06-021597-6).
Grades: K–3. Dewitt introduces young readers to what scientists know about weather, and what scientists cannot know about the weather. The unpredictable nature of weather is addressed in this picture book format that includes simple diagrams illustrating such concepts as warm front and cold front as well as pictures that illustrate types of instruments used to collect weather data.

Flow Diagram

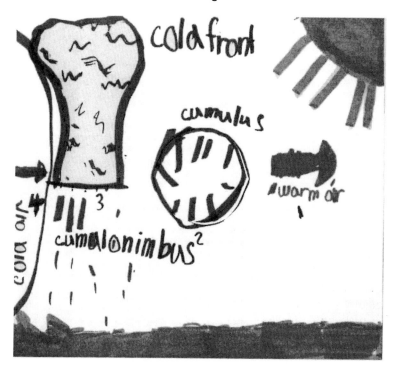

Figure 4.5. Illustration of the sequence of events that occurs when a cold front moves into an area. The warm air is pushed ahead, and cumulus clouds follow behind the warm air with the accumulation of cumulonimbus clouds and rain. The cold air usually follows the resulting thunderstorms.

Rodgers, Alan, and Angella Streluk. *Precipitation.* 2003. 32p. Chicago, Ill.: Reed Educational and Professional Publishing. (hc. 158810688-8).

Grades: 3–8. Questions answered by this book include where does rain come from, how is snow measured, and what is precipitation. Numerous charts, graphs, and diagrams illustrate such concepts as measuring rainfall, humidity, frontal systems, microbursts, and rain and snow warnings. The text includes a table of contents, a glossary, an index, and a listing of other books to read about precipitation.

Flow Diagram

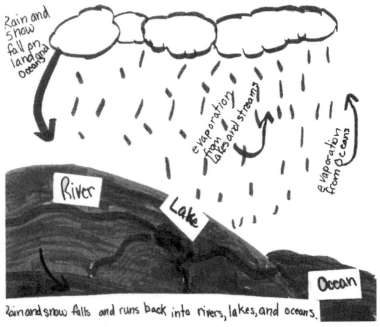

Rain and snow fall on land and oceans

evaporation from lakes and streams

evaporation from ocean

River

Lake

Ocean

Rain and snow falls and runs back into rivers, lakes, and oceans.

Figure 4.6. Depiction of the water cycle illustrating the cyclical nature of this process. The rain and snow fall on land, rivers, streams, and oceans. The arrows indicate the precipitation as well as the evaporation from rivers, lakes, and streams that goes back up into the atmosphere.

Additional Books and Resources

Cole, Joanna. *The Magic School Bus Inside a Hurricane.* Illustrated by Bruce Degen. 1995. Unp. New York: Scholastic. (hc. 0-590-44687-8).
Grades: 1–5. The mix of narrative and nonfiction that is representative of the Magic School Bus books is continued with this exploration into hurricanes with Mrs. Frizzle's class. The charts, graphs, diagrams, and pictures provide children with an array of information resources with which to learn more about this weather phenomenon. From the students' spelling list of weather words tacked to the wall to the journal

entries about lightning by Ralphie, Keesha, and Phoebe, there is a wealth of basic weather information for the novice meteorologist. Students travel along with Mrs. Frizzle's class as the bus morphs into a hot air balloon followed by an airplane, and they learn more about the sequence of events that occurs as the hurricane develops. Once the class arrives back at school, they complete and share their weather projects.

Supraner, Robyn. *I Can Read about Weather.* Illustrated by Courtney Studio and Dennis Davidson. 1997. 46p. Mahway, N.J: Troll Communications. (hc. 0-8167-4206-5).

Grades: 2–5. This text introduces children to the concept of weather with a simple dialogue that explains how all of our weather starts with the sun. The sequence of events that occurs on a hot day is discussed with an overview of clouds included. Rain, snow, and hail are described with picture illustrations. There is a brief discussion of meteorologists and resources used to forecast as well as a summary of more severe weather such as the tornado, hurricane, and blizzard.

Peacock, Graham. *Meteorology.* 1994. 32p. New York: Thomson Learning. (hc. 1-56847-194-7).

Grades: 2–8. Questions that are answered by Peacock's book include why the wind blows, what are clouds made of, and what causes thunder and lightning. Step-by-step directions are shown so that students can do simple science experiments such as how much the temperature changes in a day, measuring rainfall and observing what happens to plants in freezing weather, and turning water vapor to liquid.

Rodgers, Alan, and Angella Streluk. *Wind and Air Pressure.* 2003. 32p. Chicago, Ill.: Reed Educational and Professional Publishing. (hc. 158810690-X).

Grades: 3–8. This book answers questions about where the wind comes from, what an anemometer is, and who invented the Beaufort Scale. Other topics covered in the book are wind direction, the wind chill, using technology to monitor the wind, extreme winds, global winds, and air pressure. Photographs that further illustrate the topics are also included throughout the text. A table of contents, a glossary, and an index help the reader to easily locate information in the text. A listing of other books related to the topic is also included.

Taylor-Cork, Barbara. *Be an Expert Weather Forecaster.* 1992. 32p. New York: Aladdin Books. (hc. 0-531-17267-8).

Grades: 3–8. Pictures, photographs, diagrams, and projects are included in this weather book so that students can learn about different weather conditions, how to make weather equipment, how to record weather conditions, and how to make predictions about changes in weather.

Pringle, Laurence. *Global Warming: The Threat of Earth's Changing Climate.* 2001. 48p. New York: Seastar Books. (hc. 1-58717-009-4). Grades: 4–8. Color photographs and diagrams help to tell the story of this looming environmental problem. This thoroughly researched text defines global warming and then explains its impact on our environment and our lives. The author describes what has been done to reduce global warming and the obstacles that impede progress. A glossary and an index are included.

Everything Weather, software developed by the Weather Channel and published by Sunburst Communications, teaches weather through activities, video, photographs, interactive maps, articles, and a glossary. Designed for grades four through eight, the software helps students: a) identify various types of cloud formations and learn their importance as indicators of approaching weather, b) track hurricanes and input the latitude and longitude of a current tropical storm and instantly compare its track to the paths of major twentieth-century hurricanes, c) learn to calculate the closeness of a thunderstorm by timing the lightning, d) explore the wind-chill phenomenon, e) view tornadoes from every angle, f) create weather journals filled with a wealth of weather facts, and g) determine average precipitation, snowfall, and frequency of thunderstorms in specific cities and regions using United States and Global Climate Data.

The *Water Cycle* software for grades four through six by Tom Snyder Productions covers the topics of water cycle, condensation and evaporation, and states of matter. The software shows meteorologist Maria Hernandez taking the stand as a witness in the case of Pip Peterson's leaky pipes. Students have to decide if the pipes are really leaky or if Pip has been a victim of the water cycle.

One weather resource, http://www.weather.com, enables the user to input the ZIP Code or city name to locate weather information. The web site has information about health issues such as pollen counts, air quality forecasts, and skin protection. There is also a link to vacation resources that includes a vacation planner, daily traveler, interstate forecast, and daily driving forecast. Other available resources include special events (e.g. sporting), recreation (e.g. boats, parks), and home and garden information.

The web site Interactive Weather Information Network (http://iwin.nws.noaa.gov/iwin/graphicsversion/main.html) is provided by the National Weather Service. Viewers are able to access information about local weather, national items, and world weather. In addition, a section for national warnings provides current weather information for weather conditions around the United States. Warning categories that are available include flood, flash floods, coastal floods, tornadoes, hurricanes, severe thunderstorm, non-precipitation (e.g. fog), and winter storm.

Other web resources that are location specific include the Commonwealth Bureau of Meteorology located in Australia (http://www.bom.gov.au/), the Weather Network located in Canada (http://www.theweathernetwork.com/), the BBC Weather Center (http://www.bbc.co.uk/weather/) in the United Kingdom, and OnlineWeather.Com (http://www.onlineweather.com/) in the United Kingdom and Ireland.

The National Oceanic and Atmospheric Administration (NOAA), found at http://www.nws.noaa.gov, "provides weather forecasts and warnings in many different languages throughout a large expanse of the Pacific. This area includes the Islands of Hawaii, Guam, the Northern Mariana Islands, the Federated States of Micronesia, the Republic of the Marshall Islands, the Republic of Palau, and south to American Samoa. Chuukese, Pohnpeian, and Yapese are among the languages used by NWS forecasters in this region." Sections that can be selected include information about warnings, observations, forecasts, and education.

References

McKenna, Michael C., and Richard D. Robinson. *Teaching through Text: A Content Literacy Approach to Content Area Reading*, 2nd ed. White Plains, N.Y.: Longman, 1997.

Moline, Steve. *I See What You Mean: Children at Work with Visual Information*. York, Maine: Stenhouse, 1995.

National Science Education Standards. Washington, D.C.: National Academy Press, 1995. http://stills.nap.edu/readingroom/books/nses/ (20 Nov. 2002).

Vacca, Richard T., and Jo Anne L. Vacca. *Content Area Reading: Literacy and Learning across the Curriculum*, 7th ed. Boston, Mass.: Allyn and Bacon, 2002.

·5·
Habitats and Biomes

This chapter on habitats encourages the investigation of life forms that are found in complex environments. These environments will vary in temperature, moisture, light, and diversity, as well as other factors. The various forms of life that are found within each environment join together to make an extremely complex community of living organisms known as a biome.

Five major types of biomes that can be investigated include aquatic, desert, forest, tundra, and grassland. An exploration of habitats or biomes builds on the third strand of the *National Science Education Standards* (NSES, 1995), which requires students to have an understanding of the characteristics of organisms and their environments including adaptations and ecosystems. Graphic organizers in this chapter include picture glossaries, T-charts, and matrixes.

Picture Glossaries

Picture glossaries are simple diagrams that help the reader to identify, differentiate, or define items within a group or parts of a whole (Moline, 1995). One purpose of the picture glossary can be to classify subgroups as each relates to an overall concept. When exploring habitats, the picture glossary can be used to show the types of animals in their homes within the particular habitat or biome. The picture glossary can be used with any subject where it is useful to name its parts and understand their relative positions (Moline, 1995).

Richardson and Morgan (2003) suggest that children can create picture glossaries by using individual cards, which can then also be used to practice alphabetizing skills according to key index words. The picture glossary in this chapter is used in a broader context to look at habitats. In Chapter 2, a variation of the picture glossary, the labeled diagram, is also discussed. The labeled diagram could also be used to form a number of entries in a picture glossary. (See figures 5.1 and 5.2.)

Steps

1. Show students pictures of simple diagrams that illustrate graphic information about a topic.
2. Discuss the types of graphic information that are shown in the diagram.
3. Another option is to work with your students to draw a picture of an object, such as a bicycle (Moline, 1995).
4. The students can take turns drawing a part of the bicycle that magnifies the small details (e.g. two links in the chain or the bicycle's tire valve).
5. After students have drawn the diagram, then the class takes turns deciding what part of the bicycle was drawn. The primary goal of this part of the activity is to get students to notice details that could be represented in the diagram.
6. Once students have this concept, then discuss how the picture glossary could be used to illustrate a habitat.
7. When illustrating the habitats, the class could focus on one habitat at a time, or small groups could each be responsible for a different habitat.
8. After reading about the habitat, students could make a semantic map that lists the animals that would be shown in their habitat as well as special visual features of the habitat that could be included. For example, in figure 5.1, a student included trees, grass, and flowers to represent things around the pond.
9. Students can crosscheck the semantic map each time an animal or feature is added to the habitat.
10. Afterwards, students can create a picture glossary of the particular habitat using the semantic map resources to locate information for their glossary.

Examples

George, Lindsay Barrett. *Around the Pond: Who's Been Here?* 1996. Unp. New York: Greenwillow Books. (hc. 0-688-14376-8).

Grades: K–3. Two children follow an old deer path around a pond as they search for blackberries. Along the way, they find numerous clues about the animals that live around the pond. The story is told using a narrative format, but it has much useful information about eight different animals that can be found around the pond. The children in the story use clues they find as they are walking to identify each animal. At the end of the book, George includes a picture dictionary that shows a small picture of the animal with interesting information about each one.

Picture Glossary

Figure 5.1. After reading George's book, students could go on a field trip to a local park to take a nature walk. Ask them to record the different plants and animals they see during their walk. This same activity could be done around the school where students record the plants and animals that live around their school.

Awan, Shaila. *The Burrow Book.* Illustrated by Richard Orr. 1997.
    19p. New York: Dorling Kindersley. (hc. 0-7894-2025-2).
Grades: 1–5. This text illustrates a variety of burrows found in different
environments such as the woodland, arctic, forest, grassland, and desert. Each different environment depicts the land and the animals that
call it home. In figure 5.1, a student has drawn a cross section of burrows made by animals living in the arctic biome. The arctic ground
squirrel creates burrows underneath the ground, whereas the arctic
hare's burrow is found underneath the layer of snow covering the
ground. A gray wolf is shown above the ground as it looks for food.

Picture Glossary

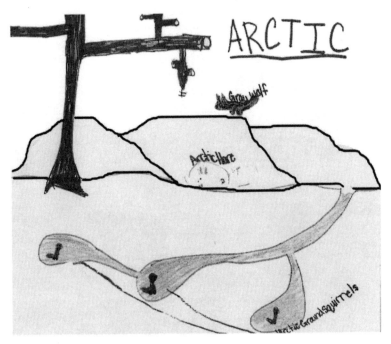

Figure 5.2. This picture glossary includes elements of a cross section
(see Chapter 9, Landforms) in the illustrations of the arctic ground
squirrels that live underground.

Additional Books and Resources

Cowcher, Helen. *Rain Forest.* 1988. Unp. New York: Farrar, Straus and Giroux. (pbk. 0-374-36167-3).
Grades: P–2. This visually appealing book provides beautiful illustrations of the animals and plants found in the rain forests. The underlying storyline shows the animals of the rain forest fleeing for their lives as machines tear down the trees of the rain forest. As the animals flee, they head to higher ground and watch as men and machines are swept away when the floods arrive.

Luenn, Nancy. *Squish! A Wetland Walk.* Illustrated by Ronald Himler. 1994. Unp. New York: Simon and Schuster. (hc. 0-689-31842-1).
Grades: P–2. A young child explores the wetland and shares the sights and sounds that he experiences along the way. Interesting information about this biome is introduced with each page that explains how big or small the wetland can be and how important the wetland is to Earth.

Yolen, Jane. *Welcome to the River of Grass.* Illustrated by Laura Regan. 2001. Unp. New York: Putnam. (hc. 0-399-23221-4).
Grades: P–4. The world of the Everglades swamp is highlighted through Yolen's text and Regan's artwork. The visual image of a "silent carpet of flowing grass" to the low-hooted singing of a barred owl helps young readers to learn about the cycle of life found in this biome. The rich illustrations will be enjoyed by children of all ages.

Gibbons, Gail. *Marshes and Swamps.* 1998. Unp. New York: Holiday House. (hc. 0-8234-1347-0).
Grades: 2–4. The wetlands biome is illustrated through Gibbons' artwork as she teaches children about how marshes and swamps differ, how important they are in the balance of nature, as well as the assortment of life that can be found within their boundaries.

———. *Exploring the Deep, Dark Sea.* 1999. Unp. New York: Little, Brown. (hc. 0-316-30945-1).
Grades: 2–8. Gibbons' book illustrates to children how humans are able to explore the ocean. Using submersibles, children are shown a variety of sea creatures that can only be seen when going underwater. The colorful illustrations include interesting facts about each animal such as those that create their own light through bioluminescence (e.g. hatchet fish, anglerfish).

George, Jean Craighead. *Everglades.* Paintings by Wendell Minor. 1995. Unp. New York: HarperCollins. (hc. 0-06-021228-4).

Grades: 3–8. Paintings by Minor vividly illustrate the nature and beauty of the Florida Everglades. The book covers the evolution of the area from its creation as a sea to a river. A storyteller takes children through the Everglades and shares the story of how the Everglades evolved, describes the plant and animal life that once thrived there, and tells them of the negative impact of humans on the life forms that used to be in such abundance.

——. *One Day in the Tropical Rain Forest.* Illustrated by Gary Allen. 1990. 56p. New York: HarperCollins. (hc. 0-690-04767-3).

Grades: 4–8. The tropical rain forest is seen through the eyes of a young boy, Tepui, who finds his home threatened one day when bulldozers and trucks arrive to level the forest. The young boy embarks on a quest to discover a nameless butterfly in order to save the rain forest. In a narrative format, Jean Craighead George tells the story of Tepui and the rain forest by writing in vivid detail about its inhabitants (e.g. a colony of ants, capuchin monkeys, scarlet macaws) to broader topics relating to the rain forest's role in Earth's ecology.

The web site The World's Biomes gives an overview of the biomes including aquatic, desert, forest, tundra, and grassland. This web site can be found at http://www.ucmp.berkeley.edu/glossary/gloss5/biome/.

Enchanted Learning hosts a web site providing an overview of biomes. This web site can be found at the following location: http://www.enchantedlearning.com/biomes/. It also includes links to the major types of biomes as well as other categories (e.g. land caves, coniferous forests, and deciduous forests).

Blue Planet Biomes has a wealth of information about biomes and was created by Elisabeth Benders-Hyde, a science aide at the West Tisbury School in Massachusetts, along with two teachers at the school, Ann and Karl Nelson. This site provides information and links about the world's biomes. The Blue Planet Biomes web site can be found at http://www.blueplanetbiomes.org/table_of_contents.htm.

Another piece of software from Tom Snyder Productions, *Rainforest Researchers,* would be appropriate for grades five through eight. Students work as teams of scientists to complete two assignments about rain forest plants. As part of the project, they explore the Indonesian rain forest for clues to complete the assignment while exploring the diversity of life in this ecosystem. In order to finish the assignments, students have to address specific scientific questions that threaten this particular biome.

Field Trip into the Sea for grades two through eight was designed by Inview and published by Sunburst Communications. This multimedia software allows students to visit a kelp forest and the rocky shore so that students learn about the plants, animals, and habitats of coastal environments. Students can use the interactive Field Guide to get detailed information or use the Organism Data Table to search and sort. The software helps students understand predatory relationships.

Rainforest Designer, also by Tom Snyder Productions, is designed for grades two through six and enables students to design rain forest habitats by assembling three-dimensional dioramas or wall-size posters. They can choose any layer of the rain forest and select from hundreds of animals, plants, people, and objects to create original rain forest scenes. Students learn about this ecosystem by selecting from such backgrounds as jungles, waterfalls, rivers, or even deforestation scenes. The software includes an online gallery (offering background information and narrated pictures) that serves as an additional resource.

T-charts

A T-chart is a two-column chart that asks students to categorize information they are reading about a topic. McKenna and Robinson (1997) state that a good approach to many factually rich reading selections is to provide students with a chart that requires them to categorize information they encounter while reading. The column headings in the chart are provided for the students prior to reading which helps establish a purpose for reading the selection. Also called a T-diagram (Cunningham, Moore, Cunningham, and Moore, 2000), this organizer can serve as a listening guide for students to help them keep a record of important information. (See figures 5.3 and 5.4.)

Steps

1. Read through the text to identify important information.
2. Create a two-column chart on butcher paper or a transparency with the category headings for each column clearly identified.
3. Discuss the columns of the chart with your students prior to reading the text. Include a representative sample for each column, so

that students have a clear understanding of what could be recorded on the chart.

4. Read the text with your students, ask them to read it with a small group, or have students read the text independently.

5. After students read the text, then discuss it with them. Add an example from the text for each column of the T-chart. Complete the rest of the chart as a class, or ask students to work with a partner to record three examples for each column of the chart.

Examples

Hannah, J., and Rick A. Prebeg. *Jungle Jack Hannah's Safari Adventure.* Photographs by Rick A. Prebeg. 1996. 45p. New York: Scholastic. (hc. 0-590-67332-X).

Grades: 2–8. Drive through the savannas of Kenya and hike into the rain forest of Uganda to learn about the animals and people that live there. Vivid photographs enable children to see the beauty of the African wilderness.

T-chart

Savannas in Kenya	Rain Forests in Uganda
• A savanna is an enormous grassland dotted with trees. • Animals - baboons, Kape buffalo, warthog, impala, lions, giraffe, ostrich, wilde beests, gerenuk, zebra. • flat-topped trees called "acacias" • cheetahs can run about 70 miles an hour. • An elephants uses its trunk to gather leaves, branches, and tree bark	• gorillas live in the Rainforest. • gorillas make a nest of leaves on the ground and high up in the trees. • the silverback is the leader of the gorillas. • the vegetation (trees, plants) is very thick. It is hard to walk.

Figure 5.3. Information about the people and animals of the savannas and the rain forest are recorded on this T-chart.

Levinson, Nancy Smiler. *Death Valley: A Day in the Desert.* Illustrated by Diane Dawson Hearn. 2001. 29p. New York: Holiday House. (hc. 0-8234-1566-X).
Grades: K–3. This book includes a lot of facts about Death Valley including the fact that it is one of the hottest places on Earth. Despite the extreme temperatures found in this desert, many animals and plants call it home. Especially designed for beginning readers, this Level 2 book uses large type with simple vocabulary to help children learn about life in the desert.

T-chart

Death Valley is one of the hottest places on Earth.	Water can be found in the desert.
Ground temp. can rise to 200 degrees. Hardly any rain falls in Death Valley. Air temp. can rise to 125 degrees.	You can get a drink from the barrel cactus by cutting off the top. It rains once or twice a year. There are springs underground.

Figure 5.4. This T-chart was used to record information about the desert.

Additional Books and Resources

Wright-Frierson, Virginia. *A Desert Scrapbook: Dawn to Dusk in the Sonoran Desert.* 1996. Unp. New York: Simon and Schuster. (hc. 0-689-80678-7).
Grades: 1–5. The plants and animals of the Sonoran Desert are shown using beautiful watercolor illustrations. Photos, labeled pictures, and journal entries are inserted within the book that provide tidbits of information about the animals and plants that can be found in this desert biome.
Cherry, Lynne. *A River Ran Wild: An Environmental History.* 1992. Unp. Orlando, Fla.: Harcourt Brace Jovanovich. (hc. 0-15-200542-0).
Grades: 3–8. The course of a river over the past six centuries is charted from the time Native Americans found a home there to the English settlers who later joined them. The Nashua River is shown as a vital re-

source that gradually becomes ecologically dead due to the growth of factories, towns, and cities along its banks. Instead of ending the story there, Cherry tells a story of hope as people join together to change how industry polluted the river. Over the years, the river was slowly cleansed, animals returned, and the river was restored to its former beauty.

Markle, Sandra. *Pioneering Frozen Worlds.* 1996. 48p. New York: Atheneum Books. (hc. 0-689-31824-3).

Grades: 3–8. Markle explores the polar realm using text and photographs to illustrate the beauty of frozen worlds. The Arctic and Antarctica are described for readers by looking at the land, water, people, and animals. Satellite images illustrate the differences in size of Antarctica in the winter versus the summer. Text narrative and photos illustrate other interesting topics, such as polar class icebreakers, dressing instructions from the *Field Manual for the U.S. Antarctic Program,* the *aurora borealis* (Northern Hemisphere) and *aurora australis* (Southern Hemisphere), space farms, joining an ice floe expedition, and testing robot space explorers.

Talbot, Hudson, and Mark Greenberg. *Amazon Diary: The Jungle Adventures of Alex Winters.* 1996. Unp. New York: Putnam Books. (pbk. 0-399-22916-7).

Grades: 3–8. This story chronicles Alex's journey as he flies to South America to visit his parents who are searching for a lost tribe of Indians. Along the way, the plane crashes and strands Alex and the pilot in the Amazon rain forest. They are rescued by the Yanomanis and live with them until the pilot recovers. Told in a diary format, the story is full of photos and drawn illustrations of Alex's recognition of another culture.

Sayre, April Pulley. *Wetlands.* 1996. 78p. New York: Henry Holt. (hc. 0-8050-4086-2).

Grades: 4–8. This text discusses a range of aquatic biomes including the North American wetlands, freshwater marshes and swamps, bogs, and coastal wetlands. It is part of the Exploring Earth's Biomes series which also includes these titles: *Desert, Grassland, Lake and Pond, River and Stream, Taiga, Temperate Deciduous Forest, Tropical Rain Forest,* and *Tundra.*

Dewey, Jennifer Owings. *Antarctic Journal: Four Months at the Bottom of the World.* 2001. 64p. New York: HarperCollins. (hc. 0-0602-8586-9).

Grades: 5–8. Writing in a journal format, Dewey shares her four-month journey spent in Antarctica. With a sketchpad and typewriter, she chronicles her experiences as she hikes on glaciers, camps on deserted islands, and sails past icebergs and whales.

Matrixes

A matrix can be used to organize and record information. It is a visual presentation of a number of categories that are compared by looking at key variables (Bromley, Irwin-DeVitis, and Modlo, 1995). The matrix can help to identify prior knowledge and helps to actively involve students in the learning process. Because of the way it is organized, the matrix can also help students to identify patterns and relationships (Bromley et al., 1995). When recording information, it is important to encourage your students to discuss the rationale they have for including certain information on the chart. This type of guide is also a useful tool for reviewing information as a study guide. (See figures 5.5 and 5.6.)

Steps–One Book

1. Prior to working with your students, identify the categories for the column headings at the top of the matrix.
2. Use the overhead, butcher paper, or a template in *Microsoft Word* to create the matrix.
3. Discuss with students the information shown on the matrix. Ask them to read or listen for examples that could be included for each column heading.
4. Students read the story or listen as it is read to them. Discuss and record examples to be included on the matrix.
5. The information on the matrix can then be used to write a short summary paragraph about the topic.
6. Students can share the summaries at the end of the activity. (See figure 5.5.)

Steps–Multiple Books

1. When using multiple books (see figure 5.6), students could work in small groups to each focus on a different book. An alternative to this format is for the whole class to study each book one at a time.
2. After looking through the book, they could write on index cards or sticky paper information that would be included for their topic.

3. During the discussion time, small groups each take one major column heading (e.g. Plants), and record the information that should be written onto the chart using index cards or sticky notes.
4. When it is time for partners or groups to report to the rest of the class, the information is easily placed on the matrix while students are presenting their information.

Examples

Greenaway, Theresa. *Tree Life*. Photographed by Kim Taylor. 1992. 29p. New York: Dorling Kindersley. (pbk. 0-7894-3475-X).
Grades: 3–8. Vivid photographs illustrate life in a tree. The accompanying narrative shares a variety of information about trees and the relationship between them and animals that use them for a food resource or call them home. Every page has numerous creatures featured that include references to common name, scientific name, location, and/or size.

Matrix

	Does it use the tree for food? How?	Does it use the tree as a home? How?
Forest Frogs		
Butterflies		
Ants		
Mini Monkey		
Woodpecker		

Figure 5.5. This tree matrix looks at different animals that use the tree to survive. Children use the categories on the matrix to record the information as they read the book.

Taylor, Barbara. *Forest Life*. Photographed by Kim Taylor and Jane Burton. 1993. 29p. New York: Dorling Kindersley. (pbk. 0-7894-3475-X).
——. *Meadow*. Photographed by Kim Taylor and Jane Burton. 1992. 29p. New York: Dorling Kindersley. (pbk. 0-7894-3475-X).
——. *River Life*. Photographed by Frank Greenaway. 1992. 29p. New York: Dorling Kindersley. (pbk. 0-7894-3475-X).

Grades: 3–8. This series of books explores life in these different habitats by looking at the animals and plants that call each one home.

Matrix

	Plants that are found here.	Animals that are found here.	What it looks like...	Interesting Features
Forest	oak trees, pine trees, mushrooms, bluebell flowers, scaly male ferns, fly agaric	owls, weasels, squirrels, eastern rosella, wood wasp, oak bush cricket,	trees, mushrooms, hardly no grass, thick trees, limbs on ground	gray squirrels can run 18 mph, and can swim good. a lot of mushrooms
Meadow	red clover, dandelion, wood cranesbill, field scabous, water avens	bumble bee, dung fly, damselfly, red-legged partridge chick, cinnabar moth, grass snake, slow worm, crab spider	grassy, flowers everywhere, tall grass, butterflys, insects	The crab spider wait to pounce on bees, a red-legged partridge chicks couldn't is water proof
Rivers	Algae, Alder, Cat tail, Rush, Roots, Catkins to Cones	Water Snake, fish, turtles, crawfish	Clear, stones in it, diff animals & plants	Minnows can only live in clean water. Some rats swim in water to find food
Trees		marble gail wasp, day gecko, Asian tree frog, Wood Ant, Marmoset	leafy	Birds hold feet close to them. Woodpeckers have very long tongues

Figure 5.6. This matrix was used to look at broader areas related to each of these particular habitats, while also looking at other features that might be present in each one (e.g. rivers, trees).

Additional Books and Resources

Arnosky, Jim. *Crinkleroot's Guide to Knowing Animal Habitats.* 2000. 32p. New York: Aladdin. (pbk. 0-689-83538-8).
Grades: P–3. Arnosky provides the illustrations for Crinkleroot and his snake, Sassafras, as a way for children to explore six different habitats.

The book enables children to look at eighty different species as they explore marshes, swamps, bogs, woodlands, roadsides, cornfields, grasslands, and drylands.

Simon, Seymour. *Deserts.* 1990. Unp. New York: William Morrow. (pbk. 0-688-15479-4).

Grades: 1–5. Simon continues his success with nonfiction by looking at deserts from Africa to Australia to the Americas. The Sahara, Sonoran, the Chihuahuan, the Great Basin, and Death Valley are described using photographs with large-print text. Simon includes a map of North American deserts, a table with annual rainfall, and a larger map of the world that highlights desert areas.

Farndon, John. *Wildlife Atlas: A Complete Guide to Animals and Their Habitats.* 2002. 176p. Pleasantville, N.Y.: Reader's Digest. (hc. 0-762-10354-X).

Grades: 1–6. Students take a tour of eight different habitats and learn how the animals that live there are able to survive. The tour includes a look at the vast Sahara, the Florida Everglades, and the Eurasian tundra. Three-dimensional maps and detailed cutaway illustrations explain how and why each habitat is able to support wildlife.

Llewellyn, Claire. *Our Planet Earth.* 1997. 77p. New York: Scholastic. (hc. 0-590-87929-4).

Grades: 1–6. Divided into four parts, this book covers the larger picture by looking at planet Earth. Included are sections covering Earth's surface, the changing planet, and life on Earth. Within each section, a variety of subtopics are addressed that provide numerous details using pictures, photos, labeled diagrams, and captions. The inclusion of cross-references, a table of contents, a glossary, and an index make it easily accessible to the reader looking for specific information. The section on the Earth's Surface includes a look at the forest, tropical rain forest, plain, desert, and polar lands biomes. The section on Life on Earth would be helpful for Chapter 6, Animals, since reptiles, birds, and mammals are also discussed.

Dorros, Arthur. *Rainforest Secrets.* 1990. Unp. New York: Scholastic. (pbk. 0-590-43368-7).

Grades: 3–8. Dorros' book covers aspects of the rain forest including temperature, plant life, animal life, and people. He illustrates the different layers of the rain forest including plant and animal life that can be found from the forest floor to the understory to the canopy. Buttresses, stilt roots, and lianas along with specific foods such as bananas, peanuts, peppers, papayas, and avocados are introduced throughout the text.

Macquitty, M. *Ocean.* Illustrated by Frank Greenaway. 1995. 64p. New York: Dorling Kindersley. (hc. 0-679-87331-7). Grades: 3–8. Part of the Eyewitness Book series, this book takes a look at a variety of ocean topics. Students read about the waves and weather, sandy and muddy bottoms, the seabed, underwater rocks, and the coral reef.

Nature Virtual Serengeti software from Tom Snyder Productions enables children to go on a virtual African safari. Students are introduced to East African climate, vegetation, and animal life. The software includes a journal, field guide, and virtual video recorder to draw conclusions about the survival of the species while gaining a greater understanding of biodiversity. Users can travel by foot, truck, boat, airplane, and hot air balloon as they develop a video documentary of their safari.

Another piece of software by Sunburst Communications, *Ecosystems*, is designed for grades four through eight. Students can investigate the concept of interdependency by exploring the energy cycles, food webs, and populations of aquatic and land environments with this dynamic science simulation. The software includes eighteen species to explore, and students test their knowledge by creating and sustaining an island ecosystem.

References

Bromley, Karen, Linda Irwin-DeVitis, and Marcia Modlo. *Graphic Organizers: Visual Strategies for Active Learning.* New York: Scholastic, 1995.

Cunningham, Patricia, Sharon Arthur Moore, James W. Cunningham, and David W. Moore. *Reading and Writing in Elementary Classrooms*, 4th ed. New York: Longman, 2000.

McKenna, Michael C., and Richard D. Robinson. *Teaching through Text*, 2nd ed. New York: Longman, 1997.

Moline, Steve. *I See What You Mean: Children at Work with Visual Information.* York, Maine: Stenhouse, 1995.

National Science Education Standards. Washington, D.C.: National Academy Press, 1995. http://stills.nap.edu/readingroom/books/nses/ (20 Nov. 2002).

Richardson, Judy S., and Raymond F. Morgan. *Reading to Learn in the Content Areas*, 5th ed. Belmont, Calif.: Wadsworth, 2003.

· 6 ·
Animals

The study of animals can take many different directions depending on the grade level. There can be a study of animals in general, a look at types of animals organized by vertebrate category (e.g. mammals, birds, fish, reptiles, and amphibians), or even a look at one specific category of animals (e.g. mammals only). A look at animals could involve family pets, animals at the zoo, animals in the wild, animals in your backyard, animals of North America, and so forth. Regardless of the direction that you choose to take, students need to determine a general definition and concept of what is meant by "animals." Pringle's *Scholastic Encyclopedia of Animals* (2001, p. 5) states that:

> Today, about 1.5 million species of both animals and plants have been discovered and named. These include about four thousand mammals, nineteen thousand fishes, about nine thousand birds, and more than ten thousand reptiles and amphibians. The largest animal group by far is insects, with nearly 800 hundred thousand names so far. And there are still many more species of animals to be discovered. Scientists estimate that there may be one million kinds in just one insect group, beetles. The total of all animal species on Earth may number several million.

The third strand of the *National Science Education Standards* (NSES, 1995), life science, addresses the characteristics of organisms and their environment. Since Chapter 2 of *Reading Comprehension* is devoted to bugs and insects, this chapter will look at animals in the science category of vertebrates. The strategies discussed include concept circles, Venn diagrams, and bio-poems.

Concept Circles

Concept circles are a type of activity that can easily be used across grade levels. They enable students to relate words conceptually to one another (Vacca and Vacca, 2002). Using concept circles "involves putting words or phrases in sections of a circle and then directing students to describe or name the concept relationship among the sections" (Vacca, Vacca, Gove, Burkey, Lenhart, and McKeon, 2003, p. 299). The idea behind this type of activity is similar to categorizing, but it incorporates a more visual format to do so. (See figures 6.1, 6.2, 6.3, and 6.4.)

Steps

1. Students can be given circles divided into four parts. Inside each section of the circle is a word or phrase. Students discuss together what would be the main idea of the circle. (See figure 6.1.) For example, in a four-part circle, the words included are *have hair, live birth, warm-blooded,* and *feed their young milk.* The main idea for this concept circle would be mammals.

2. A second option would be to give students the main idea and the concept circle with four parts filled in using key words or phrases. (See figure 6.2.) Students analyze the concept circle to identify the phrase that does not belong. In the concept circle for Guinea Pigs, the four parts are *rodent, squeaks, 8 inches long,* and *active at night.* After looking at the concept circle, students would shade in the part of the concept circle that says *active at night*, since the guinea pig is active during the day instead.

3. A third variation for concept circles is to give students the main idea with three parts of the concept circle completed. (See figure 6.3.) It is their job to identify a fourth part of the concept circle that would also reflect the main idea. In a concept circle with the main idea *horses*, three of the completed parts are *equine, neigh,* and *eat hay.* After examining the concept circle, students would need to determine a different key word or phrase to complete the fourth part of the circle.

4. A fourth option is for students to create their own concept circles. Once the circles have been created, then they could be shared with the rest of the class and made into a resource at one of the classroom center areas.

Examples

Pringle, Laurence. *Scholastic Encyclopedia of Animals.* Photographs by Norbert Wu. 2001. 128p. New York: Scholastic. (hc. 0-590-52253-1).

Grades: 1–5. Students of all ages will enjoy looking through this book. The beautiful photographs and accompanying text provide a wealth of information about animals. The largest section of the book, "Animal Profiles," is an encyclopedia about different animals organized alphabetically. Students are provided pronunciation guides along with descriptive information such as physical attributes, habitat, and means of communication. A glossary, an index, and a pronunciation guide are included.

Concept Circle—Identify Main Idea

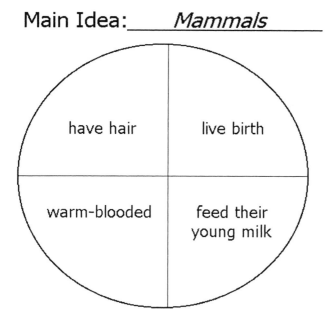

Figure 6.1. Students need to identify the main idea of the concept circle, which would be *mammals*.

Concept Circles—Shade the Part that Does *Not* Belong

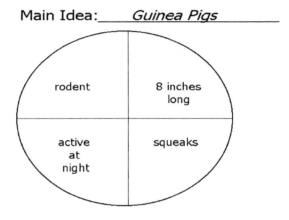

Figure 6.2. *Guinea Pigs* are active during the day, therefore *active at night* should be shaded to show it is incorrect.

Concept Circles—Identify the Missing Section

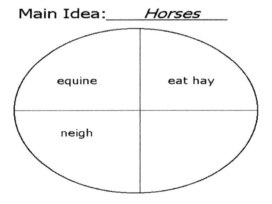

Figure 6.3. The main idea for this concept circle is *Horses*. Three of the completed parts are *equine, eat hay,* and *neigh*. Students could use any of the following to complete the concept circle: eat oats, pull heavy load, Quarter Horse, or Tennessee Walking Horse.

Concept Circle—Student-Created Concept Circles

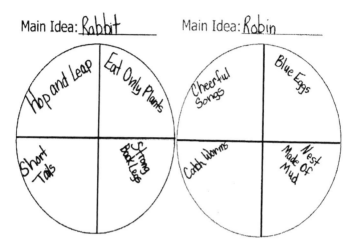

Main Idea: Rabbit   Main Idea: Robin

Figure 6.4. These two concept circles were created by a student using the *Scholastic Encyclopedia of Animals* as a resource. She selected two of the animals in the book, then used the animals as the main ideas, and completed the concept circles using the information she found in this resource.

Additional Books and Resources

Jordan, Martin, and Tanis Jordan. *Amazon Alphabet.* 1996. Unp. New York: Scholastic. (pbk. 0-590-06860-1).
Grades: P–2. The Jordans take students through the Amazon rain forest and introduce them to the many different animals that call it home. The simple format of the book uses large, full-color illustrations along with the uppercase and lowercase letters and the name of the animal that starts with that letter of the alphabet. A pronunciation guide is also included at the bottom of the page.

Leopold, Niki Clark. *K Is for Kitten.* Illustrated by Susan Jeffers. 2002. Unp. New York: G. P. Putnam's Sons. (hc. 0-399-23563-9).
Grades: P–2. Rosie the alley cat finds a home with a little girl. Her life in her new home is chronicled using an alphabet story format. Large, bold-print text with simple vocabulary will help young readers to follow along with the story or attempt it on their own.

Arnosky, Jim. *All about Alligators*. 1994. Unp. New York: Scholastic. (hc. 0-590-46788-3).
Grades: 1–5. This visually appealing book provides beautiful illustrations of the alligator. Noted naturalist Jim Arnosky takes students on a walk through nature to learn more about this type of animal.

Ganeri, Anita. *Animals in Disguise*. Illustrated by Halli Verrinder. 1995. 24p. New York: Aladdin. (pbk. 0-689-80264-1).
Grades: 1–5. Frogs, snakes, katydids, geckos, foxes, mantises, chameleons, birds, and fish are covered in this book about animals and how they disguise themselves. The trickery that these animals use is shown by using flip-over see-through pages.

Patent, Dorothy Hinshaw. *Slinky Scaly Slithery Snakes*. Illustrated by Kendahl Jan Jubb. 2000. 32p. New York: Walker and Company. (hc. 0-8027-8743-6).
Grades: 1–5. Interesting facts and information about the snake are shared throughout this text about snakes. Everything from what they look like to where they sleep, what they do to protect themselves, and more can be found in Patent and Jubb's book. Scientific names for the snakes and page numbers where each is found are also included at the back of the book.

Kalman, Bobbie, and Amanda Bishop. *The Life Cycle of a Lion*. 2002. 32p. New York: Crabtree Publishing. (hc. 0-7787-0656-7; pbk. 0-7787-0686-9).
Grades: 2–5. The lion in all its glory is shared in this book. Topics addressed include where lions live, life in the pride and in the litter, joining the pride, growing up, adult lions, top of the food chain, and dangers to lions.

Mammals. 1995. 46p. New York: Scholastic. (hc. 0-590-47654-8).
Grades: 3–8. This Voyages of Discovery book from Scholastic follows mammals from prehistoric times to the present and compares mammals across continents. The text includes art and interactive elements throughout the book. For example, students can feel the tracks that would be made by a giraffe, an antelope, a kangaroo, a cheetah, and a hare on a cardboard page. Students can mix and match the facial features of a beaver, a bear, or a chimpanzee. Students can also complete illustrations in the book by using reusable vinyl stickers.

The National Wildlife Federation's web site, http://www.nwf.org/, offers a variety of resources about wildlife, environmental education, and basic issues concerning conservation. It also has information for

kids and teens that is organized by age ranges (i.e. 1-3, 3-7, 7-13, and
13 and up).

Venn Diagrams

The compare-and-contrast text structure is a common type of expository pattern that students will encounter during their reading of content
area material (Schmidt, 1993). To organize information found in this
type of text structure, the Venn diagram can be used to describe how
two or more things are alike and different (Tompkins, 1998). This type
of diagram consists of overlapping circles. The students record similarities between the items being compared in the overlap section, and
record differences in the outer left and right parts of the circle. Where
the circles do not overlap, students record items that are different. This
type of diagram is helpful when "concepts cannot be broken down
cleanly into narrower concepts" or when overlapping is possible
(McKenna and Robinson, 1997, p. 118). (See figures 6.5 and 6.6.)

Steps

1. Discuss similarities and differences that can be identified for a
   topic. As an example, two common objects could be compared,
   such as a pen and pencil.
2. The common features shared by the pen and pencil would be written in the middle overlap section of the two circles. The pen and
   pencil can both be used to write symbols, numbers, and letters.
3. Differences between the two objects would be written in the outside left and right portions of the circle. Depending on the age
   level of the student, pictures, words, or phrases could be used to
   complete the Venn diagram.
4. Once students have an idea of how the Venn diagram works, then a
   new topic based on a text reading would be selected that relates to
   a current unit of study.
5. Discuss together as a class what would be recorded for differences
   and what would be recorded for similarities. Then, summarize the
   Venn diagram after the information has been recorded.

Examples

Glassman, Jackie. *Amazing Arctic Animals.* 2002. 48p. New York: Grosset and Dunlap. (pbk. 0-448-42844-X).
Grades: K–3. Students learn fascinating facts about Arctic animals in this All Aboard Science Reader. They read about how long winter lasts in the Arctic and what it is like, the kinds of animals that visit the Arctic in the summer, and the animals that dare to stay for the winter. Students are introduced to such vocabulary as *adaptations, blubber, harsh, huddle, prey,* and *tusks.* Interspersed throughout the book are facts about various animals such as their baby name, size at birth, and favorite foods.

Venn Diagram

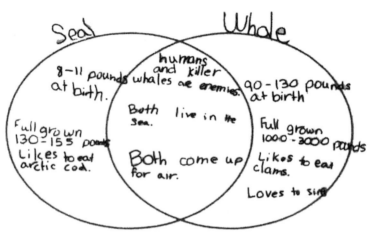

Figure 6.5. This Venn diagram compares and contrasts two arctic animals: the seal and the whale.

Arnold, Caroline. *African Animals.* 1997. 48p. New York: William Morrow. (hc. 0-688-14116-1).
Grades: 1–5. Readers discover the wide variety of animals that can be found in the African grasslands, forests, and deserts in this book. Beautiful, color photographs of the animals in their natural habitats are accompanied by descriptions of special features of the animals that make them interesting to study.

Venn Diagram

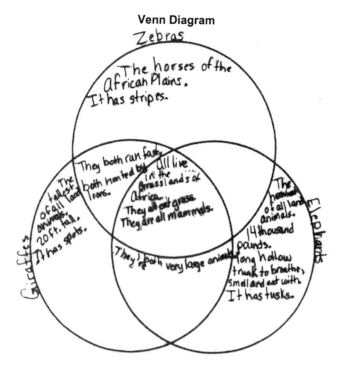

Figure 6.6. A three-topic Venn diagram that compares and contrasts three African animals: zebras, giraffes, and elephants. The student completed the diagram using the Arnold book, *African Animals*, and was able to find examples for most parts of the diagram, although the similarities between the zebra and elephant were sketchy.

Additional Books and Resources

Rau, Dana Meachen. *Pet Your Pet.* Illustrated by Jeffery Scherer. 2002. 32p. Minneapolis, Minn.: Compass Point Books. (hc. 0-7565-0175-X).
Grades: P–1. This Level B Compass Point Early Reader is geared towards developing readers. The text itself has a simple storyline that looks at different pets of children.
Carle, Eric. *"Slowly, Slowly, Slowly," Said the Sloth.* 2002. Unp. New York: Philomel. (hc. 0-399-23954-5).

Grades: P–2. Carle's text includes a foreword by Jane Goodall where she shares basic information about this creature. Carle's book uses his collage art technique to look at the daily life of the sloth. The back inset cover of the book includes illustrations of other animals that can be found in the jungles of South America.

McMillan, Bruce. *The Baby Zoo.* 1992. 40p. New York: Scholastic. (pbk. 0-590-44635-5).

Grades: P–2. McMillan includes a photograph of baby zoo animals along with a map of where they would be found in the world, their common and scientific names, as well as general information about each one. Some of the baby zoo animals include the fawn of a Bawean Deer, the foal of a Grevy's Zebra, and the pup of a California Sea Lion.

Patent, Dorothy Hinshaw. *Flashy Fantastic Rainforest Frogs.* Illustrated by Kendahl Jan Jubb. 1997. 32p. New York: Walker Publishing. (pbk. 0-590-10861-1).

Grades: 1–5. Patent looks at the variety of different frogs that can be found in the rain forest. The vibrant blues, reds, oranges, and pinks of the frogs in the illustrations bring them to life for students wishing to learn more about this particular animal.

Simon, Seymour. *Animals Nobody Loves.* 2001. 48p. New York: Sea Star Books. (hc. 1-58717-079-5).

Grades: 1–5. A variety of animals are highlighted in Simon's book that includes descriptive information and beautiful photographs. Students can read about some of nature's grossest and most fascinating survivors of the animal world. Some of the animals included are the cobra, vulture, rattlesnake, coyote, and piranha.

Singer, Marilyn. *Tough Beginnings: How Baby Animals Survive.* Illustrated by Anna Vojtech. 2001. Unp. New York: Henry Holt. (hc. 0-8050-6164-9).

Grades: 1–5. Animal babies do not have it nearly as easy as human babies do when they are born. Many must be able to stand on their own within hours of birth or risk abandonment by their mother. These animal survival stories will fascinate students of all ages.

George, Jean Craighead. *Frightful's Daughter.* Illustrated by Daniel San Souci. 2002. Unp. New York: Dutton Children's Books. (hc. 0-525-46907-9).

Grades: 3–8. George's rich text and San Souci's beautiful illustrations tell the story of a peregrine falcon named Oksi. The young falcon is rescued by Sam who helps her through her first winter. The story tells of the bond that is forged between the raptor and the boy.

Patent, Dorothy Hinshaw. *Looking at Bears.* Photographs by William Munoz. 1994. 40p. New York: Holiday House. (hc. 0-8234-1139-7). Grades: 3–8. The evolution of bears, their physical characteristics, and their habitat are explained. Different species of bears covered in the book include the American black bear, the polar bear, and the giant panda. Other topics also addressed are how bears eat, raise their young, and hibernate.

Sea World Adventures Park has an animal database located at their web site (http://www.seaworld.org/infobook.html). Resources include information about animal rescue and rehabilitation and teacher resources. In addition, links for specific animals enable readers to learn more about designated animals. For example, the link for sea turtles includes a discussion of their habitat and distribution, physical characteristics, and diet and eating habits.

Animal Planet (http://animal.discovery.com/) hosted by The Discovery Channel offers links to Mutual of Omaha's Wild Kingdom as well as to the Crocodile Hunter. Other resources include Animals A to Zoo, Fun and Games, and Pet Help.

Bio-Poems

"Perhaps it is true that great poets are born, not made, but every child can write poems and enjoy the experience" (Tompkins, 1994, p. 296). One way to expand students' concept of poetry is to explore poetry in connection to content area material that is being read (Richardson and Morgan, 2003). A type of poetry that can be used to help scaffold the poetry writing would be the bio-poem. Gere (1985) introduced the use of the bio-poem as a way for the writer to focus on himself or herself. This poetic form can be used to reflect on a large amount of material by enabling the students to synthesize what they have been studying about a concept or an event (Vacca and Vacca, 2002).

The bio-poems shown in this section are adapted to focus on animals by using word counts and parts of speech as a guide. The term "guide" is used loosely here. When the poem is actually written as a final draft, students are free to add any extra words they need to help structure the rhythmic features of the poem. Rhyming is not a requirement, although some children may opt to have theirs rhyme. Tompkins (1994, p. 252) has stated that "most children are inclined toward poetry, but when they equate poetry with rhymed verse, the poems they compose are stilted and artificial." As a support structure, a chart is used for students to collect information, which then serves as a plan for writing when they are drafting the poem. (See figures 6.7, 6.8, 6.9, and 6.10.)

Steps

1. Show students the chart that can be used to record information about the animal.
2. Select an animal to do together as a class. Record the information on the chart, then model writing the poem using the chart as a guide. The lines of the chart can be numbered as well as the template for writing to help younger children when writing the poem.
3. Once the class poem is written, then students can select their own animal along with any book or electronic resources that can assist with information.
4. Information about the animal should be recorded on the chart. Once this has been done, then students can write the first draft of the bio-poem.
5. After the first draft is written, students will need to conference for content with a peer or small group where questions that could be asked include: a) does it make sense, or b) is anything missing?
6. Students need to also have a conference that checks for capitalization, usage, punctuation, and spelling errors.
7. Once these conferences have been completed, students can proceed with writing the final draft and illustrating their poem.

Examples

Cowley, Joy. *Red-Eyed Tree Frog.* Photographs by Nic Bishop. 1999. Unp. New York: Scholastic. (hc. 0-590-87176-5).
Grades: K–3. Large-print text with beautiful photographs illustrating the red-eyed tree frog in its natural habitat helps young students read and remember the information about this interesting frog. Cowley shares with young students where this tiny rain forest frog lives and sleeps and what it eats. At the end of the book, a Did You Know section is included that provides additional pictures and information about the red-eyed tree frog.

Information Chart

Name of Animal	Red Eyed Tree frog
2 words to describe what the animal looks like	Green Shiny
3 words to describe how the animal moves	hops climbs Jumps
3 words to describe what the animal eats	moths flies spiders
2 words to describe where the animal lives	rain forest trees leavs
Name of Animal	Red eyed Tree frog

Figure 6.7. After reading *Red-Eyed Tree Frog* by Joy Cowley, this student recorded the information on the chart. The information that was used was found either through pictorial clues or narrative in the book, or by reading the additional Did You Know section at the back of the book.

Bio-Poem

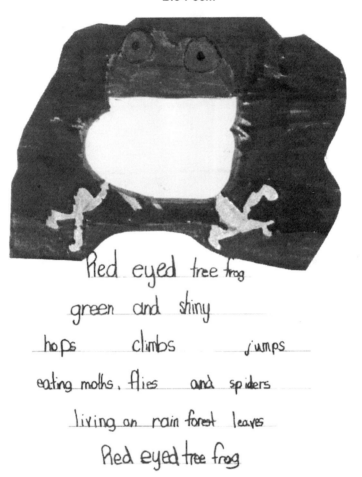

Figure 6.8. This poem about the red-eyed tree frog was written after reading the book *Red-Eyed Tree Frog* by Joy Cowley. The information chart shown in figure 6.7 was completed first and served as a guide for writing the draft of the poem.

Arnosky, Jim. *All about Turtles.* 2000. Unp. New York: Scholastic. (hc. 0-590-48149-5).

Grades: 1–5. The beautiful illustrations and informative text will appeal
to children of all ages. Arnosky's book looks at the world of turtles by
talking a little bit about different types. Land turtles, freshwater turtles,
and sea turtles are all addressed in terms of where they live, what they
eat, and how they stay warm.

Information Chart

Scientific Name of Animal	Chrysemus picta
3 adjectives to describe what the animal looks like	less than 10", green or brownish, yellow streaks
4 verbs to describe how the animal moves	Slowly, burrowing, clawing, basking
2 adjectives and 2 nouns to describe what the animal eats	aquatic insects, slimy snails
2 adjectives and 1 noun to describe where the animal lives	Slow moving river
Common Name of Animal	Painted Turtle

Figure 6.9. Information about the painted turtle was found in Arnosky's
book. Two web sites were also used. Enchanted Learning provides information about painted turtles and can be found at
www.enchantedlearning.com/subjects/turtle/Paintedturtle.sthml. Another web resource for this student was found at the Alien Earth web
site, http://www.alienexplorer.com/ecology/Ecology.html, which offers
a 600-article database on mammals, pond life, and basic ecology. Notice that the student used one adverb and three verbs instead of four
verbs.

Bio-Poem

Chrysemys picta
Small, greenish, yellow streaks
Slowly, burrowing, clawing, and basking
Eating aquatic insects, and slimy snails
Living in a slow moving river
Painted Turtle

Figure 6.10. This bio-poem was written about painted turtles using the information chart in figure 6.9 as a guide.

Additional Books and Resources

Rylant, Cynthia. *The Whales.* 1996. Unp. New York: Blue Sky Press. (hc. 0-590-58285-2).
Grades: P–3. The simple rhythmic format of this book wavers between poetry and informative text. Children will love Rylant's paintings done in acrylics using natural sea sponges as each depicts the whales as beautiful and gentle creatures of the sea.

Markle, Sandra. *Down, Down, Down in the Ocean.* Illustrated by Bob
   Marstall. 1999. 32p. New York: Walker and Company. (hc. 0-
   8027-8654-5).
Grades: K–3. Markle takes a look at animals found in the ocean by going from the surface to the floor. She identifies adaptations that many
of these sea creatures have made in order to live where they do in the
ocean.
Gibbons, Gail. *Bats.* 1999. Unp. New York: Holiday House. (hc. 0-
   8234-1457-4).
Grades: 1–5. Gibbons tells the story of bats as being shy, gentle creatures that live on every continent except Antarctica. She looks at the
many different kinds of bats as well as how they fit into our world.
Blake, Robert J. *Togo.* 2002. Unp. New York: Philomel. (hc. 0-399-
   23381-4).
Grades: 3–8. The true story of one of the bravest dogs called on to help
deliver the serum that would save Alaska from a life-threatening out-
break of diphtheria. Seppala and his dogsled team were led by Togo
over 350 miles for their part of the journey. The author states that for
many people the annual Iditarod Race is in commemoration of this serum run from 1925.
Goodman, Susan E. *Animal Rescue: The Best Job There Is.* 2000. 48p.
   New York: Aladdin. (pbk. 0-689-81795-9).
Grades: 3–8. This Ready to Read Level 3 book tells the story of how
animals are rescued during natural disasters such as fires, floods, and
volcanic eruptions. The book includes true stories about John Walsh
and how he and his team rescue animals in the jungle, during wartime,
and after earthquakes.
Kalman, Bobbie. *The Life Cycle of a Wolf.* 2002. 32p. New York:
   Crabtree Publishing. (hc. 0-7787-0657-5; pbk. 0-7787-0687-7).
Grades: 3–8. Kalman tells the story of the wolf using photographs, diagrams, maps, and other illustrations. Students will find out where
wolves live, how they are part of a pack, stages in their life cycle, how
they join a pack, how they talk to each other, and how they prepare for
birth. The table of contents, glossary, and index help readers to easily
locate specific information.
Sacks, Janet, Polly Goodman, and Steve Parker. *Animals and Art
   Activities.* 2002. 48p. New York: Crabtree Publishing. (hc. 0-7787-
   1108-0; pbk. 0-7787-1136-6).
Grades: 3–8. This book offers photographs, informative text, and activities for students to do as a way of exploring the world of animals.
Birds, zebras, snakes, sheep, porcupines, and much more are high-

lighted. Teachers and students will especially enjoy the activities that are included, which use a step-by-step format along with a materials list required to complete the project.

References

Buehl, Doug. *Classroom Strategies for Interactive Learning*, 2nd ed. Newark, Del.: International Reading Association, 2001.

Gere, Anne Ruggles. *Roots in the Sawdust: Writing across the Disciplines*. Urbana, Ill.: National Council of Teachers of English, 1985.

McKenna, Michael C., and Richard D. Robinson. *Teaching through Text: A Content Literacy Approach to Content Area Reading*, 2nd ed. White Plains, N.Y.: Longman, 1997.

National Science Education Standards. Washington, D.C.: National Academy Press, 1995. http://stills.nap.edu/readingroom/books/nses/ (20 Nov. 2002).

Pringle, Laurence. *Scholastic Encyclopedia of Animals*. New York: Scholastic, 2001.

Richardson, Judy S., and Raymond F. Morgan. *Reading to Learn in the Content Areas*, 5th ed. Belmont, Calif.: Wadsworth/Thomson, 2003.

Schmidt, Marion B. "The Shape of Content: Four Semantic Map Structures for Expository Paragraphs." In *Teacher to Teacher: Strategies for the Elementary Classroom*, edited by Mary W. Olson and Susan P. Homan, 140–144. Newark, Del.: International Reading Association, 1993.

Tompkins, Gail E. *50 Literacy Strategies: Step by Step*. Upper Saddle River, N.J.: Merrill Prentice Hall, 1998.

——. *Teaching Writing: Balancing Process and Product,* 2nd ed. Upper Saddle River, N.J.: Prentice Hall, 1994.

Vacca, Jo Anne L., Richard T. Vacca, Mary K. Gove, L. Burkey, L. A. Lenhart, and Christine McKeon. *Reading and Learning to Read*, 5th ed. Needham Heights, Mass.: Allyn and Bacon, 2003.

Vacca, Richard T., and Jo Anne L. Vacca. *Content Area Reading: Literacy and Learning across the Curriculum*, 7th ed. Boston, Mass.: Allyn and Bacon, 2002.

Section 2
SOCIAL STUDIES

Introducing a variety of trade books with different reading levels into the social studies curriculum gives students opportunities to find books on their reading levels. Allington's (2002) observations of exemplary teachers found that they use texts that match their students' reading levels and they provide instructional supports for their students. These instructional supports may be comprehension strategies or other literacy activities that extend students' learning. Combining social studies trade books with literacy activities helps students focus on the content and helps them make connections between the content in their textbooks and in the trade books (Kincade and Pruitt, 1996). Reading books aloud and sharing the illustrations is one activity that helps develop students' literacy skills as they learn social studies content (Button, 1998). The chapters in this section contain comprehension strategies that can provide the instructional support students need as they learn social studies content.

The National Council for the Social Studies developed *Curriculum Standards for Social Studies* (NCSS, 1994) as guidelines for the design of social studies programs. These standards encompass ten thematic strands:

1. culture;
2. time, continuity, and change;
3. people, places, and environment;
4. individual development and identity;
5. individuals, groups, and institutions;
6. power, authority, and governance;
7. production, distribution, and consumption;

8. science, technology, and society;
9. global connections;
10. civic ideals and practices.

Social studies promotes civic competence and is both multidisciplinary and interdisciplinary (NCSS, 1994). For example, thematic strand seven includes production, distribution, and consumption, concepts which also are taught in mathematics classes as students learn about money and the economy.

These thematic strands are woven into the stories and text found in children's books. Quality children's literature encourages students to develop emotional connections between themselves and the people and events they are studying (Krey, 1998). Lists of notable social studies books can be found at http://www.socialstudies.org/resources/notable.

Chapters in the social studies section include American history, states, landforms, the world, cultures, and biographies. The chapters contain comprehension strategies for use before reading, during reading, and after reading. Also included are strategies for vocabulary building.

References

Allington, Richard L. "You Can't Learn Much from Books You Can't Read." *Educational Leadership* 60, no. 3 (Nov. 2002): 16–19.

Button, Kathryn. "Linking Social Studies and Literacy Development through Children's Books." *Social Studies and the Young Learner* 10, no. 4 (March/April 1998): 23–25.

Kincade, Kay M., and Nancy E. Pruitt. "Using Multicultural Literature as an Ally to Elementary Social Studies Texts." *Reading Research and Instruction* 36 (Fall 1996): 18–32.

Krey, DeAn M. "Children's Literature in the Social Studies." *National Council for the Social Studies Bulletin 95* (1998).

National Council for the Social Studies. *Curriculum Standards for Social Studies.* 1994. http://www.ncss.org/standards/ (20 Nov. 2002). Ten thematic strands on pp. 109–110 reprinted with permission from *Expectations of Excellence: Curriculum Standards for Social Studies,* © National Council for the Social Studies.

· 7 ·
American History

Using children's literature in the social studies class enables the teacher to share stories with children (Edgington, 1998). Further, Edgington contends that literature contains details and passion that capture students' interests, qualities not often found in textbooks. These books enable students to learn about history and to respond emotionally to the characters and the events (Ross, 1994). As students read about America's past and reflect on what they have read, they develop connections between their lives and the past. They discover how things change over time and the continuity between the past and the present. Encouraging students to talk to their parents and relatives about the past helps them make personal connections between America's past and their own lives. These connections make learning more meaningful to the students and motivates them to learn about their past.

Time, continuity, and change are encompassed by thematic strand two of the *Curriculum Standards for Social Studies* (NCSS, 1994). For example, when studying about Colonial America students learn about the first Thanksgiving. They discover that this holiday feast was first celebrated a long time ago and that the tradition continues today. They make connections between the first Thanksgiving celebration and their own Thanksgiving celebrations. They also discover how the celebration has changed over time. They enjoy participating in classroom reenactments of the first Thanksgiving complete with costumes and a feast. Additionally, they enjoy learning about life in Colonial America and comparing the Pilgrims' and Native Americans' lives to their own. Timelines, problem-solution charts, and character comparison charts help students understand and remember what they read about America's past.

Timelines

Timelines enable students to visualize sequences of events, to show logical connections between events, and to depict growth and development over time. (See figures 7.1 and 7.2.) Timelines may be drawn to indicate fixed amounts of time between events or they may be more fluid and simply reflect progression over time. One way to introduce timelines is by having students create a timeline of events in their own lives starting with their birth and including memorable events, such as a special birthday, holidays, or their first day of school. The ages of the students and their reading levels should be considered when determining how many events to include on the timeline. Once older students are familiar with timelines, they work with partners to create timelines as they read.

Steps

1. Read the book to determine what dates or events to include on the timeline.
2. For younger students the teacher can create a timeline template for them to complete. Older students can be shown an example of a timeline and then they can create their own.
3. Explain to the students that some authors organize their text based on events that happen over time.
4. Tell the students that as the story is read aloud they are to note events that happened during the story.
5. Begin reading the story and stop after the first few pages to record the first event. Continue in this manner until the end of the book.
6. At the end of the book, provide the students with an opportunity to discuss the book and the events recorded on the timeline.

Examples

Stutson, Caroline. *Cowpokes.* Illustrated by Daniel San Souci. 1999. Unp. New York: Lothrop, Lee & Shepard Books. (hc. 0-688-13973-6).
Grades: P–2. At daybreak, the cowpokes sleepily drag themselves out of their bedrolls and get dressed. The end of the day finds them sitting under the stars strumming guitars around a campfire. Amusing colorful

illustrations accompanied by brief phrases and sentences chronicle the cowpokes' day.

After the book has been read aloud, younger students can complete a simple timeline such as the one below that was created with *Inspiration* software. Students enjoy creating timelines on the computer with software programs such as *Inspiration, Kidspiration,* or *Timeliner.* Students also enjoy drawing timelines on banner paper taped to the wall or sprawled along the floor.

Timeline

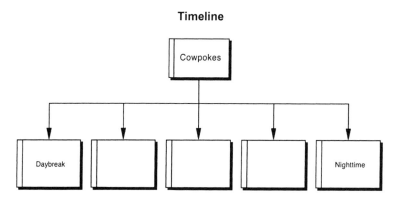

Figure 7.1. As the book is read aloud, the teacher pauses to record three things that the cowpokes did during the day. For older students, more blocks can be added to the timeline to record all of the events mentioned in the story. Students can also draw pictures of the events and tape them together to make a visual timeline.

Schanzer, Rosalyn. *How We Crossed the West: The Adventures of Lewis & Clark.* 1997. Unp. Washington, D.C.: National Geographic Society. (hc. 0-7922-3738-2).
Grades: 4–8. Excerpts from these intrepid explorers' journals enable readers to experience the excitement of the journey from Missouri to the Pacific Ocean. The journal entries capture the trials and tribulations faced by these explorers as they charted unexplored territory and discovered the beauty of the landscapes and wildlife that they encountered. Colorful, very detailed American folk art style illustrations fill the pages of this book and provide additional interesting details. The end pages contain a map showing the route Lewis and Clark followed.

Timeline

May 14, 1804	Lewis & Clark set off for their expedition
August 29, 1804	violent storms Sergeant Pryor, 5 chiefs & 70 men arrived
November 4, 1804	Mr. Charbonneau" wished to be hired as an iterpiter
February 11, 1805	Sacagawea and Charbonneau had a little boy
June 11, 1805	found rivers called the Marias
August 17, 1805	saw Indians coming
November 7, 1805	They found Pacific Ocean
March 23, 1806	Been in same place since December 7 1805
July 26, 1806	he saw 8 indians & invited them to camp that night
September 20, 1806	They found a white settlement they haven't seen one in 2 yrs.
September 23, 1806	passed there old camp at Wood River & it was a short distance from Saint Louis

Figure 7.2. As the student read the book, she recorded events on this brief timeline depicting events in Lewis and Clark's journey across America. Completing the timeline as she read gave her a focus for her reading.

Additional Books and Resources

January, Brendan. *Explorers of North America.* 2000. 47p. New
  York: Children's Press. (hc. 0-516-21629-5; pbk. 0-516-27195-4).
Grades: K–2. In A.D. 1000 Leif Eriksson landed on Canada's shore and
so began the history of the exploration of North America. This easy-to-
read book with color illustrations briefly describes the explorations of
those intrepid explorers who came after Eriksson. Resources for learning more, a brief glossary, and an index conclude the book. This book
is from the A True Book series.

Turner, Ann. *Katie's Trunk.* Illustrated by Ron Himler. 1992. Unp.
  New York: Macmillan Publishing. (hc. 0-02-789512-2).
Grades: K–3. After the Boston Tea Party, things begin to change and
the air becomes filled with an unspeakable tension. Katie is called a
"Tory" and she is not sure what that means. When the rebels come Katie's family hides in the woods, but Katie runs back to the house and
hides in a trunk. Discovered by one of the rebels, Katie learns that there
is good in every group.

Hopkinson, Deborah. *Sweet Clara and the Freedom Quilt.* Paintings
  by James Ransome. 1993. Unp. New York: Alfred A. Knopf. (hc.
  0-679-82311-5).
Grades: 1–4. Clara's sewing skills earn her a place in the Big House as
a seamstress. When she overhears two slaves talking about needing a
map to find the Underground Railroad, she decides to make a map using the leftover pieces of material in her scrap bag. She quietly gathers
information from other slaves and begins to create a map disguised as a
quilt. When the quilt is finished she and her friend Jack set out to find
their way north on the Underground Railroad leaving the quilt behind
to show others the way. Rich, powerful paintings beautifully portray
this emotional story.

Stein, R. Conrad. *The Great Depression.* 1993. 32p. Chicago: Children's Press. (hc. 0-516-06668-4).
Grades: 3–6. Here is the story of a dark period in American history;
however, the author points out that not everyone was poor and destitute
through the years of the depression. The haunting photographs and illustrations tell the story in ways words cannot. An index is included in
the book. This book is from the Cornerstones of Freedom series.

Feinstein, Stephen. *The 1960s: From the Vietnam War to Flower
  Power.* 2000. 64p. Berkeley Heights, N.J.: Enslow. (hc. 0-7660-
  1426-6).

Grades: 3 and up. People, art, sports, politics, environmental issues, and scientific advances during the 1960s are examined in this brief history. Captioned black-and-white photographs help students visualize the events described in the text. When creating a timeline of this decade students can interview relatives and add their personal comments about the events portrayed. A timeline, a collection of resources for additional learning, and an index are included. This book is from the Decades of the 20th Century series.

Fremon, David K. *Japanese–American Internment in American History.* 1996. 128p. Springfield, N.J.: Enslow. (hc. 0-89490-767-0).
Grades: 4 and up. Throughout the book students read about the personal experiences of Japanese Americans detained in internment camps. The reasons behind the internment are presented as is information on legal proceedings that sought to redress the injustice. The book concludes with a timeline, chapter notes, books for further reading, and an index. This book is from the In American History series.

Gay, Kathlyn, and Martin Gay. *Korean War.* 1996. 64p. New York: Henry Holt. (hc. 0-8050-4100-1).
Grades: 5 and up. While the book contains details about the reasons for the war and information on the battles, it is most notable because it puts a human face on the war. Black-and-white photographs and quotes from participants provide details that make the text memorable and enhance understanding. The book begins with a chronology and a map. It concludes with resources for learning more and an index. This book is from the Voices from the Past series.

Inspiration 7.0 and *Kidspiration* concept mapping software enable students to brainstorm ideas and then effortlessly organize them. *Kidspiration* software is for grades kindergarten through five and *Inspiration* is for grades six and up. This software is available on CD-ROM for both Macintosh and Windows computers from Inspiration Software, Inc.

With *TimeLiner 5.0,* students create multimedia timelines with graphics, video, and sound. As students enter the event and the date, the program arranges them in chronological order. This program is easy and fun to use. This software is appropriate for grades one and up and is available on CD-ROM for both Macintosh and Windows computers from Tom Snyder Productions.

Infoplease.com from the Family Education Network provides resources for teachers, parents, and students on related topics such as history, government, business, and culture. The site has a search engine and is located at http://www.infoplease.com.

Problem–Solution Charts

Understanding the different text structures authors incorporate into their writing aids in the retention and recall of the material. One way to foster understanding of text structures is by creating visual representations (Vacca and Vacca, 2002). Problem–solution is one type of text structure that readily lends itself to a visual representation. Completing problem-solution charts focuses students' attention as they read. Once they have completed the charts students need opportunities to discuss them. They may discover that the problems faced by the characters are similar to ones they have had to face in their own lives and this helps them develop empathy for the characters and make connections to their own lives (Monson, 1992). The problem-solution charts presented here depict only one solution. (See figures 7.3 and 7.4.) Additional solution boxes can easily be added to the charts to show how characters tried one or more solutions before actually solving their problem.

Steps

1. Set the stage for this activity by introducing the reading selection and asking students what types of problems they think the characters may encounter.
2. Introduce the problem-solution chart to the students.
3. As you read the book, have students raise their hands when they think they have heard a problem and a possible solution. Record their responses on the chart.
4. Provide students an opportunity to discuss the completed charts.
5. Once older students become familiar with this activity, they can complete the charts on their own or with a partner.

Examples

Calhoun, Mary. *Flood*. Illustrated by Erick Ingraham. 1997. Unp. New York: Morrow Junior Books. (hc. 0-688-13919-1).

Grades: P–1. In this story based on the Midwest floods of 1993, a ficti-
tious family carefully watches the river level, moves furniture to the
second floor of the house, and makes plans to leave. When the levee
breaks, they are forced to leave behind their farm and house.

Problem–Solution Chart

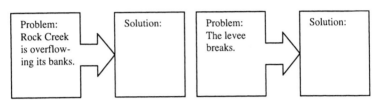

Figure 7.3. When confronted by problems brought on by the rising waters, the family in this story finds solutions.

Wright, Courtni C. *Wagon Train: A Family Goes West in 1865.* Illustrated by Gershom Griffith. 1995. Unp. New York: Holiday House.
(hc. 0-8234-1152-4).
Grades: K–4. This is the story of an African American family and their
long, difficult journey in a wagon train from Virginia to California
along the Oregon Trail. They encounter many hardships or problems,
such as Pa's rattlesnake bite. An author's note at the beginning of the
book contains background information about African Americans' mi-
grations west.

Problem–Solution Chart

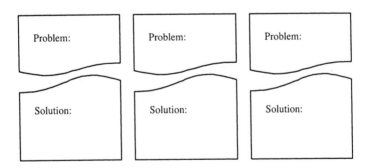

Figure 7.4. A blank chart such as this one can be used with older students.

Additional Books and Resources

Howard, Ellen. *The Log Cabin Quilt.* Illustrated by Ronald Himler. 1996. Unp. New York: Holiday House. (hc. 0-8234-1247-4).

Grades: P–3. After Mam dies, Pap and Granny gather the children and some of their belongings into a covered wagon and move from Carolina to the woods of Michigan. When the cold north wind blows through the cracks in the log cabin, Elvirey comes up with a unique solution to the problem.

Anderson, Joan. *Cowboys: Roundup on an American Ranch.* Photographs by George Ancona. 1996. 47p. New York: Scholastic. (hc. 0-590-48424-9).

Grades: 1–4. Color photographs help tell the story of the spring cattle roundup on a family ranch in New Mexico. The family members and the cowboys they hire spend two weeks gathering the cattle and returning them to the ranch. This is a tribute to America's hardworking, dedicated cowboys. The book contains a glossary.

Kroeger, Mary Kay, and Louise Bordon. *Paperboy.* Illustrated by Ted Lewin. 1996. 33p. New York: Clarion Books. (hc. 0-395-64482-8).

Grades: 1–4. In 1927 Jack Dempsey was expected to win his boxing match with Gene Tunney. Willie, a young paperboy, was ready to sell papers on the streets of Cincinnati after the fight to earn money to help support his family. When Dempsey lost, Willie was the first paperboy to appear at the newspaper office, but no one wanted to buy papers. Undaunted, he returned the next day to the newspaper office to collect papers to sell and was rewarded for his unfailing efforts to sell papers.

Wilder, Laura Ingalls. *Hard Times on the Prairie.* Illustrated by Renée Graef. 1998. 72p. New York: Harper Trophy. (hc. 0-06-027792-0; pbk. 0-06-442077-9).

Grades: 2–3. Fires, grasshoppers, and blizzards presented hardships to this indomitable family as they made their home on the prairie. With determination and hard work, they overcame the hardships. This book is A Little House Chapter Book, which was adapted from an original Little House novel.

Blashfield, Jean F. *Women at the Front: Their Changing Roles in the Civil War.* 1997. 63p. New York: Franklin Watts. (hc. 0-531-20275-5).

Grades: 3–6. During the Civil War women disguised as men fought alongside men. They also nursed the injured, sewed uniforms, cooked

food, spied on the other side, and kept farms and businesses in opera-
tion. One was a doctor. Their work helped to change the way society
perceived women's roles. Photographs, illustrations, and short biographies interspersed throughout the text provide interesting details that
aid in understanding this crucial time in American history. A timeline
of the Civil War, a listing of resources for additional information, and
an index are included. This book is from the First Books series.

Calabro, Marian. *The Perilous Journey of the Donner Party.* 1999.
    192p. New York: Clarion Books. (hc. 0-395-89910-3).
Grades: 4–8. The Donner party left Springfield, Illinois, in April 1846
setting out in search of a better life in California. Survivors' letters and
diaries tell the story of a tragic band of travelers beset by seemingly
insurmountable hardships. A list of the members of the Donner party,
reproductions, photographs, and maps enhance the story. At the end of
the book are a letter from a survivor, a chronology, a roster of the dead,
resources for further research, a bibliography, and an index.

The Donner party web site contains links to a variety of resources,
such as a map of the route, information on ordering the video, an interview with Rick Burns who wrote and co-produced the video, and a
teacher's guide. This site is part of the PBS American Experience web
site and is located at http://www.pbs.org/wgbh/amex/donner/.
    Crossing the Plains, 1865 is a web site that contains excerpts from
Sarah Raymond's diary as she crossed the plains with her family. The
site is located at http://www.ibiscom.com/plains.htm.

Character Comparison Charts

One type of text structure authors use to organize their writing is comparison–contrast. Completing character comparison charts helps students become aware of how authors develop and describe characters.
(See figures 7.5 and 7.6.) As they read, students can note character
traits and make comparisons between the characters in the story or between a character in the story and themselves. As they look for character traits remind them that authors use dialogue, description, and action
to tell readers about characters (Monson, 1992). Looking for comparisons as they read actively involves students in their reading. This active
involvement has the potential to increase their comprehension of the
material they are reading. Additionally, as they develop an under-

standing of how authors use comparisons to develop characters, they can be encouraged to create comparison charts for characters in stories they are writing.

Steps

1. Read the story and decide on which characters the students will compare or if they will compare the character to themselves.
2. Create the character comparison chart.
3. Introduce the reading selection and the chart to the students.
4. Read the story aloud to the students.
5. Ask them for descriptions of the characters. Model for them how to return to the text to find support for their responses.
6. Record their responses on the chart.
7. Discuss the similarities and differences they discovered.

Examples

Wiles, Deborah. *Freedom Summer.* Illustrated by Jerome Lagarrigue. 2001. Unp. New York: Atheneum Books for Young Readers. (hc. 0-689-83016-5).
Grades: K–3. The Civil Rights Act of 1964 forbids segregation and two young boys, Joe and John Henry, are thrilled because now they can swim together in the local pool. They learn that laws do not change feelings and that their friendship defies the racism in the hearts of many of the townsfolk. An author's note begins the text and explains that the story is based on real events.

Character Comparison Chart

	Joe	John Henry
What do they look like?		
What do they like to do?		
What do they do when they go to the store?		
How do they feel about the pool being closed?		

Figure 7.5. Encourage students to return to the text and illustrations to find support for their responses. Once the chart is completed, allow ample time for the students to discuss the chart and reflect on the book.

Waters, Kate. *Giving Thanks: The 1621 Harvest Feast.* Photographs
    by Russ Kendall. In cooperation with Plimoth Plantation. 2001.
    40p. New York: Scholastic. (hc. 0-439-24395-5).
Grades: 2–4. Large color photographs depict this reenactment of the
first Thanksgiving shared by the Pilgrims and the Wampanoag. The
feast unfolds through the eyes of Dancing Moccasins, a fourteen-year-
old Wampanoag, and Resolved, a six-year-old Pilgrim. The book includes additional information about the harvest feast, the actors, and
Plimoth Plantation. At the end of the book is a list of books for further
reading and a glossary.

Character Comparison Chart

Dancing Moccasins	Resolved
How are the characters similar?	
How are they different?	

Figure 7.6. After completing this chart, students can be encouraged to
compare themselves to Dancing Moccasins and Resolved.

Additional Books and Resources

Schroeder, Alan. *Carolina Shout.* Illustrated by Bernie Fuchs. 1995.
    Unp. New York: Dial Books for Young Readers. (hc. 0-8037-
    1676-1).
Grades: 1–3. Delia lives in Charleston, South Carolina, and everywhere
she goes she hears music in the streets. Her sister Bettina does not hear
the music. The music Delia hears is the street vendors calling as they
sell their wares, men singing as they work, and children making up
rhymes as they play. Lush oil paintings accompany the rhythmic text.

Waters, Kate. *On the Mayflower: Voyage of the Ship's Apprentice & a Passenger Girl.* Photographs by Russ Kendall. 1996. 40p. New York: Scholastic. (hc. 0-590-67308-4).

Grades: 2–4. Neither the ship's apprentice nor the passenger girl have family with them on the voyage to the New World. They become fast friends and each has a different perspective on the trip. The color photographs were taken aboard the *Mayflower II,* a reproduction of the original *Mayflower.* Additional information and a diagram of the *Mayflower* are located at the end of the book as is a glossary.

Sinnott, Susan. *Charley Waters Goes to Gettysburg.* Photographs by Dorothy Handelman. 2000. Unp. Brookfield, Conn.: The Millbrook Press. (hc. 0-7613-1567-5).

Grades: 2–5. This photographic essay portrays a Civil War reenactment at Gettysburg. The main character is an eight-year-old boy, Charley Waters, who participates in the reenactment as a soldier in the Union Army. Students can compare his everyday life with his life as a soldier. The book concludes with a glossary and books for further reading.

Yin. *Coolies.* Illustrated by Chris K. Soentpiet. 2001. Unp. New York: Philomel Books. (hc. 0-399-23227-3).

Grades: 3–5. During the mid-1800s, Chinese immigrants came to America to build the railroad. This is the story of two brothers who came to the land of opportunity to work and to send money back to their family in China. The book concludes with an author's note that provides additional details about these Chinese immigrants and a bibliography.

Sandler, Martin W. *Presidents.* 1995. 94p. New York: HarperCollins. (hc. 0-06-024534-4).

Grades: 3–6. Photographs and illustrations portray the presidents as leaders, family men, and pet owners. This informative book with short paragraphs provides intimate glimpses into the lives of men who held the highest office in the land. This is a Library of Congress Book.

West, Delno C., and Jean M. West. *Braving the North Atlantic: The Vikings, the Cabots and Jacques Cartier Voyage to America.* 1996. 86p. New York: Atheneum Books for Young Readers. (hc. 0-689-31822-7).

Grades: 4–8. Viking sagas contain the first clues about explorers of the North Atlantic. The authors caution readers about the accuracy of the tales. The book is filled with fascinating facts and information about these intrepid explorers. A chronology, black-and-white pictures, and maps enhance the text. The book concludes with a glossary, books for further reading, and an index.

The *Civil War: Two Views* CD-ROM from Clearvue requires students' active involvement as they explore text, pictures, and videos depicting the Civil War and its aftermath. The software is available for both Macintosh and Windows platforms.

The American Memory: Historical Collections for the National Digital Library is sponsored by the Library of Congress and contains a searchable database of documents, pictures, and other resources. This site is located at http://memory.loc.gov/ammem/amhome.html.

Primary source documents are featured on the Civil War web site at http://www.ibiscom.com/cwfrm.htm. These documents provide powerful reminders of the horrors of war and give students personal accounts of the war.

References

Edgington, William D. "The Use of Children's Literature in Middle School Social Studies: What Research Does and Does Not Show." *The Clearing House* 72, no. 2 (Nov./Dec. 1998): 121–125.

Monson, Dianne. "Realistic Fiction and the Real World." In *Invitation to Read: More Children's Literature in the Reading Program*, edited by Bernice E. Cullinan, 24–39. Newark, Del.: International Reading Association, 1992.

National Council for the Social Studies. *Curriculum Standards for Social Studies*. 1994. http://www.ncss.org/standards/ (20 Nov. 2002).

Ross, Elinor P. *Using Children's Literature across the Curriculum*. Phi Delta Kappa Educational Foundation Fastback No. 374. Bloomington, Ind.: Phi Delta Kappa Educational Foundation, 1994.

Vacca, Richard T., and Jo Anne L. Vacca. *Content Area Reading: Literacy and Learning across the Curriculum*, 7th ed. Boston: Allyn and Bacon, 2002.

· 8 ·
The United States

Learning about the fifty states introduces students to different regions of the United States, each with its own geographic features, customs, cultural traditions, and climate. Students build on their personal experiences as they learn about distant and less familiar places (Wunder, 1995). A quick survey of the students in the classroom can uncover students who have lived in different states or who have friends and relatives living in different states. Some students may have taken family vacations to other states. To utilize students' personal connections to the states, make them the classroom experts on those states. Students can share their knowledge and experiences about living in or visiting other states with their classmates. They may have photographs or movies to share with their classmates. Their parents, friends, or relatives may be willing to make presentations to the class on the states.

As they learn about the different regions and the states in those regions, students discover the interconnections between people and the environment. This encompasses thematic strand three of the *Curriculum Standards for Social Studies* (NCSS, 1994), which is people, places, and environments. As students learn about the history of each of the states, they discover how the states have changed over time and students develop an appreciation of the past. Time, continuity, and change are encompassed in thematic strand two of the *Curriculum Standards for Social Studies* (NCSS, 1994). To assist students in understanding and remembering what they learn about the states, these comprehension strategies are included in this chapter: connection stems, book bits, and pyramids.

Connection Stems

When children make connections between the texts they read and their own lives, they develop a greater understanding of what they read and the text becomes personally meaningful to them. Connection stems give students a structure to use as they read, reflect, and make connections (McLaughlin and Allen, 2002). Children first learn to make connections between the books they read and their lives, and then they begin to make connections between their reading and the world (Harvey and Goudvis, 2000). Making connections between what they read and the world is a skill that develops gradually. Teachers and librarians can model this skill as they share books with students by making connections between the books and events that are taking place in the world. By reading completed connection stems, teachers and librarians learn about students' prior knowledge and experiences that can be utilized to help students understand new material. Connection stems are used when reading either expository or narrative text. (See figures 8.1 and 8.2.)

Steps

1. Share the connection stems with the students before reading the text aloud.
2. Encourage them to think of connections as you read the text aloud.
3. After reading, think aloud while you complete the connection stems.
4. Encourage the students to share any connections they can make to the text.
5. Read another text aloud and have the students work with a partner to complete the connection stems.
6. Older students can work with partners or in small groups to read texts and complete connection stems. Working together gives students opportunities to discuss, develop, and refine their connections.
7. Provide the students with opportunities to share their connection stems with the class. Have students raise their hands when a classmate shares a connection stem similar to one they have made. Encourage the students to discuss these similar connections.

Examples

Dubois, Muriel L. *Wyoming: Facts and Symbols.* 2000. 24p. Mankato, Minn.: Hilltop Books. (hc. 0-7368-0529-X).
Grades: K–2. Wyoming has a rich supply of natural resources including oil, coal, and natural gas. This state is also known for ranching and farming. Each year millions of tourists visit its two national parks, Yellowstone and Grand Teton. A map of Wyoming and a list of fast facts start young readers on their journey of discovery. Descriptions of the state's symbols contain additional information about the Equality State. The book concludes with places to visit, resources for learning more, and an index. This book is from the States and Their Symbols series.

Connection Stems

1. That picture reminds me of
2. I saw something like that when
3. If I were there, I would
4. I wish that
5. I remember when
6. I felt

Figure 8.1. For younger students there may be fewer connection stems and they may be encouraged to use pictures rather than words to illustrate their connections.

Murphy, Claire Rudolf. *A Child's Alaska.* Photographs by Charles Mason. 1994. 47p. Portland, Ore.: Alaska Northwest Books. (hc. 0-88240-457-1).
Grades: 3–6. When you finish reading this book, you want to make Alaska your next vacation destination. Breathtaking color photographs of the people, the animals, and the landscape let you know that this is a very special place. The engaging text makes comparisons between the lower forty-nine states and Alaska, which helps readers make connections between their lives and the lives of Alaskan children. A glossary concludes the book.

Connection Stems

That reminds me of *when Allisons dog had puppies.*

I remember when *I watched the Coca Cola commercial.*

I have a connection *with Alaska because some of Allisons friends live there.*

I had an experience like that when *I drove under the green light*

I saw something like that when *I went to North Carolina.*

I felt *cold when I saw the boys swimming in Alaska.*

If I were there, I would *play in the snow*

I wish that *I could go there.*

Write your own connections below:

It would be neat to pick berries there

Figure 8.2. The students who worked on these connection stems selected the book because one of them has friends who live in Alaska. As they read, both of the girls made connections between the people and places in the book and their own lives.

Additional Books and Resources

Crane, Carol. *L Is for Lone Star: A Texas Alphabet.* Illustrated by Alan Stacy. 2001. Unp. Chelsea, Mich.: Sleeping Bear Press. (hc. 1-58536-019-8).
Grades: 1–4. Lush illustrations, engaging poems, and fact-filled text motivate readers to learn about Texas. Younger readers may be confused by the illustrations on some of the pages, such as pictures of

Lyndon Johnson and an astronaut on the Moon on the "H" page. The text explains that Houston is the Space Capital and the space center is named after President Johnson. Questions and answers at the end of the book provide additional facts about the state.

La Doux, Rita C. *Iowa.* 1992. 71p. Minneapolis, Minn.: Lerner Publications. (hc. 0-8225-2724-3).

Grades: 3–5. Facts about the history, geography, people, and environment of Iowa are included in this small, easy-to-hold book. The book concludes with a timeline, famous people, facts, a pronunciation guide, a glossary, and an index. From the Hello USA series.

Fradin, Dennis B. *Pennsylvania.* 1994. 64p. Chicago, Ill.: Children's Press. (hc. 0-516-03838-9).

Grades: 3–6. Travel through the Keystone State and discover its history, its cities, its people, and its spectacular landscapes all within the pages of this book. Students find familiar faces in the gallery of famous Pennsylvanians. A glossary and an index are included. This book is one of the From Sea to Shining Sea series.

Gravelle, Karen. *Growing Up in a Holler in the Mountains: An Appalachian Childhood.* 1997. 64p. New York: Franklin Watts. (hc. 0-531-11452-X).

Grades: 3–6. Ten-year-old Joseph Ratliff lives in Stephens Branch Hollow in northeastern Kentucky and readers explore Appalachia with the help of Joseph and his family. Readers learn about the social lives, customs, and economy of the region through narrative text accompanied by color photographs. A glossary, resources for learning more about Appalachia, and an index are included. This book is from the Growing Up in America series.

Bjorklund, Ruth. *Kansas.* 2000. 144p. New York: Benchmark Books. (hc. 0-7614-0646-8).

Grades: 4–8. The book opens with a sweeping view of a field of grain and then three pages later readers are face-to-face with a very muddy piglet. The geography, history, economy, and people of the state are featured in the text. Maps, charts, sidebars, and diagrams support the text and contain a great deal of useful information. A state survey, resources for learning more, and an index are included. This book is from the Celebrate the States series.

Freedman, Nancy. *California.* 1998. 120p. New York: Henry N. Abrams. (hc. 0-8109-5552-0).

Grades: 4–8. Perhaps the motto "Eureka" (I have found it!) best sums up the state of California. Artwork and photographs capture the beauty and excitement of California's natural and manmade wonders. The landscapes, the history, the commerce, the culture, and the seasons are a few of the topics covered in the book. From the Art of the State series.

National Inspirer software sends teams of students scurrying across the United States on a scavenger hunt to locate resources and commodities. This program is perfect for the one-computer classroom. A teacher's guide is included. This software is appropriate for grades four to twelve and is available on CD-ROM for both Macintosh and Windows computers from Tom Snyder Productions.

Book Bits

Book bits are phrases or sentences from the reading selection that are read aloud before reading the text (Yopp and Yopp, 2001). These small bits of information stimulate students' curiosity and motivate them to read the text. Additionally, they activate students' prior knowledge on the topic, encouraging them to make connections between the text and their prior experiences. Using book bits, students think aloud and make predictions about the text before reading. (See figures 8.3 and 8.4.)

Steps

1. Read the book and decide on the phrases and sentences in the text to use for the book bits.
2. Write the phrases and sentences on slips of paper. Make one book bit for each child.
3. Students read their book bits to themselves and reflect on what they have read.
4. Students then move around the room reading their book bits aloud to each other. During this time students only read their book bits, they do not discuss them.
5. After students have heard most of the book bits, they reflect on what they have heard and then discuss their reflections in small groups or write about their reflections. As they reflect, the students make predictions about the text.
6. Students read the text or listen to the text as it is read aloud.
7. After reading, students discuss the book bits and where they were found in the text.

Examples

Davis, Kenneth C. *Don't Know Much about the 50 States.* Illustrated by Renée Andriani. 2001. 61p. New York: HarperCollins. (hc. 0-06-028607-5).
Grades: 1–4. Clever questions and answers tell readers interesting, unusual details about the states and make learning fun. Jokes, riddles, definitions, quotes, and humorous cartoon illustrations are scattered among the questions and answers. The nickname, the year of statehood, the capital, the flower, and the bird are given for each state. The endpapers feature a map of the United States and a list of the thirteen original colonies.

Book Bits

"daytime at night"
"has a fountain of youth"
"tallest trees on Earth"
"spied on the British disguised as a school teacher"
"can grow thirty feet tall"

Figure 8.3. These intriguing bits of information encourage students to read and learn about people and places in the fifty states in order to find out more about them. Sharing book bits with their classmates encourages students to work together to determine which state the information is describing.

Pollack, Pamela. *Virginia, the Old Dominion.* 2002. 48p. Milwaukee, Wis.: World Almanac Library. (hc. 0-8368-5125-0; pbk. 0-8368-5293-1).
Grades: 3–8. Mountains on Virginia's western border gradually slope down to the Atlantic Coastal Plain on its eastern border. It is home to the Blue Ridge and Allegheny mountain ranges, part of the Appalachian mountain chain. The book has an appealing, colorful layout that combines just the right amount of text, sidebars, photographs, charts, graphs, and maps to hold readers' attention as they learn about the birthplace of colonial leaders and presidents. An index concludes the book. This book is from the World Almanac Library of the States series.

Book Bits

> "Tobacco farming had exhausted the land."
> "give me liberty or give me death"
> "in the rough shape of a triangle"
> "tenth state to ratify the Constitution"
> "Booker T. Washington was born here"
> "epicenter of the Civil War"

Figure 8.4. These book bits give students clues about what they will be learning about Virginia.

Additional Books and Resources

Kummer, Patricia K. *New Jersey.* 1998. 48p. Mankato, Minn.: Capstone Press. (hc. 1-56065-529-1).
Grades: 2–4. Beginning with a set of fast facts this book contains a brief introduction to New Jersey. Chapters provide information about the land, the people, the history, the economy, and the landmarks to visit. A timeline, a list of famous citizens, a glossary, resources for learning more, and an index are included. This book is from the One Nation series.
Fradin, Dennis B., and Judith Bloom Fradin. *Delaware.* 1994. 64p. Chicago, Ill.: Children's Press. (hc. 0-516-03808-7).
Grades: 3–6. Since Delaware was the first state to sign the United States Constitution, it is nicknamed the First State. After reading a brief history of the state, students take a quick tour of the state to discover famous landmarks. A glossary and an index are included. This book is one of the From Sea to Shining Sea series.
Sirvaitis, Karen. *Tennessee.* 1991. 71p. Minneapolis, Minn.: Lerner Publications. (hc. 0-8225-2722-2).
Grades: 3–6. This concise text takes readers on a trip around the state, recounts the history of the state, shares information about the economy, and describes how the citizens are preserving their environment. A timeline, a list of famous people, brief facts, a glossary, and an index conclude the book. From the Hello USA series.
Brill, Marlene Targ. *Michigan.* 2000. 144p. New York: Benchmark Books. (hc. 0-7614-0418-8).
Grades: 4–8. Michigan is composed of two peninsulas surrounded by glistening water and rich with natural resources. Being the home to

General Motors and Ford Motor Company earned this state the nickname Motor Capital of the World. A state survey, resources for learning more, and an index are included. From the Celebrate the States series.

Rubel, David. *Scholastic Atlas of the United States.* 2000. 144p. New York: Scholastic. (hc. 0-590-72562-9).

Grades: 4–8. An introduction on how to use the atlas helps readers become acquainted with the format of the book. Brightly colored maps, charts, graphs, photographs, and succinct text present basic facts about the states. The sections of the book correspond to the regions of the United States: New England, Mid-Atlantic, South, Midwest, Great Plains, Mountain, Southwest, and Pacific. Appendices, a glossary, and an index conclude the book.

Shirley, David. *Alabama.* 2000. 144p. New York: Benchmark Books. (hc. 0-7614-0648-4).

Grades: 4–8. From mountain to shore is how the author describes the geography of this southern state. Chapters on the history, government, and economy contain basic, factual information. It is the chapters on the people, their achievements, and the state's landmarks that contain information on the heart and the soul of the state. Maps, charts, sidebars, and diagrams are included. A state survey, resources for learning more, and an index are included. From the Celebrate the States series.

Pyramids

Completing expository or narrative pyramids provides students with a quick way to summarize their reading (Waldo, 1991). The information in the pyramid varies depending on the books used. Teachers and librarians tailor the pyramids to meet their objectives. (See figures 8.5 and 8.6.) When students have completed their pyramids, they need opportunities to use them to extend what they have learned. Rather than using these graphic organizers as closed-end assignments, teachers can use the organizers to assist students as they think, discuss, and write about what they have learned (Preller, 2000). Once students become familiar with pyramids, they can be encouraged to create pyramids before writing summaries and to use as study aids when they prepare for tests. After reading a book, students can create pyramids for their classmates to complete.

Steps

1. Select a book, decide on the information in the book to include on the pyramid, and create a blank pyramid.
2. Introduce the pyramid to the students and then read the story aloud.
3. Have the class complete the pyramid, returning to the story to locate the information they need.
4. Using the information on the chart, have a student do an oral summary of the story.
5. Older students can complete pyramids with a partner or in a small group. They can then use the pyramids to write a brief summary of the book.

Examples

Bedard, Michael. *The Divide.* Illustrated by Emily Arnold McCully. 1997. Unp. New York: A Doubleday Book for Young Readers. (hc. 0-385-32124-4).
Grades: K–3. When she was a young girl, Willa Cather's family moved to the Nebraska prairie. She did not want to leave her familiar surroundings and she at first resisted being in her new home. However, as the seasons of the year unfolded, she developed a fondness for the wide expanses and made friends with the other settlers.

Narrative Pyramid

Character's name

Two words describing the character

Three words stating the problem

Four words describing one event

Five words describing the solution to the problem

Six words describing the setting

Figure 8.5. The number of rows to include on the pyramid varies based on the reading ability of the students and whether they are working alone, in small groups, or in a large group.

La Doux, Rita C. *Louisiana*, 2nd ed. 2002. 83p. Minneapolis, Minn.: Lerner Publications. (hc. 0-8225-4065-7; pbk. 0-8225-4145-9).

Grades: 3–5. Travel the bayous to learn about the history, the economy, the cultures, and the wetlands in the southern part of the state. Then, travel the winding country roads through the pine forests in the northern part of the state to discover a different history, economy, and culture. The book concludes with a timeline, famous people, facts, a pronunciation guide, a glossary, and an index. This book is from the Hello USA series.

Expository Pyramid

Line 1 – name of the state
Line 2 – names of two cities
Line 3 – three words describing the geography (rivers, mountains, etc.)
Line 4 – four words describing the people and where they came from
Line 5 – five words describing the state's landmarks
Line 6 – six words about the state's symbols
Line 7 – seven words about famous people from the state
Line 8 – eight words describing what you like best about the state

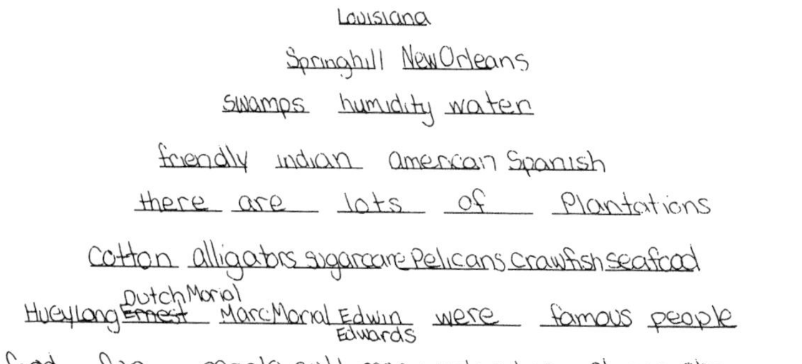
Louisiana
Springhill NewOrleans
swamps humidity water
friendly indian american Spanish
there are lots of Plantations
cotton alligators sugarcane Pelicans crawfish seafood
HueyLong ~~Ernest~~ DutchMorial MarcMorial Edwin Edwards were famous people
food fun people cultures animals citys stores shopping

Figure 8.6. The students who completed this pyramid alternated between listing items and writing sentences on the lines. Names that could have spanned two lines they squeezed onto one line.

Additional Books and Resources

Feeney, Kathy. *West Virginia: Facts and Symbols*. 2000. 24p. Mankato, Minn.: Hilltop Books. (hc. 0-7368-0528-1).

Grades: 2–3. Basic facts about West Virginia and its symbols are included in this introductory volume. Colorful drawings and photographs fill the left side of each two-page spread. Known as the Mountain State, it is also known for the spectacular views from its mountainsides. Places to visit, a glossary, resources for learning more, and an index are included. This book is from the States and Their Symbols series.

Illinois. 1996. 48p. Mankato, Minn.: Capstone Press. (hc. 1-56065-353-1). Grades: 2–3. Fast facts about Illinois begin this introductory look at The Land of Lincoln. Color photographs and illustrations accompany the succinct text. A timeline, famous people, a glossary, resources for learning more, and an index conclude the book. This book is from the One Nation series.

Kuedee, Jaycee. *How to Draw Missouri's Sights and Symbols.* 2002. 32p. New York: PowerKids Press. (hc. 0-8239-6081-1). Grades: 2–5. The engaging narrative text is accompanied by color photographs and directions for drawing Missouri's sights and symbols. The book includes a listing of state facts, a glossary, an index, and web sites. This book is from the A Kid's Guide to Drawing America series.

Elish, Dan. *Vermont.* 2000. 144p. New York: Benchmark Books. (hc. 0-7614-0146-6). Grades: 4–8. Vermont is known for its spectacular fall foliage and delicious maple syrup. This state is also known for another sweet treat, Ben and Jerry's Ice Cream. Words and color photographs describe the history, government, economy, people, and landmarks. A state survey, resources for learning more, and an index are included. This book is from the Celebrate the States series.

Goldberg, Jake. *Hawaii.* 1998. 144p. New York: Benchmark Books. (hc. 0-7614-0203-9). Grades: 4–8. Swaying palm trees and breaking ocean waves only begin to tell the story of our fiftieth state. This state is composed of islands filled with magnificent waterfalls, lush tropical foliage, active volcanoes, and a royal heritage. The text describes the geography, history, economy, and people of the state. Maps, charts, sidebars, and diagrams complement the text. A state survey, resources for finding out more, and an index are included. This book is from the Celebrate the States series.

Wills, Charles. *A Historical Album of Georgia.* 1996. 64p. Brookfield, Conn.: The Millbrook Press. (hc. 0-7613-0035-X; pbk. 0-7613-0125-9). Grades: 4–8. The muted, dark colors of the cover illustration set the context for this historical look at Georgia from its earliest beginnings to the present. Illustrations, photographs, and maps help to tell the story of the last of the original thirteen colonies. A gazetteer, a resource guide, and an index are included. This book is from the Historical Albums series.

Maps of the states and a list of state facts are on the U.S. State Facts web site located at http://www.educationamerica.net/facts/index. At the bottom of the list of facts is the state web site where students can find out more information on the state. Information on this web site is useful for students interested in completing expository pyramids or comparing and contrasting states.

References

Harvey, Stephanie, and Anne Goudvis. *Strategies that Work: Teaching Comprehension to Enhance Understanding.* Portland, Maine: Stenhouse, 2000.

McLaughlin, Maureen, and Mary Beth Allen. *Guided Comprehension: A Teaching Model for Grades 3–8.* Newark, Del.: International Reading Association, 2002.

National Council for the Social Studies. *Curriculum Standards for Social Studies.* 1994. http://www.ncss.org/standards/ (20 Nov. 2002).

Preller, Paula. "Fostering Thoughtful Literacy in Elementary Classrooms." *English Update* (Spring 2000): 1, 7.

Waldo, Brenda. "Story Pyramid." In *Responses to Literature: Grades K–8*, edited by James M. Macon, Diane Bewell, and Mary Ellen Vogt, 23–24. Newark, Del.: International Reading Association, 1991.

Wunder, Susan. "Addressing the Curriculum Standards for Social Studies with Children's Literature." *Social Studies and the Young Learner* 8, no. 2 (Nov.–Dec. 1995): 4–7.

Yopp, Ruth Helen, and Hallie Kay Yopp. *Literature-Based Reading Activities*, 3rd ed. Needham Heights, Mass.: Allyn and Bacon, 2001.

· 9 ·
Landforms

As students learn about the environment and landforms, they also learn about the impact of people on the environment. Thematic strand three of the *Curriculum Standards for Social Studies* (NCSS, 1994) is people, places, and environments. It may be very difficult for students to grasp geographical concepts when they have never seen them, but picture books can help students develop these geographical concepts (Farris and Fuhler, 1994; Kincade and Pruitt, 1996). Comprehension strategies in this chapter include cross sections, maps, and tables.

Cross Sections

Cross sections allow students to visualize and analyze the interior of structures. By analyzing and discussing cross sections students develop an understanding of what lies beneath the surface. (See figures 9.1 and 9.2.) One way to assess their understanding is to have them talk or write about what they learned from the cross section (Moline, 1995). After reading a descriptive text, such as how lava is formed, students can draw and label diagrams to demonstrate their understanding.

Steps

1. Project a cross section for all of the students to see, such as the inside of a mountain.
2. Have students carefully examine the cross section.
3. Ask them to describe what they see and record their observations on the board or chart paper.

139

4. Divide the students into groups of three or four and provide each group with one-half of an apple, a pear, or an orange.
5. Have each member of the group draw a cross section of the fruit, labeling the parts.
6. Ask group members to compare their cross sections and discuss what they observed.
7. Then, have the students examine cross sections in books related to geography.
8. Provide them with time to draw a cross section of one of the landforms they have seen.
9. Discuss their cross sections and then display them in the classroom.

Examples

Gans, Roma. *Let's Go Rock Collecting.* Illustrated by Holly Keller. 1997. 32p. New York: HarperCollins. (pbk. 0-06-445170-4).
Grades: K–3. Children are familiar with rocks, but they probably have not thought much about where they come from. Here is an introduction to rocks that explains to students how rocks are formed and gives students ideas for starting their own rock collections. This book is from the Let's-Read-and-Find-Out Science series.

Cross Section

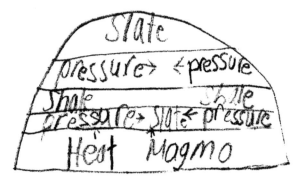

Figure 9.1. This child drew a cross section showing how rocks are formed.

Knapp, Brian. *Earthquakes and Volcanoes, Vol. 4.* 2000. 72p.
   Danbury, Conn.: Grolier Educational. (hc. 0-7172-9496-X).
Grades: 4–8. There are chapters on earthquakes, landforms, volcanoes,
and eruptions in this volume. The descriptions and explanations of
these mighty forces of nature are well written and easily understood by
readers. Spectacular color photographs and detailed, labeled diagrams
highlight key points in the text. The book concludes with a glossary
and a set index. From the Earth Science: Discovering the Secrets of the
Earth set.

Cross Section

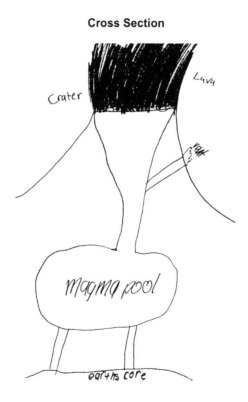

Figure 9.2. This child drew and labeled a cross section of a volcano to
help him remember the parts of a volcano, many of which are hidden
beneath the earth's surface. Students can be encouraged to use cross
sections such as this one for study guides when preparing for a test.

Additional Books and Resources

Klingel, Cynthia, and Robert B. Noyed. *The Grand Canyon.* 2000.
32p. Chanhassen, Minn.: The Child's World. (hc. 1-56766-825-9).
Grades: K–2. Gorgeous color pictures showcase the natural beauty of
the Grand Canyon. This brief text describes the history, formation, and
appearance of the canyon. Information is also provided on sights to see
when traveling there for a vacation. A glossary, an index, and resources
for learning more conclude the book. This is from the Wonder Books
series.

Redmond, Jim, and Ronda Redmond. *Landslides and Avalanches.*
2002. 32p. Austin, Tex.: Steck-Vaughn. (hc. 0-7398-4704-X).
Grades: 1–3. These powerful forces of nature and the destruction they
cause are described and explained. Captioned color photographs and
diagrams enhance the brief succinct text. Included in the book are a
glossary, resources for obtaining additional information, and an index.
This book is from the Nature on the Rampage series.

Bradley, Catherine. *Life in the Mountains.* 2001. 32p. Chicago, Ill.:
World Book. (hc. 0-7166-5221-8).
Grades: 1–4. This is an introductory look at mountain features and
mountain inhabitants. It is filled with appealing color photographs and
illustrations. Included in the book is a Native American tale about the
discovery of fire. The book concludes with a true–false quiz, a glossary
and an index, and resources for learning more. From the World Book
Ecology set.

Sauvain, Philip. *Rivers and Valleys.* 1995. 32p. Minneapolis, Minn.:
Carolrhoda Books. (hc. 0-87614-996-4).
Grades: 2–6. Rivers, valleys, waterfalls, gorges, dams, floods, and river
wildlife are all explored in this interactive book that contains activities
for readers to help them understand the concepts presented. Clear, colorful diagrams and photographs further explain the text. A mapping
activity, a glossary, and an index are included. This book is from the
Geography Detective series.

Clifford, Nick. *Incredible Earth.* 1996. 44p. New York: DK Publishing. (hc. 0-7894-1013-3).
Grades: 3–6. Glorious, color photographs and diagrams of cross sections and three-dimensional models fill the pages of this intriguing
book depicting Earth's landforms. A glossary and an index are included
in the book. This book is from the DK Inside Guides series.

Knapp, Brian. *Landforms, Vol. 6.* 2000. 72p. Danbury, Conn.: Grolier Educational. (hc. 0-7172-9498-6).
Grades: 4–8. Striking color photographs and detailed color diagrams spring from the pages of this book. They capture the readers' attention and draw them into learning about landforms, weathering, erosion, and faults. The book concludes with a glossary and a set index. From the Earth Science: Discovering the Secrets of the Earth set.

Volcano Live has cameras focused on volcanoes around the world. The images are updated every few minutes. The link for kids has information for students and teacher resources. There is even a link for breaking news stories about volcanoes. This wonderful resource is located at http://www.volcanolive.com/.

Maps

Maps are often first introduced in geography class as students develop an understanding of the physical world and their place in the world. Maps can be used to move from place to place and to indicate changes over time. Maps help readers manage the text and aid in understanding the text (Ranson, 1995). Using maps to show children where stories take place helps them make connections between the story and the geographical locations and ensures deeper comprehension and meaningful learning (Kincade and Pruitt, 1996). Students enjoy drawing their own maps and these maps can be used to assess their understanding of the material presented in the social studies classroom. (See figures 9.3 and 9.4.)

Steps

1. Model for the students how to create a simple map of the classroom by drawing the map on the blackboard or on a transparency on the overhead projector.
2. Provide the students with books to read with a partner or with a small group of students.
3. Have the students draw a map of a place in the book. Encourage students to return to the book and look for details to include in their map.
4. Work with younger students to refine the map of the classroom or a map of a place in a familiar story.

Examples

Dorros, Arthur. *Follow the Water from Brook to Ocean.* 1991. 32p.
   New York: HarperCollins. (hc. 0-06-021598-4; pbk. 0-06-445115-1).
Grades: K–3. Where do rivers begin and where do they end? Readers
journey along with a band of intrepid explorers as they follow a brook
as it becomes a river and ultimately ends up in an ocean. Watercolor
illustrations and clear, succinct text introduce readers to the wonders of
rivers. This book is from the Let's-Read-and-Find-Out Science series.

Map

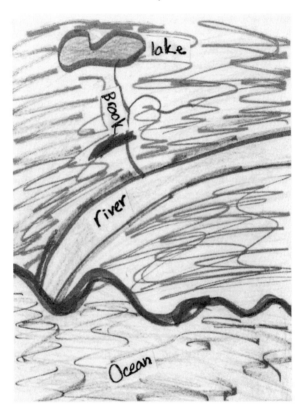

Figure 9.3. This child has drawn a map to show how a brook becomes a
river and eventually spills into the ocean.

Steele, Philip. *Islands.* 1996. 32p. Minneapolis, Minn.: Carolrhoda
  Books. (hc. 0-87614-997-2).
Grades: 2–6. Islands are fascinating, exotic landforms surrounded by
water. Readers learn how they are formed and what plants and animals
grow on islands. This book contains questions and activities that engage students and encourage them to think about what they are learning. Photographs and diagrams are interspersed throughout the text.
The book concludes with a mapping activity, a glossary, and an index.
This book is from the Geography Detective series.

Map

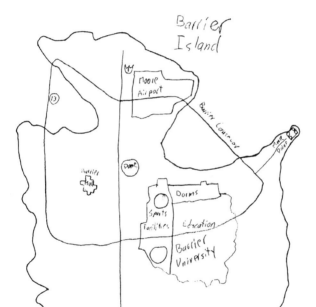

Figure 9.4. After reading about islands, this student designed his own
private island. Students can also include a map key, a compass rose,
and a scale bar in their maps.

Additional Books and Resources

Leedy, Loreen. *Mapping Penny's World.* 2000. 32p. New York: Henry
    Holt. (hc. 0-8050-6178-9).
Grades: 1–3. After learning about maps in school, Lisa draws a map of
her bedroom. Then, she creates a series of maps of her dog Penny's
world. One shows Penny's favorite places to hide things and another
shows Penny's favorite places to spend time. The clear text and
brightly colored illustrations present the concepts in an easy-to-
understand format that has children wanting to create their own maps of
familiar places.
George, Linda, and Charles George. *The Natchez Trace.* 2001. 32p.
    New York: Children's Press. (hc. 0-516-22006-3; pbk. 0-516-
    25959-8).
Grades: 2–5. This fascinating look at the Natchez Trace and the people
who traveled it includes the gruesome deeds of some of the notorious
travelers who tortured and killed fellow travelers. Photographs and illustrations depict this once important trade route. A glossary, a timeline, and an index are included. This book is from the Cornerstones of
Freedom series.
Gallant, Roy A. *Dance of the Continents.* 1999. 80p. New York:
    Benchmark Books. (hc. 0-7614-0962-9).
Grades: 3–6. This book contains an introduction to plate tectonics and
the resulting changes in the earth's shape. Color photographs, illustrations, maps, and diagrams are used to extend the text. A glossary,
books for further reading, and an index are included. This book is from
the Story of Science series.
——.*Geysers: When Earth Roars.* 1997. 63p. New York: Franklin
    Watts. (hc. 0-531-20288-7; pbk. 0-531-15838-1).
Grades: 3–6. Readers learn about the formation of geysers, their locations, how they work, and why some of them are extinct. Color photographs, diagrams, and maps help to explain and document the wonder
of geysers. The book concludes with a glossary, resources for additional research, and an index.
Glicksman, Jane. *Cool Geography: Miles of Maps, Wild Adventures,
    Fun Activities, Facts from Around the World.* Illustrated by Ruta
    Daugavietis. 1998. 96p. New York: Price Stern Sloan. (pbk. 0-
    8431-7442-0).
Grades: 3–6. This fun, interactive book actively engages children as
they learn about geography and drawing maps. The book concludes

with the answers to the brain busters located throughout the book, geography at a glance, a glossary, and an index.

Leacock, Elspeth, and Susan Buckley. *Places in Time: A New Atlas of American History.* Illustrated by Randy Jones. 2001. 48p. Boston, Mass.: Houghton Mifflin. (hc. 0-395-97958-7).
Grades: 3–6. Within the pages of the book readers encounter bird's-eye views of America's historical sites featuring a variety of landforms. The book begins with Cahokia, the city of the sun, as it might have looked in 1200 and ends with Lakewood, a suburb in southern California, as it looked in 1953. Included in the book are notes about each of the sites and an index.

Neighborhood Map Machine software has children practicing their map-making skills as they create maps of their neighborhoods. The program includes a slide show feature for students to use to present their maps to their classmates. A teacher's guide is included. This software is appropriate for grades one to six and is available on CD-ROM for both Macintosh and Windows computers from Tom Snyder Productions.

Tables

Tables enable students to record information in an organized format that helps them as they learn and remember what they have read. Tables are one way to present a large quantity of information in a visual format (Harris and Sipay, 1990). Placing the text in a table requires students to revisit the text and to restructure the text. Restructuring the text enables them to make comparisons and aids in the retention of the material. Students benefit from direct instruction and modeling as they learn to locate information in the text to record in tables. Creating their own tables helps students develop an appreciation for and an understanding of the tables they encounter in books. (See figures 9.5 and 9.6.)

Steps

1. Preview the book and determine the key concepts to include in the table.
2. Create the table using a word processing software program or draw a large table on bulletin board paper.

3. Introduce the book and the table to the students.
4. Explain to the students that recording information on the table will help them organize and remember the information presented in the book.
5. Complete the table while reading the book.
6. After reading, have the students discuss the information they recorded in the table.

Examples

Brimner, Larry Dane. *Valleys and Canyons.* 2000. 47p. New York: Children's Press. (hc. 0-516-21569-8; pbk. 0-516-27193-8).
Grades: K–3. This basic book describes the different kinds of valleys in clear, easy-to-understand text. Simple explanations tell students how valleys are formed. Striking color photographs showcase spectacular valleys and canyons from around the world. A glossary and an index are included. This book is from the A True Book series.

Table

Types of Valleys					
How They Are Formed					

Figure 9.5. As they read the book, students complete the table indicating the types of valleys and how they are formed. For younger students this is a large-group activity with the table completed as the teacher reads the book aloud.

Malam, John. *Highest Longest Deepest: A Fold-out Guide to the World's Record Breakers.* Illustrated by Gary Hinks. 1996. 41p. New York: Simon & Schuster Books for Young Readers. (hc. 0-689-80951-4).
Grades: 3–6. Mountains, lakes, glaciers, rivers, caves, and coral reefs are just some of the landforms explored in this book. This is a book that entices students to read and linger as they read the text and examine the artwork. Beautiful, detailed color illustrations, photographs, and diagrams on foldout pages present a visual feast for the eyes. The end

pages contain a map of the world for students to use to locate the landforms as they read about them in the text. The book concludes with a glossary, information on the maps in the book, and an index.

Table

Landform	Location	Animals	Plants	People
mountain				
lake				
glacier				
river				
coral reef				

Figure 9.6. Older students enjoy working with partners as they complete this table. Working with a partner provides them an opportunity to discuss what they are reading and learning.

Additional Books and Resources

Gallant, Roy A. *Minerals.* 2001. 48p. New York: Benchmark Books. (hc. 0-7614-1039-2).
Grades: K–3. This introductory book describes minerals and explains how they are formed. Color photographs illustrate the beauty and wonder of minerals. The book concludes with instructions for growing a crystal garden, a glossary, books and web sites for learning more, and an index. This book is from the Kaleidoscope series.
——. *Sand on the Move: The Story of Dunes.* 1997. 64p. New York: Franklin Watts. (hc. 0-531-20334-4; pbk. 0-531-15889-6).
Grades: 3–6. This is an intriguing look at moving, noisy sand dunes. The book contains information on their composition, types of dunes, how they move, noises they make, plants and animals that inhabit them, and where to find them. The book concludes with a glossary, an index, and books for further reading. This book is from the A True Book series.

Maynard, Christopher. *Why Do Volcanoes Erupt?: Questions Children Ask about the Earth.* 1997. Unp. New York: DK Publishing. (hc. 0-7894-1532-1).
Grades: K–3. From high in the sky to deep under ground the earth is filled with wonders to explore. This short book answers young children's questions about the earth in simple-to-understand language surrounded by color photographs.

Walker, Sally M. *Glaciers: Ice on the Move.* 1990. 47p. Minneapolis, Minn.: Carolrhoda Books. (hc. 0-87614-373-7).
Grades: 3–6. Concise diagrams and informative text describe how glaciers form and move. Spectacular color photographs contain breathtaking views of these icy giants. Information is also included on how and why scientists study glaciers. The book concludes with a glossary and an index. This book is from the A Carolrhoda Earth Watch Book series.

Downs, Sandra. *Shaping the Earth: Erosion.* 2000. 64p. Brookfield, Conn.: The Millbrook Press. (hc. 0-7613-1414-8).
Grades: 4–8. Wind, rain, waves, and glaciers are all shaping the earth and this book describes how these powerful forces over time shape the contours of the earth's surface. Color photographs and sidebars provide additional information and enhance the descriptions provided in the text. The book includes a glossary, recommended resources, and an index. This book is from the Exploring Planet Earth series.

Patent, Dorothy Hinshaw. *Shaping the Earth.* Photographs by William Muñoz. 2000. 88p. New York: Clarion Books. (hc. 0-395-85691-4).
Grades: 4–8. The spreading of the sea floor along the Mid-Atlantic Ridge and plate tectonics are some of the forces changing the earth. Other forces described in the book include volcanoes, geysers, glaciers, rivers, wind, animals, and mankind. Descriptive, informative text and beautiful color photographs explain how these forces shape the earth. The book concludes with a glossary, resources for further research, and an index.

The United States Geological Survey web page has links to information on mapping, volcanoes, landslides, and earthquakes. The information on this site enhances material presented in the classroom and provides additional information for students who want to learn more. Under the link for geology publications are resources for teachers. This web site is located at http://www.geology.usgs.gov/index.html.

Rice University hosts the Glacier web site, which contains links to information on Antarctica's glaciers and links to curriculum resources for teachers. This site houses an extensive collection of resources and it takes a while to navigate through all of them, but it is well worth the time as the resources are excellent. This web site is located at http://www.glacier.rice.edu.

References

Farris, Pamela J., and Carol J. Fuhler. "Developing Social Studies Concepts through Picture Books." *The Reading Teacher* 47, no. 5 (Feb. 1994): 380–387.

Harris, Albert J., and Edward R. Sipay. *How to Increase Reading Ability: A Guide to Developmental and Remedial Methods.* White Plains, N.Y.: Longman, 1990.

Kincade, Kay M., and Nancy E. Pruitt. "Using Multicultural Literature as an Ally to Elementary Social Studies Texts." *Reading Research and Instruction* 36 (Fall 1996): 18–32.

Moline, Steve. *I See What You Mean: Children at Work with Visual Information.* York, Maine: Stenhouse, 1995.

National Council for the Social Studies. *Curriculum Standards for Social Studies.* 1994. http://www.ncss.org/standards/ (20 Nov. 2002).

Ranson, Clare. "Cartography in Children's Literature." Paper presented at the annual meeting of the International Association of School Librarianship, Worcester, England, July 1995.

· 10 ·
The World

Using children's literature in the social studies class transports readers to other times and places (Button, 1998). Before they begin their armchair travels, they can locate the countries on a large map of the world. Students in the classroom from other countries can share their special knowledge of that country with their classmates. The books in this section showcase different countries around the world and motivate children to learn more about these countries. As students read and learn about other countries, they notice similarities and differences among the countries, and they develop their critical thinking skills as they make comparisons. Comparing America to other countries provides students with opportunities to develop an appreciation of their own country and the countries they study. Including both fiction and nonfiction books provides students opportunities to learn about countries from different perspectives as does providing them with several books on the same country.

As they learn about other countries, students begin to make connections between their lives and the lives of children in other parts of the world. Studying about the world encompasses thematic strand nine of the *Curriculum Standards for Social Studies* (NCSS, 1994), which is global connections. Learning about other countries helps students begin to develop an understanding of how national interests affect global priorities. As students learn about other countries teachers and librarians can talk to them about current world events found in newspaper headlines and on the evening news. List–group–label, contrast charts, and book charts help students build on their prior knowledge and make connections.

List–Group–Label

List–group–label requires students to categorize words and aids in vocabulary development. Categorizing helps students relate words and concepts to their prior learning, which helps them remember new vocabulary (Tierney and Readence, 2000). List–group–label activates students' prior knowledge about a topic and motivates them to look for connections between words as they read (Taba, 1971). They develop their critical thinking skills as they make decisions about how to group and label a list of words. As they discuss the words and groupings with other students they refine their own ideas and begin to develop an appreciation for others' ideas. The students' groupings aid teachers and librarians as they discern whether the students have the background knowledge they need to comprehend the text. (See figures 10.1 and 10.2.)

Steps

1. Prior to reading the text, the students brainstorm a list of words related to the topic.
2. The teacher writes the words on the board and then reads aloud the list of words.
3. Students then work with partners or in cooperative groups to arrange the list into categories or groups that have something in common.
4. Once they have grouped the words, they decide on a label for the groups of words.
5. Students then share their groupings with the class and explain why they grouped the words as they did.
6. Students read the text and then reexamine their groupings, making any changes they think necessary.

Examples

Onyefulu, Ifeoma. *Emeka's Gift: An African Counting Story.* 1995. Unp. New York: Cobblehill Books. (hc. 0-525-65205-1).
Grades: P–2. Set in a village in southern Nigeria, the story follows a young boy as he travels to his grandmother's house. On his way, he daydreams about all of the wonderful things he sees that would make a perfect gift for his grandmother. When he arrives empty-handed, he

learns that he has in fact brought her the best present of all. Bright, colorful photographs show the objects he sees in the village.

List–Group–Label

Word List:

Okoao (spinning game)	baskets
brooms	hats
necklaces	beads
ishaka (musical instruments)	dried seeds
water pots	tomatoes
pestles and mortars	plastic containers

Group:
   baskets
   water pots
   pestles and mortars
   plastic containers
	Group:
	   necklaces
	   hats
	   beads
	   dried seeds

Label: holds things	Label: things to wear

Figure 10.1. Notice that not all of the brainstormed words fit into the two groups. Students need to know that they do not have to use all of the words in the list. They can also be encouraged to think of different ways to group and label the words.

Armentrout, David, and Patricia Armentrout. *Treasures from Italy.* 2001. 48p. Vero Beach, Fla.: The Rourke Book Company. (hc. 1-55916-292-9).

Grades: 3–5. This brief book is a wonderful introduction to a topic unfamiliar to many students. It is just the book to get them started on an exploration of this fascinating country and its impact on present times. Examining antiquities is one way to make connections between our past and present. A timeline of the Roman Empire is included as are color photographs. A pronunciation guide, a glossary, books for further reading, and an index are included. This book is from the Treasures from the Past series.

List–Group–Label

Word List

Senate	baths	slaves	Forum	steam room
Christians	emperor	temples	chariots	Colosseum
traders	athletes	tax collector	Pompeii	Pantheon
empire	markets	aqueducts	horses	Amphitheater
Mt. Vesuvius	basilicas	gladiators	circus	mosaic

Group: aqueducts
baths
steam room

Label: water things

Group: athletes
chariots
horses
traders
circus
gladiators

Label: things to do with athletes

Group: Christians
temples
basilicas

Label: religion

Group: empire
emporer
tax collector
slaves
senate

Label: rich people

Figure 10.2. Lively discussions accompanied the forming of these groups and labels.

Additional Books and Resources

Oppenheim, Shulamith Levey. *The Hundredth Name.* Illustrated by Michael Hays. 1995. Unp. Honesdale, Penn.: Boyds Mills Press. (hc. 1-56397-694-3).

Grades: 1–4. This magical, mystical story is set in Muslim, Egypt, along the banks of the Nile River. Salah worries about his sad camel. He learns from his father that man only knows ninety-nine names for Allah, but that there are one hundred names for Allah. So one night Salah slips outside and prays to Allah to reveal the hundredth name to his camel. The next morning his camel is holding his head high with a look of infinite wisdom spread across his face.

Morrison, Marion. *Cuba.* 1998. 48p. Austin, Tex.: Raintree Steck-Vaughn. (hc. 0-8172-4796-3).
Grades: 2–5. In Cuban schools students learn academic subjects as well as how to grow plants. Readers learn about the culture, land, and climate of Cuba. Color photographs, illustrations, and maps help portray this island in the Caribbean. A glossary, a list of additional books to read, and an index are included. From the Country Insights series.

Ancona, George. *The Past.* 2002. 48p. Tarrytown, N.Y.: Benchmark Books. (hc. 0-7614-1330-8).
Grades: 3–6. Succinct text, photographs, and reproductions provide a brief examination of Mexico's turbulent history. Readers learn that just as America fought England for independence, Mexico fought Spain for independence. A timeline, a glossary, a list of books for finding out more, and an index are included. From the Viva Mexico! series.

Rubin, Susan Goldman. *Fireflies in the Dark: The Story of Friedl Dicker-Brandeis and the Children of Terezin.* 2000. 48p. New York: Holiday House. (hc. 0-8234-1461-2).
Grades: 4–6. When Friedl Dicker-Brandeis, artist and art therapist, was notified that she was being sent to Terezin concentration camp, she packed her art supplies because she knew that drawing and painting would comfort the children. The haunting artwork of the children depicts the horrors they experienced in the camp and their hope for the future. References and an index conclude the book.

Clare, John D., ed. *Industrial Revolution.* 1994. 64p. San Diego, Calif.: Gulliver Books. (hc. 0-15-200514-5).
Grades: 4–8. Information about the Industrial Revolution is followed by information on its impact on society. Photographs and illustrations with detailed captions help students understand the changes in society brought about by the Industrial Revolution. An index concludes the book, which is from the Living History series.

Goodwin, William. *Saudi Arabia.* 2001. 111p. San Diego, Calif.: Lucent Books. (hc. 1-56006-783-2).
Grades: 4–8. The economy of this desert kingdom was dramatically altered during the 1930s when American geologists discovered vast oil deposits. The geography of the country is described as well as its religious, political, and cultural values. A chronology, books for further reading, a bibliography, and an index are included. This book is from the Modern Nations of the World series.

The Destruction of Pompeii, 79 A.D. web site has letters from Pliny the Younger describing the eruption. Links on the site take students to an illustrated history of the Roman Empire and pictures of Pompeii. This site is located at http://www.ibiscom.com/pompeii.htm.

Information on the Terezin Memorial is located on the International Coalition of Historic Site Museums of Conscience web site at http://www.sitesofconscience.org/terezin.html. There are links to information on what happened at Terezin, the exhibits at the museum, descriptions of programs at the museum, ongoing issues in the world today, and other museums.

Contrast Charts

Contrast charts introduced before reading activate students' prior knowledge and, used during reading, focus students' attention (Yopp and Yopp, 2001). As students learn about other countries, they recognize similarities and differences among the countries in their customs, landforms, languages, and occupations. Having students looking for contrasts between countries and cultures helps them develop an understanding of cultural similarities and differences (Kincade and Pruitt, 1996). As students discuss what they have learned, they compare the information gleaned from different books, confirm what they have learned, and develop new perspectives (Ross, 1994). Contrast charts require students to restructure the material in the text, which aids in comprehension. (See figures 10.3 and 10.4.)

Steps

1. Explain to students that contrasting information is one organizational strategy used by authors.
2. Provide them with a contrast chart.
3. Model how to find ideas in the text that support the contrast.
4. Have the students read the text, complete the contrast chart, and discuss the contrasts they noted.

Examples

Oberman, Sheldon. *The Always Prayer Shawl.* Illustrated by Ted Lewin. 1994. Unp. Honesdale, Penn.: Boyds Mills Press. (hc. 1-878093-22-3).

Grades: 1–4. When Adam and his family leave Czarist Russia his grandfather gives him his prayer shawl. It had originally belonged to Adam's great-great-grandfather. In America, things are different, but his prayer shawl is the same. Over the years, Adam replaces parts of the shawl and mends the shawl so that one day he can give it to his grandson.

Contrast Chart

	Russian Farm	American City
Heat	Chopped wood	Turned a dial
Travel	Horse and wagon	Car
Education	Grandfather's house	School
Language	Russian	English
Housing	House	Apartment
Work	Farm	Factory

Figure 10.3. Students compared Adam's life on a Russian farm with his life in an American city.

Platt, Richard. *Castle Diary: The Journal of Tobias Burgess, Page.* Illustrated by Chris Riddell. 1999. 64p. Cambridge, Mass.: Candlewick Press. (hc. 0-7636-0489-5).
Grades: 3–8. In 1285, eleven-year-old Toby Burgess spent a year as a page in his uncle's castle. His diary entries describe the daily life of a page and what it was like to live in a castle. Colorful, humorous illustrations highlight the entries. Notes for the reader, a glossary, an index, and a bibliography are included.

Contrast Chart

	Castle Page	American Child
Bed	Pallet with straw mattress	Bed with foam mattress
Riding	Horses	Bikes
Sports	Tournament	Rodeo
Writing	Wax tablet	Tablet of paper
Poultry	Stuffed and roasted peacock	Stuffed and roasted turkey
Christmas	Holly and mistletoe	Holly and mistletoe

Figure 10.4. This contrast chart shows the differences between the life of a castle page and the life of an American child.

Additional Books and Resources

Brandenburg, Jim. *Sand and Fog: Adventures in Southern Africa.*
1994. 44p. New York: Walker. (hc. 0-8027-7476-8).
Grades: 2–5. Each chapter contains glorious photographs of the people,
the land, and the animals of Namibia. From deserts to oceans, from
penguins to elephants, from shipwrecked galleons to piles of sparkling
diamonds, Namibia is a study in contrasts.

Wright, Rachel. *Paris, 1789: A Guide to Paris on the Eve of the
Revolution.* 1999. 32p. New York: Kingfisher. (hc. 0-7534-5183-2).
Grades: 3–6. Travel back in time to explore the dazzling city of Paris
just before the French Revolution. This sightseer's guide is filled with
colorful illustrations and short, descriptive paragraphs. The author contrasts the lifestyles of the poor and the wealthy. A survival guide, a
souvenir quiz, a foldout map, and an index are included.

Hinds, Kathryn. *Medieval England.* 2002. 79p. New York: Benchmark Books. (hc. 0-7614-0308-6).
Grades: 4–8. Hinds uses contrast charts to help readers understand life
in Medieval England. There is a chart contrasting the comforts of home
in a village, in a town, and in a castle. Another chart contrasts the lives
of boys and girls born in a country village. Maps, illustrations, photographs, and reproductions enhance the text. A timeline, a glossary,
books for further reading, web sites, a bibliography, and an index are
included. From the Cultures of the Past series.

Blumberg, Rhoda. *Shipwrecked! The True Adventures of a Japanese
Boy.* 2001. 80p. New York: HarperCollins. (hc. 0-688-17484-1).
Grades: 4 and up. In the 1800s, Japan did not allow foreigners to land
on its shores and if Japanese left, they were not allowed to return.
Manjiro, a fourteen-year-old fisherman, was shipwrecked and rescued
by American whalers. This intriguing true story tells of his life in
America and, after many years, his eventual return to Japan. Rich de-
tails are included about the nineteenth-century cultures of Japan and
America. An author's note and resources for additional research are
included at the end of the book.

Pullman, Philip. *The Firework-Maker's Daughter.* Illustrated by S.
Aelig Gallagher. 1999. 97p. New York: Arthur A. Levine Books.
(hc. 0-590-18719-8).
Grades: 5–8. Lila's father teaches her to make fireworks, but he refuses
to tell her the final secret needed to become a true firework-maker.
With the help of a friend, she discovers the final secret is that she must

journey to Razvani the Fire-Fiend and exchange three gifts for royal sulphur. The determined, fearless Lila sets off alone on the perilous journey. This is an amusing, suspenseful novel from beginning to end.

Walgren, Judy. *The Lost Boys of Natinga: A School for Sudan's Young Refugees.* 1998. 44p. Boston, Mass.: Houghton Mifflin. (hc. 0-395-70558-4).

Grades: 5–8. Walgren, an award-winning photojournalist, traveled to Natinga in southern Sudan and documented the lives of approximately two thousand young male refugees at a camp protected by the Sudanese People's Liberation Army. Daily they face the threat of war, disease, and famine. However, they understand the importance of education and do not let the lack of books, paper, or pencils keep them from learning.

Book Charts

Book charts enable students to organize information from several books (Yopp and Yopp, 2001). Using multiple sources and a variety of genres fosters students' comprehension of the concepts and content (Roser and Keehn, 2002). Additionally, using more than one source to gather information requires students to summarize, synthesize, compare, and evaluate (Preller, 2000). Book charts enable students to make comparisons between the characters, settings, problems, and solutions found in different books. (See figure 10.5.) They can also be used by students to make comparisons between the lives of children in different countries. (See figure 10.6.) Book charts require students to use higher-order thinking skills as they think about and draw comparisons between the books.

Steps

1. Create a large chart with several categories and enough room for several books. The number of categories and the number of books depend on the ages and reading levels of the students.
2. After reading each book, have students discuss the books and work together to decide on the information to go into the categories.
3. Write the information in the categories.
4. Once the charts are completed, provide the students with opportunities to discuss the charts and the comparisons they made.

Examples

Kimmel, Eric A. *Asher and the Capmakers: A Hanukkah Story.* Illustrated by Will Hillenbrand. 1993. Unp. New York: Holiday House. (hc. 0-8234-1031-5).
Grades: P–3. Asher volunteers to go out in the snow and borrow an egg from a neighbor so his mother can make potato latkes. He gets lost in a blizzard where he meets up with capmaking fairies and joins them on a magical flight to Jerusalem. After what seems like only a fortnight, he returns home with an egg and discovers he has been gone seven years.

Polacco, Patricia. *Rechenka's Eggs.* 1988. Unp. New York: Philomel Books. (hc. 0-399-21501-8).
Grades: P–3. All winter long Babuska paints eggs for the Easter Festival. She rescues an injured goose, who accidentally breaks all of the decorated eggs. For several mornings thereafter, Babuska awakens to discover the goose has laid a beautiful, decorated egg and Babuska once again has eggs for the festival.

Book Chart

Title	Character	When	Problem	Solution
Asher and the Capmakers	Asher	The night before Hanukkah in Eastern Europe.	He gets lost trying to borrow an egg for his mother to make latkes.	When he returns home with the egg seven years have passed.
Rechenka's Eggs	Old Babuska	About two weeks before the Easter Festival in Moskva.	Her goose breaks all the eggs she has decorated for the festival.	The goose, Rechenka, lays beautiful, decorated eggs.

Figure 10.5. In this chart, comparisons have been made between two folktales.

Ross, Michael Elshon. *Children of Puerto Rico.* Photographs by Felix Rigau. 2002. 48p. Minneapolis, Minn.: Carolrhoda Books. (hc. 1-57505-522-8).
Grades: 3–5. The book begins with a brief history of Puerto Rico and then readers meet children living in different areas of this island coun-

try. For example, readers meet Gabriel from Sabana Grande whose great-grandmother remembers when the U.S. soldiers came and freed the people from Spanish domination. A pronunciation guide and an index are included. From The World's Children series.

Staub, Frank. *Children of Sierra Madre.* 1996. 48p. Minneapolis, Minn.: Carolrhoda Books. (hc. 1-87614-943-3).

Grades: 3–5. The Sierra Madre range is located on the western side of Mexico. The lives and cultures of the people are described by children who live in different areas of the mountain range. A pronunciation guide and an index are included. From The World's Children series.

——. *Children of the Yucatan.* 1996. 48p. Minneapolis, Minn.: Carol-rhoda Books. (hc. 1-87614-943-3).

Grades: 3–5. Color photographs and short paragraphs contain a wealth of information about this Mexican state. Children from Yucatan tell readers about the culture, the environment, and the people. Additional information about Yucatan and the Maya, a pronunciation guide, and an index conclude the book. From The World's Children series.

Book Chart

Book Title	Location	Children's Activities	Celebrations	Occupations
Children of Puerto Rico	Caribbean island	flying kites, riding horses, playing sports	*fiesta patronales* (festival of the patron saints)	salesman, forest supervisor, teacher
Children of Sierra Madre	western side of Mexico	caring for farm animals, fishing, riding mules	Fiesta of the Virgin of Guadalupe, Easter	farmer, teacher, brick maker, tour guide
Children of the Yucatan	Yucatan Peninsula in Mexico	caring for farm animals, fishing, playing sports	*el dia de los muertos* (Day of the Dead)	teacher, salesman, fisherman

Figure 10.6. This chart enabled students to organize information they learned about children living in different countries.

Additional Books and Resources

McKay, Lawrence, Jr. *Journey Home.* Illustrated by Dom Lee and
    Keunhee Lee. 1998. Unp. New York: Lee & Low Books. (hc. 1-
    880000-65-2).
Grades: K–5. Mai accompanies her mother, Lin, as she returns to Vietnam in search of her birth family. Together mother and daughter search
to find their family with their only clue being the kite found with Lin
when she was left on the doorstep of the orphanage. Together they discover a new country and a new home.
Garcia, Guy. *Spirit of the Maya: A Boy Explores His People's Myste-
    rious Past.* Photographs by Ted Wood. 1995. 47p. New York:
    Walker. (hc. 0-8027-8379).
Grades: 2–5. Twelve-year-old Kin's family honors their Lacando'n
heritage. As direct descendants of the Maya, the males wear their hair
long and wear long white robes. One Saturday morning Kin rides with
his father to the ruins of Palenque and there discovers an appreciation
and understanding of his heritage.
Knoll, Donna L. *France.* 2002. 64p. Mankato, Minn.: Bridgestone
    Books. (hc. 0-7368-1077-3).
Grades: 2–5. Scenic photographs, maps, charts of fast facts, and illustrations combined with succinct text introduce students to France. The
geography, history, economy, and people of France are described in
separate chapters. A timeline, a glossary, a bibliography, web sites, and
an index are included. Using this book along with others from the
Countries and Cultures series would provide students with a wealth of
information to use to complete a book chart.
Wilson, Laura. *How I Survived the Irish Famine: The Journal of Mary
    O'Flynn.* 2001. 36p. New York: HarperCollins. (hc. 0-06-029534-1).
Grades: 2–5. Set in the 1840s, this is the fictionalized journal of a
twelve-year-old girl's journey to America to escape the Irish famine.
Photographs of Irish scenery and rooms filled with authentic artifacts
illustrate the journal. Readers become engrossed in the story and develop empathy for the Irish immigrants. An introduction, an afterword,
an index, a glossary, and places to visit are included in the book.
Kuklin, Susan. *Kodomo: Children of Japan.* 1995. 48p. New York:
    G.P. Putnam's Sons. (hc. 0-399-22613-3).
Grades: 3–6. This photographic trip to Japan focuses on the everyday
lives of three children in Hiroshima and four children in Kyoto. In
school they learn math with an abacus and don white gowns and masks

to serve their classmates lunch. After-school activities include taking classes in kendo, judo, English, or calligraphy. A glossary is included.

Marx, Trish. *One Boy from Kosovo.* Photographs by Cindy Karp. 2000. 24p. New York: HarperCollins. (hc. 0-688-17732-8). Grades: 3–8. Evocative pictures and descriptive narrative present the grim realities of living in a refugee camp. Twelve-year-old Edi and his family fled Kosovo to the safety of the Brazda refugee camp. While living in a tent with other relatives, the family attempts to maintain their daily routines. The book ends with an epilogue saying that when the war ended the family returned to their home.

The Lonely Planet web site has a wealth of information on regions and countries throughout the world, all contained in a searchable database. This site is a travel guide; however, it also contains information about the history, the culture, and the environment of the countries. This site's address is http://www.lonelyplanet.com/destinations.

References

Button, Kathryn. "Linking Social Studies and Literacy Development through Children's Books." *Social Studies and the Young Learner* 10, no. 4 (March/April 1998): 23–25.

Kincade, Kay M., and Nancy E. Pruitt. "Using Multicultural Literature as an Ally to Elementary Social Studies Texts." *Reading Research and Instruction* 36 (Fall 1996): 18–32.

National Council for the Social Studies. *Curriculum Standards for Social Studies.* 1994. http://www.ncss.org/standards/ (20 Nov. 2002).

Preller, Paula. "Fostering Thoughtful Literacy in Elementary Classrooms." *English Update* (Spring 2000): 1, 7.

Roser, Nancy L., and Susan Keehn. "Fostering Thought, Talk, and Inquiry: Linking Literature and Social Studies." *The Reading Teacher* 55, no. 5 (Feb. 2002): 416–426.

Ross, Elinor P. *Using Children's Literature across the Curriculum.* Phi Delta Kappa Educational Foundation Fastback No. 374. Bloomington, Ind.: Phi Delta Kappa Educational Foundation, 1994.

Taba, Hilda. *Teacher's Handbook for Elementary Social Studies*, 2nd ed. Reading, Mass.: Addison-Wesley, 1971.

Tierney, Robert J., and John E. Readence. *Reading Strategies and Practices: A Compendium*, 5th ed. Needham Heights, Mass.: Allyn and Bacon, 2000.

Yopp, Ruth Helen, and Hallie Kay Yopp. *Literature-Based Reading Activities*, 3rd ed. Needham Heights, Mass.: Allyn and Bacon, 2001.

· 11 ·
Cultures

Sharing multicultural literature with students enables them to comprehend, appreciate, and celebrate differences among cultures (Bishop, 1992). Students develop empathy and tolerance as they discover similarities between cultures and find they share common human characteristics. Students in the classroom who come from other countries enjoy sharing their country and culture with their classmates. Multicultural literature exposes students to other perspectives and helps them recognize the cultural diversity in their classroom (Kincade and Pruitt, 1996). The illustrations in multicultural literature are important because they portray unfamiliar people, places, and events. Seeing these images enhances students' understanding of the culture. Learning about other cultures encompasses the first thematic strand of the *Curriculum Standards for Social Studies* (NCSS, 1994).

Folktales reveal the traditions, values, and humor of different cultures (Bishop, 1992). Similar folktales are found in different countries and comparing and contrasting them helps students develop an appreciation for their own and other cultures. Children use their prior knowledge about folktales to comprehend folktales from other countries. Students from other countries enjoy telling their classmates about folktales from their country that are similar to ones they read in class. Using different genres in the social studies classroom and providing students time to explore, question, and discuss the texts motivates them to become actively involved in their learning. Word wheels, polar opposites, and sequence of events are the comprehension strategies presented in this chapter to help students understand and remember what they learn about different cultures.

Word Wheels

Word wheels enable students to organize information about how people from different countries share similar experiences (Yopp and Yopp, 2001). Word wheels graphically display the commonalities between the experiences of people in different countries. (See figures 11.1 and 11.2.) Once students have completed their word wheels, they need opportunities to discuss and share their work. Discussions enable students to develop and refine their understanding as they compare and evaluate their ideas with those of their peers (Preller, 2000). Students develop a mutual understanding of different cultures as they work together to learn about people and cultures across the globe.

Steps

1. Draw a circle in the middle of the board and write the common element in the circle.
2. Draw circles with connecting links around the first circle.
3. Tell the students that they are going to discover how people in different cultures share common experiences.
4. Introduce the book to the students.
5. After reading the selection, have students discuss the common experiences and decide what to put in the surrounding circles.
6. Students can then discuss the completed word wheels and the similarities between the countries. During the discussion encourage students to make connections between their personal experiences and the experiences of people in other countries.

Examples

Singer, Marilyn. *On the Same Day in March: A Tour of the World's Weather*. Illustrated by Frané Lessac. 2000. Unp. New York: HarperCollins. (hc. 0-06-028187-1; pbk. 0-06-443528-8).
Grades: P–3. Readers travel around the world observing the weather in each locale. They discover that hail, a twister, fog, sun, and rain are all occurring on the same day in March somewhere in the world. Included in the book are maps of the world that show the locations of the cities. An author's note on seasons around the world concludes the book.

Word Wheel

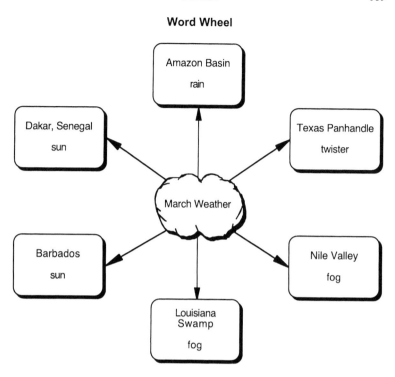

Figure 11.1. This word wheel shows students that places that are very far apart may be having very similar weather on a given day, such as the fog in the Nile Valley and the Louisiana swamp. After completing this word wheel, students can visit a weather Internet site such as http://www.weather.com/common/welcomepage/world.html to find out the current weather in these locations.

Ganeri, Anita. *Wedding Days: Celebrating Marriage.* 1998. 30p. New York: Peter Bedrick Books. (hc. 0-87226-287-1).
Grades: 1–5. The Hindu, Buddhist, Sikh, Jewish, Christian, and Muslim faiths celebrate a couple's commitment with weddings. Brief paragraphs provide details as to the customs followed in each ceremony. Colorful borders surround the pages that are filled with colorful pictures and illustrations. Students read about a variety of wedding traditions, each reflecting the religious beliefs of the participants. Students enjoy talking about weddings they have attended and comparing them to the ones in the book. This book is from the Life Times series.

Word Wheel

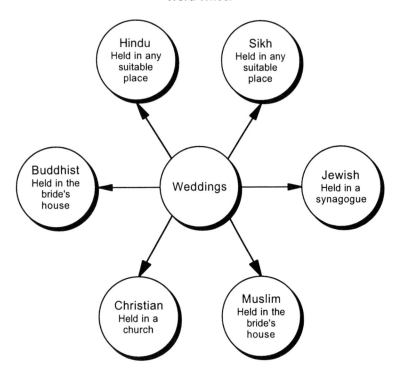

Figure 11.2. The religion of the couple dictates where the wedding is held, ranging from churches to houses to any suitable place.

Additional Books and Resources

Morris, Ann. *Families.* 2000. 32p. New York: HarperCollins. (hc. 0-688-17198-2).
Grades: P–2. Color photographs depict families from around the world at work and at play, loving and caring for one another. A wide variety of family constellations and cultures are showcased in this photographic essay that shows all families are different and that they are also the same. An index and a map show where each family lives.
Lankford, Mary D. *Birthdays Around the World.* Illustrated by Karen Dugan. 2002. 32p. New York: HarperCollins. (hc. 0-688-15431-X).

Grades: 3–6. Birthdays are celebrated around the world and descriptions of celebrations in Finland, Malaysia, Mexico, the Netherlands, New Zealand, the Philippines, and Sweden are highlighted. Readers delight in discovering the similarities in birthday celebrations and they also find new ideas for celebrating their own birthdays. A bibliography and an index are included.

Lorenz, Albert, with Joy Schleh. *House: Showing How People Have Lived Throughout History with Examples Drawn from the Lives of Legendary Men and Women.* 1998. Unp. New York: Harry N. Abrams. (hc. 0-8109-1196-5).

Grades: 3–6. Peek inside dwellings that span time and the globe to learn about the cultures of the people who reside within. Visit Jefferson's Monticello, a whale ship, a Barcelona apartment house built in the early 1900s, the Russian Mir space station, and a collection of other houses. The book concludes with additional information about dwellings and the people within.

Knight, Margy Burns. *Talking Walls.* Illustrated by Anne Sibley O'Brien. 1992. Unp. Gardiner, Maine: Tilbury House. (hc. 0-88448-102-6; pbk. 0-88448-154-9).

Grades: 3–7. By looking carefully at walls from around the world, readers learn about the different cultures responsible for the walls. Full-page color illustrations show children reacting to the walls as they search them for meaning. The text briefly tells the significance of the walls and more detailed information is presented at the end of the book. The sequel to the book is *Talking Walls: The Stories Continue.*

Yale, Strom. *Quilted Landscape.* 1996. 80p. New York: Simon and Schuster Books for Young Readers. (hc. 0-689-80074-6).

Grades: 3–10. These are the stories of twenty-six young immigrants from eleven to seventeen who are learning English and adjusting to a new culture. Their words, photographs, poems, and drawings personalize their stories and help readers make connections between their lives and the lives of these determined immigrants. Sidebars containing facts about the immigrants' countries, a list of books for further reading, notes on the sources, and an index are included.

Millard, Anne. *A Street through Time: A 12,000-Year Walk through History.* Illustrated by Steve Noon. 1998. 32p. New York: DK Publishing. (hc. 0-7894-3426-1).

Grades: 4–8. Students become armchair time travelers as they turn the pages of this book and watch the buildings and the people change through the ages. The detailed illustrations invite readers to examine them closely as they search for clues about life in other times and places. The book ends with a time-traveling quiz and a glossary.

Talking Walls multimedia software is based on the book by the same name. It contains videos and links to web sites that contain information on different cultures. This software is appropriate for grades three and up and is available on CD-ROM for both Macintosh and Windows computers from Edmark.

Polar Opposites

Polar opposites encourage students to think critically about the characters as they describe them (Yopp and Yopp, 2001). This activity requires students to rank the characters based on two opposing characteristics. (See figures 11.3 and 11.4.) As students attempt to describe the characters, they should be encouraged to return to the text and find support for their choices. As they make decisions about characters from other cultures, they should be encouraged to think about the cultural influences that may affect the characters' actions. Multicultural literature introduces students to the challenges and problems of other people, which helps them develop an understanding of the cultural influences on others' lives (Goforth, 1998).

Steps

1. Select a character.
2. Create a list of the character's traits.
3. Create a second list of the opposites of those traits.
4. Place the traits and their opposites on a three to five point continuum.
5. After reading the story, have the students rank the character by marking an X on the continuum and giving reasons for their rankings.

Examples

Geeslin, Campbell. *How Nanita Learned to Make Flan.* 1999. Unp. New York: Atheneum Books for Young Readers. (hc. 0-689-81546-8).

Grades: K–3. Nanita's father is a shoemaker who is too busy making shoes for other people to make her a pair. With her First Communion coming up she decides to make herself a pair of shoes. The rainbow-colored shoes she makes are enchanted and they take her to the distant house of a ranchero. He makes her work from dusk to dawn and she learns to make flan before eventually returning home to her father.

Polar Opposites

Nanita was				
a hard worker	____	____	____	lazy.
Nanita was				
a good cook	____	____	____	a bad cook.
Nanita was				
glad to be home	____	____	____	sad to be home.

Figure 11.3. After reading the story, students place an X on one of the three lines on each continuum to describe Nanita.

McMahon, Patricia. *Chi-Hoon: A Korean Girl.* Photographs by Michael F. O'Brien. 1993. 48p. Honesdale, Penn.: Boyds Mills Press. (hc. 1-56397-026-0).
Grades: 2–6. Readers follow along as Chi-Hoon goes through her week trying to be a dutiful daughter in order to win one of the prizes given out each Monday to dutiful students. Narrative text with excerpts from Chi-Hoon's diary is complemented by color photographs showing everyday life in Korea as seen through the eyes of this eight-year-old.

Polar Opposites

Chi-Hoon is				
dutiful	_____	_____	_____	_____mischievous
respectful	_____	_____	_____	_____disrespectful
studious	_____	_____	_____	_____unintellectual
adventurous	_____	_____	_____	_____fearful
loving	_____	_____	_____	_____hateful
happy	_____	_____	_____	_____sad

Figure 11.4. Notice that this grid has five gradients for each characteristic. Students should be encouraged to find support for their decisions in the text and to discuss their decisions with their classmates.

Additional Books and Resources

Bunting, Eve. *Going Home*. Illustrated by David Diaz. 1996. Unp.
    New York: HarperCollins. (hc. 0-06-026296-6; pbk. 0-06-443509-1).
Grades: P–3. This is the story of a family of migrant farmworkers and
their trip home to Mexico to spend Christmas with their extended family. The parents came to America in search of a better life with more
opportunities for their children, but one day they will return to live in
Mexico. Dark, colorful pictures depict the trip home and the celebration.

McCully, Emily Arnold. *The Orphan Singer*. 2001. Unp. New York:
    Arthur A. Levine Books. (hc. 0-439-19274-9).
Grades: K–3. A long time ago in Venice, Italy, the Dolcis realized that
their baby daughter was a gifted singer. Knowing that they could not
afford to provide the musical training she needed, they left her at an
orphanage where she would receive the finest musical training. This is
a heartrending story of parents determined to do what is best for their
child. Elegant tempera and watercolor paintings fill the pages.

Bercaw, Edna Coe. *Halmoni's Day*. Illustrated by Robert Hunt. 2000.
    Unp. New York: Dial Books for Young Readers. (hc. 0-8037-
    2444-6).
Grades: 1–4. Magnificent oil paintings illustrate this moving story of a
Korean grandmother's affection for her American granddaughter. Jennifer is afraid that Halmoni will embarrass her at Grandparents' Day
because she is different from the other grandparents. Jennifer's mother
translates as Halmoni tells the class about her father and how Jennifer
reminds her of him. Jennifer realizes what a special grandmother she
has.

Louie, Ai-Ling. *Yeh-Shen*. Illustrated by Ed Young. 1982. Unp. New
    York: Philomel Books. (hc. 0-399-20900-X).
Grades: 1–4. This Cinderella story is based on one from ancient China.
When Yeh-Shen's father dies, her stepmother treats her harshly. Rather
than having a fairy godmother to look after her, Yeh-Shen has a fish
that takes care of her. Woven into each of the pastel watercolor illustrations is an image of a fish.

Zucker, David. *Uncle Carmello*. Illustrated by Lyle Miller. 1993.
    Unp. New York: Macmillan Publishing. (hc. 0-02-793760-7).
Grades: 1–4. Spending the day with gruff Uncle Carmello in Boston's
Little Italy introduces David to his Italian American heritage and helps
him appreciate and understand Uncle Carmello. Colorful, detailed wa-

tercolor illustrations accompany this heartwarming story of a special relationship.

Mercredi, Morningstar. *Fort Chipewyan Homecoming: A Journey to Native Canada.* 1997. 48p. Minneapolis, Minn.: Lerner Publications. (hc. 0-8225-2659-X; pbk. 0-8225-9731-4).
Grades: 3–8. In this photo essay readers join twelve-year-old Matthew Dunn as he travels to Fort Chipewyan to visit relatives, to learn the traditions of his North American Indian heritage, and to participate in Treaty Days. A word list and books for further reading are included.

Sequence of Events

Examining organizational patterns in text such as sequence of events helps children see how events in the story are connected. Paying attention to the sequence of events as the text progresses helps students remember what they read. Completing concept maps that show the sequence of events requires students to reflect on the text and to restructure the text, which leads to a deeper understanding of what they have read. (See figures 11.5 and 11.6.) Concept mapping software such as *Inspiration* or *Kidspiration* can be used to create charts for students to complete. Learning about other cultures helps students develop an understanding of themselves and others (Wunder, 1995). As students read about other cultures, they need opportunities to reflect on what they have learned and to discuss what they have learned with their classmates. Discussion has the potential to enhance their understanding.

Steps

1. Read the text and make note of the sequence of events.
2. Create a diagram to record the events.
3. Project a copy of the diagram on the board or provide each child with a copy. Explain the diagram to the students.
4. Tell the students that as you read the book aloud, they are to listen for the major events in the story.
5. As you come to a major event in the story, stop reading and record the event on the diagram.
6. When the story is finished, provide the students an opportunity to discuss the sequence of events.

7. Older students can return to the story and fill in details to describe the events.

8. The students can use the completed diagrams to retell the story to a partner.

Examples

Takabayashi, Mari. *I Live in Tokyo.* 2001. Unp. New York: Houghton Mifflin. (hc. 0-618-07702-2).
Grades: P–2. Spend a year with Mimiko and learn something new about the Japanese culture every month of the year. Childlike drawings and succinct text take readers on a cultural journey through the sights and sounds of Tokyo. The book ends with some Japanese words and phrases.

Sequence of Events

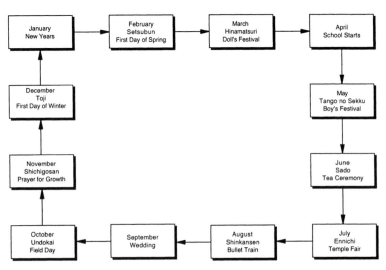

Figure 11.5. This diagram depicts the cyclical nature of the Japanese holidays celebrated each year.

Hoyt-Goldsmith, Diane. *Potlatch: A Tsimshian Celebration.* Photographs by Lawrence Migdale. 1997. 32p. New York: Holiday House. (hc. 0-8234-1290-3).

Grades: 1–5. The Tsimshians are Northwest Coast Native Americans, who celebrate their culture and heritage through potlatch ceremonies. The potlatch is explored through the eyes of a thirteen-year-old boy, David, who is participating in his first one. Color photographs capture the celebration, which involves a feast, raising totem poles, dedicating regalia and adopting new names, dancing, and giving gifts. A glossary and an index are included.

Sequence of Events

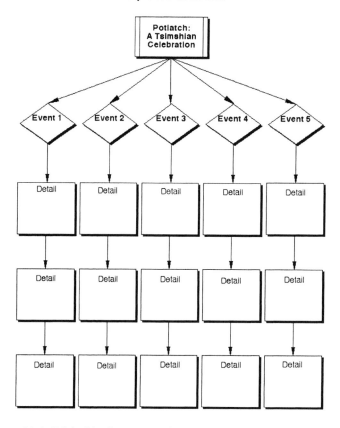

Figure 11.6. With this diagram students record the important events of the potlatch and provide details to describe the events. Encourage them to return to the text as they fill in the details.

Additional Books and Resources

Wells, Rosemary. *Yoko.* 1998. Unp. New York: Scholastic. (pbk. 0-439-10472-6).
Grades: P–1. When the other students make fun of Yoko's sushi and red bean ice cream, Mrs. Jenkins decides that an International Food Day is just the celebration needed to expose her students to a variety of international dishes. This is a delightful story with adorable characters, who discover that what might at first seem like an unusual food can actually be a tasty treat.

Lewin, Ted. *Sacred River.* 1995. Unp. New York: Clarion Books. (hc. 0-395-69846-4).
Grades: P–3. Pilgrims flock to Benares, India, to the sacred waters of the Ganges River for purification and salvation. Luminous watercolor paintings capture the bright colors of the women's flowing saris and the muted solemnity of this spiritual journey.

Bertrand, Diane Gonzales. *Family, Familia.* Illustrated by Pauline Rodriguez Howard. 1999. Unp. Houston, Tex.: Piñata Books. (hc. 1-55885-269-7; pbk. 1-55885-270-0).
Grades: 1 and up. Daniel is reluctant to attend the family reunion because he does not want to sit around listening to old people tell stories. Amidst the food and the music he meets a cousin his age and they spend the rest of the day together. By the end of the story he has developed a new appreciation for his large family. This story is told in both English and Spanish.

Breckler, Rosemary. *Sweet Dried Apples: A Vietnamese Wartime Childhood.* Illustrated by Deborah Kogan Ray. 1996. Unp. Boston, Mass.: Houghton Mifflin. (hc. 0-395-73570-X).
Grades: 1–4. Surrounded by the devastation of war, this Vietnamese family struggles to survive and to take care of their neighbors. This book is based on a true story about a Vietnamese family's flight to safety.

Ancona, George. *Charro: The Mexican Cowboy.* 1999. Unp. San Diego, Calif.: Harcourt Brace. (hc. 0-15-201047-5; pbk. 0-15-201046-7).
Grades: 4–8. The horsemanship and skills of male charros and female charras are showcased at La Charreria, a rodeo-like competition. Readers familiar with rodeos recognize the events shown in the photographs, such as roping bulls and riding wild horses. A charro's glossary is included.

Malone, Michael. *A Guatemalan Family.* 1996. 64p. Minneapolis, Minn.: Lerner Publications. (hc. 0-8225-3400-2).
Grades: 4–8. Fleeing Guatemalan guerrillas and searching for a better life, Don José made his way to America. Family members joined him and together they started new lives. Color photographs enhance the story of this family's flight and their life in America where they keep alive their Guatemalan traditions. This book is from the Journey between Two Worlds series.

References

Bishop, Rudine Sims. "Extending Multicultural Understanding." In *Invitation to Read: More Children's Literature in the Reading Program*, edited by Bernice E. Cullinan, 80–91. Newark, Del.: International Reading Association, 1992.

Goforth, Frances S. *Literature and the Learner*. Belmont, Calif.: Wadsworth, 1998.

Inspiration Ver. 7.0, Inspiration Software, Inc., Portland, Ore.

Kidspiration, Inspiration Software, Inc., Portland, Ore.

Kincade, Kay M., and Nancy E. Pruitt. "Using Multicultural Literature as an Ally to Elementary Social Studies Texts." *Reading Research and Instruction* 36 (Fall 1996): 18–32.

National Council for the Social Studies. *Curriculum Standards for Social Studies*. 1994. http://www.ncss.org/standards/ (20 Nov. 2002).

Preller, Paula. "Fostering Thoughtful Literacy in Elementary Classrooms." *English Update* (Spring 2000): 1, 7.

Wunder, Susan. "Addressing the Curriculum Standards for Social Studies with Children's Literature." *Social Studies and the Young Learner* 8, no. 2 (Nov.–Dec. 1995): 4–7.

Yopp, Ruth Helen, and Hallie Kay Yopp. *Literature-Based Reading Activities*. Needham Heights, Mass.: Allyn and Bacon, 2001.

· 12 ·
Biographies

As they read biographies, children learn about different times and places and make connections between their lives and the lives of others. This correlates with thematic strand four of the *Curriculum Standards for Social Studies* (NCSS, 1994), individual development and identity. Biographies help children identify with others and examine the personal and historical contexts of people's lives. Within the pages of these books students meet individuals who have overcome hardships and adversity, and pursued their dreams, and who will serve as role models for students as they pursue their goals. Further, biographies enable children to explore the lives of individuals who have made significant contributions to society, which correlates with thematic strand ten of the *Curriculum Standards for Social Studies* (NCSS, 1994), civic ideals and practices. As students read and discuss biographies, they find role models to emulate and they develop an understanding of the importance of citizenship.

Authentic biographies present facts pertaining to the subjects' lives while fictionalized biographies present dramatizations based on facts. Selecting biographies for classroom use requires a careful examination of the subject, of the accuracy of the information, of the characterization, of the theme, of the style of writing, and of the format including illustrations. Character analysis webs, story retellings, and cause and effect charts are strategies that help students understand forces that affect people's lives. Discussions, role-playing, and story retellings are interactive strategies that enable students to construct meaning from books (Morrow, Sharkey, and Firestone, 1993).

Character Analysis Webs

Character analysis webs enable students to record pertinent information about the subject of the biography as they read (Bromley, 1996). Students record character traits on the webs and provide documentation to support their analysis. (See figures 12.1 and 12.2.) This activity requires students to become actively engaged in reading and rereading the text. Recognizing character traits requires students to critically think about the person and this can be modeled by the teacher or librarian in a large group setting. This modeling includes locating passages in the text to demonstrate the techniques authors use to introduce character traits, such as dialogue passages, descriptive details, and dangerous, humorous, or unusual situations (Monson, 1992).

Steps

1. Draw a circle in the middle of the board writing the name of the person in the circle.
2. Explain to students that as the biography is read they are to listen carefully and decide on words that describe the person's personality. For example, the person may be shy, stubborn, studious, or brave.
3. After reading the story, discuss the traits the students think describe the person.
4. Write the traits in circles linked to the main circle.
5. Have the students return to the story to find evidence to support their decisions.
6. Write the supporting details in circles linked to the traits used to describe the person.

Examples

Wallner, Alexandra. *Betsy Ross.* 1994. 32p. New York: Holiday House. (hc. 0-8234-1071-4).
Grades: K–3. At a time when few women owned their own businesses, Betsy Ross supported her family with the earnings from her upholstery shop. This hardworking seamstress outlived three husbands and two of her seven children. The book concludes with an author's note regarding

the controversy about whether or not she sewed the first United States flag and directions for folding a five-point star.

Character Analysis Web

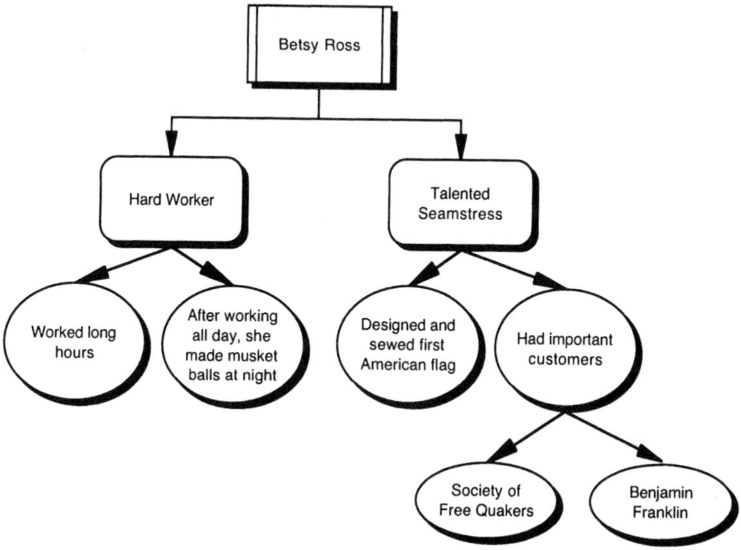

Figure 12.1. First students decided on two characteristics to describe Betsy Ross, *hard worker* and *talented seamstress*. Then, students returned to the text to find details to support the character traits. These details were written in the circles linked to the traits. *Inspiration* concept mapping software was used to create this web. A similar web could be drawn on the chalkboard or butcher paper.

Jeffrey, Laura S. *Barbara Jordan: Congresswoman, Lawyer, Educator.* 1997. 112p. Berkeley Heights, N.J.: Enslow. (hc. 0-89490-692-5).

Grades: 4–8. Through hard work, self-discipline, and the support of her parents, Barbara Jordan became an inspiration to others. The separate but equal education that she received as an African American did not adequately prepare her for the life she wanted to lead. Throughout her years in college and law school she worked until late at night to keep up with her classmates and to excel. She dedicated her life to helping others. Her eloquent, powerful speaking voice made people stop, listen, and heed her words. The book includes a chronology, books for further reading, and an index.

Character Analysis Web

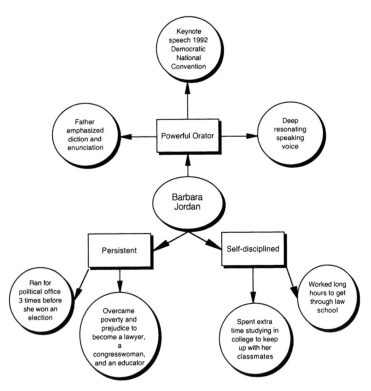

Figure 12.2. After students decide on character traits, they return to the text to find supporting details to add to the character analysis.

Additional Books and Resources

Adler, David A. *A Picture Book of Amelia Earhart.* Illustrated by Jeff Fisher. 1998. Unp. New York: Holiday House. (hc. 0-8234-1315-2). Grades: 2–4. Amelia Earhart's courage, strong will, and determination enabled her to follow her dreams with little regard for what others thought of her. She was one of the first women pilots and the first woman to fly alone across both the Atlantic and Pacific Oceans. Colorful illustrations accompany the appealing text. This book is from the Picture Book Biography series.

Jordan, Roslyn M., and Deloris Jordan. *Salt in His Shoes.* Illustrated by Kadir Nelson. 2000. Unp. New York: Simon and Schuster Books for Young Readers. (hc. 0-689-83371-7).

Grades: 2–4. Michael Jordan's hard work, resolve, and belief in himself helped him become a great basketball player. As a young child, he was concerned about growing tall enough to play basketball, so his mother sprinkled salt in his shoes to help him grow. This book was co-authored by his mother and his sister.

Fisher, Leonard Everett. *Marie Curie.* 1994. Unp. New York: Macmillan Publishing. (hc. 0-02-735375-3).

Grades: 2–5. Dark, foreboding black-and-white illustrations chronicle the life of this brilliant woman scientist who dedicated her life to her research. She fought against sexism and prejudice throughout her life. She was awarded the Nobel Prize in physics and chemistry. The book begins with a chronology of her life and ends with additional information about her life.

Adler, David A. *B. Franklin, Printer.* 2001. 126p. New York: Holiday House. (hc. 0-8234-1675-5).

Grades: 4–8. Benjamin Franklin was a printer, a writer, a scientist, an inventor, and one of the founding fathers. His curiosity, tenacity, and love of reading served him well throughout his life. Included in the book are chronologies, web sites, a bibliography, and an index.

Lang, Paul. *Maria Tallchief: Native American Ballerina.* 1997. 128p. Berkeley Heights, N.J.: Enslow. (hc. 0-89490-866-9).

Grades: 4 and up. Maria Tallchief was the first Native American prima ballerina in the United States. Her strong character and dedication to ballet helped assure her career successes. She was a member of the Osage tribe and the book contains a chapter on their history. The book includes a chronology, a glossary, books for further reading, and an index. This book is from the Native American Biographies series.

Rayfield, Susan. *Pierre-Auguste Renoir.* 1998. 92p. New York: Harry N. Abrams. (hc. 0-8109-3795-6).

Grades: 6–10. Renoir's optimistic, enthusiastic outlook is evident in the bright colors in his paintings. He is considered to be the founder and leader of the French Impressionists. The book is lavishly illustrated with his paintings and concludes with a list of illustrations and an index.

The America's Story from America's Library web site features a link called Meet Amazing Americans. This page contains links to photographs and information on a collection of notable Americans. This web site is available at http://www.americaslibrary.gov and is maintained by the Library of Congress.

Story Retelling

Story retelling actively engages children with the text as they construct their own interpretations of the text (Morrow, 1989). This active involvement improves children's comprehension of the text. Retellings require students to examine the text again and restructure the text as they clarify their understanding (Moss, Leone, and Dipillo, 1997). Retellings can be either written or oral and can be used to assess children's comprehension of the text. Younger students can draw pictures as they listen to a story and older students can take notes as they read. Using these pictures and notes students retell the story. (See figures 12.3 and 12.4.) They also enjoy using puppets or simple props as they retell stories.

Steps

1. To familiarize students with the technique the teacher or librarian can begin by retelling a familiar story.
2. Then, read a biography aloud to the students having them draw pictures or record events in the person's life while reading.
3. Have one or two children retell the story to the class using their drawings or notes.
4. Have the rest of the class retell the story to a partner.
5. Older students can read a biography on their own, recording notes as they read. They can then either use the notes for an oral retelling or for writing a short summary of the biography.

Examples

Adler, David A. *A Picture Book of Abraham Lincoln.* Illustrated by John Wallner and Alexandra Wallner. 1989. Unp. New York: Trumpet Club. (pbk. 0-440-84746-X).

Grades: K–3. Readers learn about the sixteenth president of our country from his birth in Kentucky in 1809 to his assassination in 1865. The book highlights major events in Lincoln's life including his service in the House of Representatives and the Senate, and as president.

Story Retelling

Figure 12.3. In order to retell the story of Abraham Lincoln's life, this student drew pictures of what she felt were the important events.

Stein, R. Conrad. *Chuck Yeager Breaks the Sound Barrier.* 1997. 32p. New York: Children's Press. (hc. 0-516-20294-4; pbk. 0-516-26137-1).

Grades: 3–6. This natural aviator became a pilot when he was nineteen. He was a bomber pilot during World War II and was shot down behind enemy lines. The French underground safely transported him to neutral

---

Spain. Some credit his breaking the sound barrier for making space travel possible. This book is from the Cornerstones of Freedom series.

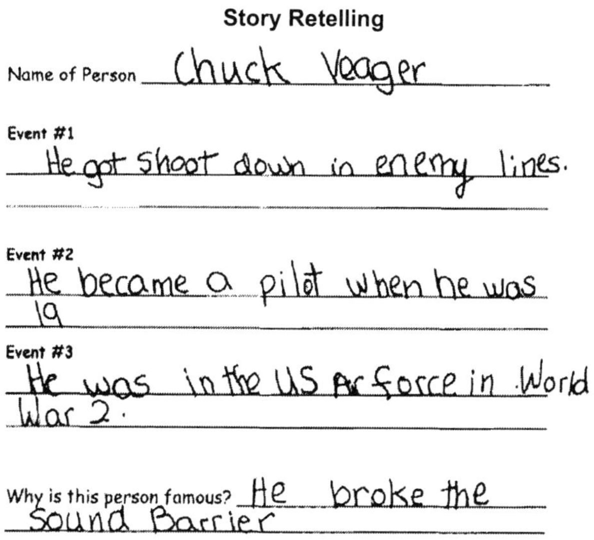

Story Retelling

Name of Person Chuck Yeager

Event #1
He got shoot down in enemy lines.

Event #2
He became a pilot when he was 19

Event #3
He was in the US Air force in World War 2.

Why is this person famous? He broke the Sound Barrier

Figure 12.4. As students work on their own to gather information they may not always get the events of the person's life in the correct order as noted in the above example. They can work with a partner to go back to the text and check the order of the events.

Additional Books and Resources

Winter, Jonah. *Frida.* Illustrated by Ana Juan. 2002. Unp. New York: Arthur A. Levine Books. (hc. 0-590-20320-7).
Grades: P–2. Frida Kahlo, a Mexican artist, escaped from loneliness and pain by painting. As a child, she was bedridden with polio and when she recovered, she walked with a limp. As a teenager, she was in a bus accident and was confined to bed. Her inspiring story unfolds with vibrant, whimsical illustrations reflecting her Mexican heritage.
Brown, Don. *One Giant Leap: The Story of Neil Armstrong.* 1998. Unp. Boston: Houghton Mifflin. (hc. 0-395-88401-2).
Grades: 1–4. Lyrical narrative and rich, pastel illustrations tell the story of the first man to set foot on the moon. His passion for flying and his determination to learn to fly led him to become a pilot before he could

drive a car. This is the story of a boyhood dream that led to stellar accomplishments.

Thomas, Joyce Carol. *I Have Heard of a Land.* Illustrated by Floyd Cooper. 1995. Unp. New York: Joanna Cotler Books. (pbk. 0-06-443617-9).

Grades: 1–4. In 1999, this book was named both a Coretta Scott King Honor Book for Illustration and a Notable Children's Trade Book in Social Studies. African Americans and women received free land in the Oklahoma territory during the 1880s. Using her own family history, the author tells the story of a single African American pioneer woman who settled in Oklahoma. The lyrical text is enhanced by muted full-page illustrations. An author's note concludes the book.

Krull, Kathleen. *Wilma Unlimited: How Wilma Rudolph Became the World's Fastest Woman.* Illustrated by David Diaz. 1996. Unp. San Diego: Harcourt Brace. (hc. 0-15-201267-2).

Grades: 2–4. This amazing runner overcame the effects of polio that crippled her left leg to become an Olympic champion. In order to do this she spent hours doing exercises and withstood excruciating pain. She was determined to be able to run again.

Whitelaw, Nancy. *Clara Barton: Civil War Nurse.* 1997. 128p. Springfield, N.J.: Enslow. (hc. 0-89490-778-6).

Grades: 4–8. Clara Barton worked as a nurse during the Civil War, founded the Red Cross, and fought for equal rights. She accomplished these things even though she suffered from debilitating depression. A glossary, books for further reading, and an index are included. This is one of the Historical American Biographies series.

Aliki. *William Shakespeare & the Globe.* 1999. 48p. New York: HarperCollins. (hc. 0-06-027821-8).

Grades: 4 and up. Written in acts rather than chapters, this blend of literature, history, biography, archaeology, and architecture is a rich introduction to this famous bard. Included in the book are a list of his works, a chronology, a collection of words and expressions, and places to visit.

Diary Maker software includes three multimedia diaries written by young girls in three different times and three different places. One of the diaries is by Anne Frank. With this program, students create their own multimedia diaries. The software is appropriate for grades five to nine and is available on CD-ROM for both Macintosh and Windows computers from Scholastic.

The American History web site contains links to biographies of famous Americans. The brief biographies are grouped alphabetically, and they can be found using the site's search engine. This web site is located at http://americanhistory.about.com/cs/biographiesmenu/.

Cause and Effect

Finding cause and effect relationships in text helps readers comprehend and remember what they read. Cause and effect relationships can be troublesome for readers as the cause and the effect may not appear in the same sentence, or even on the same page. These relationships may be inferred and the effect may come before the cause (Harris and Sipay, 1990). Examining biographies for cause and effect relationships enables students to see how experiences or events in characters' lives influence other events in their lives. (See figures 12.5 and 12.6.)

Steps

1. Select and read a biography making note of the cause and effect patterns.
2. Create a cause and effect chart listing three or four causes.
3. Share the chart with the class.
4. Read the causes aloud to the students and explain that as you read the book aloud they are to listen to determine the effects. When they think they know an effect, they are to raise their hands so the effect can be added to the chart.
5. As students become familiar with finding cause and effect, longer charts can be created and students can be given blank cause and effect charts to complete as they read on their own or with a partner.

Examples

Cooney, Barbara. *Eleanor.* 1996. Unp. New York: Viking. (hc. 0-670-86159-6).
Grades: K–5. This poignant tale of Eleanor Roosevelt tugs at the readers' heartstrings and enables them to understand how she developed the compassion and strength of character for which she was known. Born into a wealthy family, she learned at an early age that she was expected to help those less fortunate. Detailed illustrations beautifully portray the engrossing narrative.

Cause and Effect

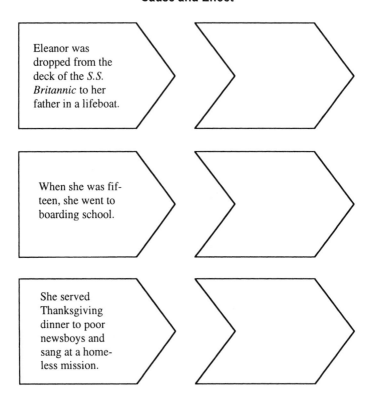

Figure 12.5. This chart provides students with the cause and they fill in the effect after reading and discussing the story.

Towle, Wendy. *The Real McCoy: The Life of an African-American Inventor.* Illustrated by Wil Clay. 1993. Unp. New York: Scholastic. (hc. 0-590-43596-5).

Grades: 1–6. Elijah McCoy was born the son of slaves who escaped to Canada via the Underground Railroad; this intelligent, tenacious inventor did not let racial prejudice stop him from patenting over fifty inventions. One of his patents was for an oil cup that was superior to others created by his competitors. Therefore, people began to ask for "the real McCoy," and this may be the origin of this well-known expression. Luminous illustrations help tell the story of this noted inventor.

Cause and Effect

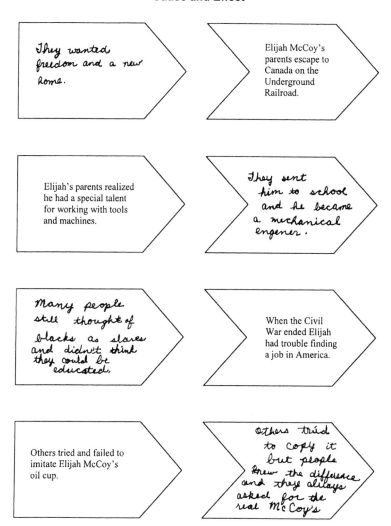

They wanted freedom and a new home.

Elijah McCoy's parents escape to Canada on the Underground Railroad.

Elijah's parents realized he had a special talent for working with tools and machines.

They sent him to school and he became a mechanical engener.

Many people still thought of blacks as slaves and didn't think they could be educated.

When the Civil War ended Elijah had trouble finding a job in America.

Others tried and failed to imitate Elijah McCoy's oil cup.

Others tried to copy it but people knew the difference and they always asked for the real Mc Coy's

Figure 12.6. This chart requires students to locate both causes and effects. As students become proficient at locating cause and effect, they can complete blank charts.

Additional Books and Resources

Raphael, Elaine, and Don Bolognese. *Daniel Boone: Frontier Hero.*
1996. Unp. New York: Scholastic. (hc. 0-590-47900-8).
Grades: 2–5. Color illustrations fill the pages of this biography of an
American frontier hero. Daniel Boone faced the hardships and hazards
of frontier life and made a home for his family, first in North Carolina
and then in Kentucky. Instructions for drawing people, a Conestoga
wagon, a canoe, and a log cabin are included. This book is from the
Drawing America series.

Turner, Ann. *Abe Lincoln Remembers.* Illustrated by Wendell Minor.
2001. Unp. New York: HarperCollins. (hc. 0-06-027577-4).
Grades 2 and up. The author cautions that this book is a work of fiction
based on historical facts rather than a biography. It is included here
because this somewhat sentimental look at Lincoln's life gives students
a different perspective from which to view this famous president. The
author explores Lincoln's thoughts and feelings about the events that
shaped his life and affected American history.

Camp, Carole Ann. *Sally Ride: First American Woman in Space.*
1997. 104p. Berkeley Heights, N.J.: Enslow. (hc. 0-89490-829-4).
Grades: 4–8. Sally Ride was the first American woman to travel into
space. She flew as a Mission Specialist and one of her jobs was to manipulate the robotic arm as it released and captured a satellite. Black-
and-white photographs complement the captivating text. The book includes a chronology, books for further reading, and an index. This book
is from the People to Know series.

Krull, Kathleen. *Lives of the Presidents: Fame, Shame (and What the
Neighbors Thought).* Illustrated by Kathryn Hewitt. 1998. 96p. San
Diego: Harcourt Brace. (hc. 0-15-200808-X).
Grades: 4–8. This anecdotal look at the presidents complete with cari-
catures of them provides glimpses into their less presidential sides.
Their bad habits, ailments, attitudes, and odd sleeping habits are ex-
posed. They are presented as fathers, husbands, neighbors, and pet
owners. The book ends with a selected bibliography.

Hart, Philip S. *Up in the Air: The Story of Bessie Coleman.* 1996. 80p.
Minneapolis, Minn.: Carolrhoda Books. (hc. 0-87614-949-2).
Grades: 4 and up. During a time when there were no black pilots and
few women pilots, Bessie Coleman pursued her dream to become a
pilot. Compelling black-and-white photographs enhance this poignant

biography of a woman who became the first African American woman
to fly a plane.

Pinkney, Andrea Davis. *Let It Shine: Stories of Black Women Freedom Fighters.* Illustrated by Stephen Alcorn. 2000. 107p. San Diego: Gulliver Books. (hc. 0-15-201005-X).
Grades: 4 and up. The ten freedom fighters in this book are Sojourner
Truth, Biddy Mason, Harriet Tubman, Ida B. Wells-Barnett, Mary
McLeod Bethune, Ella Josephine Baker, Dorothy Irene Height, Rosa
Parks, Fannie Lou Hamer, and Shirley Chisholm. These courageous
women fought against inequality, oppression, prejudice, and fear. In the
process, they made the world a better place to live. The book concludes
with suggestions for further reading.

References

Bromley, Karen D'Angelo. *Webbing with Literature: Creating Story
Maps with Children's Books*, 2nd ed. Boston, Mass.: Allyn and
Bacon, 1996.

Harris, Albert J., and Edward R. Sipay. *How to Increase Reading Ability*, 9th ed. White Plains, N.Y.: Longman, 1990.

Monson, Dianne L. "Realistic Fiction and the Real World." In *Invitation to Read: More Children's Literature in the Reading Program,*
edited by Bernice E. Cullinan, 24–39. Newark, Del.: International
Reading Association, 1992.

Morrow, Leslie Mandel. "Using Story Retelling to Develop Comprehension." In *Children's Comprehension of Text*, edited by K.
Denise Muth, 37–58. Newark, Del.: International Reading Association, 1989.

Morrow, Leslie Mandel, Evelyn Sharkey, and William Firestone.
"Promoting Independent Reading and Writing through Self-
Directed Literacy Activities in a Collaborative Setting." Reading
Research Report No. 2. Athens, Ga.: National Reading Research
Center (Spring 1993).

Moss, Barbara, Susan Leone, and Mary Lou Dipillo. "Exploring the
Literature of Fact: Linking Reading and Writing through Information Trade Books." *Language Arts* 74 (Oct. 1997): 418–429.

National Council for the Social Studies. *Curriculum Standards for Social Studies.* 1994. http://www.ncss.org/standards/ (20 Nov. 2002).

Section 3
MATHEMATICS

Children's literature is a natural starting point for learning mathematics concepts (Moyer, 2000). As children listen to stories they discover mathematics in natural contexts. Discussions about the books give students opportunities to investigate and discuss the mathematics concepts and relate them to their own lives. These books provide students with pictorial representations that help them see the connections between concrete and abstract math concepts and help them understand math problem solving in everyday situations (Lowe and Matthew, 2000). When selecting mathematics trade books, Austin (1998) cautions against those that neither entertain nor inform but rather instruct. These books sacrifice the story to teach mathematics content and often include workbook-like activities.

The National Council of Teachers of Mathematics' *Principles and Standards for School Mathematics* (NCTM, 2000) focus on both content and processes in the mathematics curriculum. The first five standards encompass the following content:

1. number and operations,
2. algebra,
3. geometry,
4. measurement, and
5. data analysis and probability.

Standards six through ten concentrate on the following processes:

6. problem solving,
7. reasoning and proof,
8. communication,
9. connections, and

10. representations.

An online version of the standards complete with interactive examples and a variety of resources for implementing them is available at http://standards.nctm.org/.

Combining reading and mathematics has the potential to enhance student learning in the mathematics classroom. For this to occur these three components must be integrated into the classroom: 1) a wide variety of mathematical texts in different textual formats, 2) transactional reading strategies that actively involve students in reading, and 3) a curricular framework that supports meaningful learning using a variety of communication systems (Siegel and Borasi, 1992). The chapters in this section contain annotations of a wide variety of fiction and nonfiction books, a collection of reading strategies that actively involve students in exploring mathematical content, and opportunities to use a variety of communication systems to explore mathematics concepts. Chapters in this section include numbers and operations, time, money, and problem solving.

References

Austin, Patricia. "Math Books as Literature: Which Ones Measure Up?" *The New Advocate* 11, no. 2 (Spring 1998): 119–133.

Lowe, Joy L., and Kathryn I. Matthew. "Exploring Math with Literature." *Book Links* 9, no. 5 (May 2000): 58–62.

Moyer, Patricia S. "Communicating Mathematically: Children's Literature as a Natural Connection." *The Reading Teacher* 54, no. 3 (Nov. 2000): 246–255.

National Council of Teachers of Mathematics. *Principles and Standards for School Mathematics.* 2000. Reston, Va.: National Council of Teachers of Mathematics. http://standards.nctm.org/ (20 Nov. 2002). Ten standards on pp. 197–198 reprinted with permission from *Principles and Standards for School Mathematics*, copyright 2000, by the National Council of Teachers of Mathematics. All rights reserved.

Siegel, Marjorie, and Rafaella Borasi. "Toward a New Integration of Reading in Mathematics Instruction." *Focus on Learning Problems in Mathematics* 14, no. 2 (Spring 1992): 18–36.

· 13 ·
Numbers and Operations

The *Principles and Standards for School Mathematics* (NCTM, 2000) numbers and operations standard involves developing number sense and becoming proficient in addition, subtraction, multiplication, and division computations. Number concepts develop gradually and to facilitate this development children need experiences with numbers, time to reflect on these experiences, and opportunities for communicating with others about their experiences (Shaw and Blake, 1998). Having children discuss books and work with the mathematical concepts presented in the books provides them with time to communicate and make connections (Moyer, 2000). As students' understanding of numbers develops, they move from working with concrete objects to pictorial representations to abstract reasoning. Careful examination of the illustrations in children's books often reveals that the illustrator has woven the mathematical concepts into them (Moyer, 2000). The bold, colorful illustrations found in these books assist students as they move from concrete objects to pictures and again as they move from pictures to abstract reasoning. Vocabulary prereading charts, "I wonder" statements, and examining the features of nonfiction text are the comprehension strategies introduced in this chapter.

Vocabulary Prereading Charts

For students to learn content vocabulary they need teacher guidance in the selection of the words to learn, the learning must involve active processing, and they need instruction on how to use context clues and outside aids to learn the words (Blachowicz and Fisher, 2000). As students learn mathematics, they encounter familiar words with unfamiliar meanings such as *face, point, table,* and *set.* They also encounter strange unfamiliar words such as *hypotenuse, parabola,* and *triskaidekaphobia.* For deep, meaningful understanding to occur, students need strategies for learning mathematics vocabulary.

Vocabulary prereading charts help students focus on key vocabulary words they encounter as they read. Prior to reading, students write down what they think the words mean. During reading as they encounter the words, they can confirm whether the definition they wrote down matches the definition in the book. This activity actively involves students in their reading and focuses their attention on word meanings as they read. (See figures 13.1 and 13.2.)

Steps

1. Read the text and select vocabulary words that are key to the students' understanding of the material.
2. Create a three-column chart. Label the columns "words," "meaning before reading," and "meaning after reading."
3. In the first column write the vocabulary words and leave the other two columns blank for the students to complete.
4. Prior to reading the book, read aloud the words in the first column.
5. Then, ask the students to write down in the second column the definitions of any of the words they think they know. Some students may prefer to draw pictures to illustrate the meaning of the words. If they do not know a word, they can skip it.
6. During reading, stop when a word in column one is encountered. Have the students look at what they wrote or drew in column two and discuss any additions or corrections. These can be recorded in column three. Students who left column two blank can record the definition in column three.
7. After reading, provide students with time to discuss their responses and clarify any misunderstandings.

Examples

Leedy, Loreen. *Mission: Addition.* 1997. 32p. New York: Holiday House. (hc. 0-8234-1307-1).

Grades: K–3. Chatty, cheerful animal cartoon characters from Miss Prime's class are busy solving addition mysteries. Six mysteries are waiting to be solved and young readers solve them using simple addition. The answers to the mysteries are at the end of the book. In the chart below are some addition vocabulary words that are introduced in the book.

Vocabulary Prereading Chart

Word	Meaning before reading	Meaning after reading
addition fact	Plusing 2 numbers (11)=2	
addend	second number you write in a problem 3+(2)=5	
sum	the total 7+3=(10)	

Figure 13.1. As shown in this example, the student knew the words prior to reading the book.

Schwartz, David. *G Is for Googol: A Math Alphabet Book.* Illustrated
by Marissa Moss. 1998. 57p. Berkeley, Calif.: Tricycle Press. (hc.
1-883672-58-9).

Grades: 4–8. This is more than a math alphabet book; it is also a mini
math dictionary. Each letter of the alphabet has its own math term, a
definition of the term, and zany illustrations to help students understand
the math term. The text contains explorations to help students understand and use the terms.

Vocabulary Prereading Chart

Word	Meaning before reading	Meaning after reading
Googol	A werid tip of math	A one with 1 hardred zeo
Tessellate	*(drawing of tessellated triangles)*	There is no gap below the shape like this
Venn Diagram	*(two overlapping circles)*	Same *(two overlapping circles)*
Symmetry	When you fold an object it will match the other side	Same *(symmetry figures)*
Obtuse	An Angle with a line of 175° or above 90°	Same *(obtuse angle drawing)*

Figure 13.2. This student noted which words she knew by writing the
word "same" on the line between the columns. She decided to offer
additional information in the third column after reading the definitions.

Additional Books and Resources

Murphy, Stuart J. *Henry the Fourth.* Illustrated by Scott Nash. 1999. 40p. New York: HarperCollins. (hc. 0-06-02761-X).
Grades: P–2. Henry and his canine friends are in a dog show and this is the context for introducing students to the concept of ordinal numbers. Text, illustrations, and diagrams help young students understand first, second, third, and fourth. Students can easily retell this story and demonstrate their understanding of ordinals. This book is from the Math-Start series.

Schlein, Miriam. *More than One.* Illustrated by Donald Crews. 1996. Unp. New York: Scholastic. (pbk. 0-590-10734-8).
Grades: P–2. A pair, a dozen, a family, and a school are examples of when one is more than one. This is an introduction to the concept of sets in a readable, fun book that presents the concept in contexts familiar to young students. Crews' watercolor illustrations help the students grasp the meanings of the words.

Adler, David A. *How Tall, How Short, How Far Away.* Illustrated by Nancy Tobin. 1999. Unp. New York: Holiday House. (hc. 0-8234-1375-6).
Grades: P–3. *Digit, span, cubit, customary system,* and *metric system* are some of the terms defined in this exploration of units of measure. Hands-on activities to try at school and at home have students exploring measurement and comparing their results. Bright, colorful illustrations spill across the pages and entice readers to try out the different activities.

Ledwon, Peter, and Marilyn Mets. *Midnight Math: Twelve Terrific Math Games.* 2000. 32p. New York: Holiday House. (hc. 0-8234-2530-9).
Grades: 1–5. What better way to learn math vocabulary and practice math skills than by playing games using ordinary objects such as playing cards and dice? The comic book–style layout and the engaging animal characters appeal to readers, who find the games both fun and challenging. The answers and variations of the games are found on the last page of the book.

Adler, David A. *Fraction Fun.* Illustrated by Nancy Tobin. 1996. Unp. New York: Holiday House. (hc. 0-8234-1259-8; pbk. 0-8234-1341-1).
Grades: 2–3. Adler introduces fractions using contexts familiar to children: sharing half of a granola bar and dividing a pizza into pieces. The

terms *numerator* and *denominator* are explained and illustrated. Following the brief introduction to fractions are activities to involve the students in hands-on explorations of fractions. Vibrant, colorful illustrations draw readers into the book and help explain the concepts.

Tang, Greg. *The Best of Times.* Illustrated by Harry Briggs. 2002. Unp. New York: Scholastic. (hc. 0-439-21044-5).

Grades: 3–4. An author's note at the beginning of the book explains that its purpose is to help students develop an intuitive understanding of multiplication. Rather than having students memorize times tables, Tang presents simple multiplication strategies in rhyming verse for them to learn. Bold, colorful, computer-generated cartoon illustrations add a humorous touch to learning how to multiply.

The *Math Rock* software program includes games, videos, and songs that reinforce a variety of math skills. Students move through five levels of difficulty as they learn about equations, sequence, geometric shapes, and other mathematics concepts. This software is appropriate for grades one to five and is available on CD-ROM for both Macintosh and Windows computers from the Learning Company.

The *How Many Bugs in a Box?* software program is based on the pop-up book of the same name written by David A. Carter and a copy of the book is included. The computer reads the book aloud to the children and they can also access eight different games which help them develop a variety of skills including counting, sequencing, visual discrimination, and number matching. This software is appropriate for grades prekindergarten to three and is available on CD-ROM for both Macintosh and Windows computers from Simon and Schuster Interactives.

"I Wonder" Statements

Self-questioning before and during reading actively involves students in making sense of what they are reading. Students write their questions in Wonder Books, nonfiction notebooks where they record questions about things that interest them, questions that occur to them as they read, and questions that lead to research (Harvey and Goudvis, 2000). McLaughlin and Allen (2002) suggest having students develop "I wonder" statements before and during reading using both nonfiction and fiction books. (See figures 13.3 and 13.4.) Students can develop the statements in large groups, small groups, or with partners depending on the age levels of the students. As teachers model wondering and express their passion for topics, they encourage their students to be curious and to develop their own passions, which can lead to engaged learning (Harvey, 2002).

Steps

1. The teacher introduces this activity by modeling how to develop "I wonder" statements using a children's literature selection.
2. Hold up the book and wonder aloud about the cover of the book. These statements or questions should include not only the information on the cover of the book but also about life experiences or events related to the book.
3. Read a few pages of the book and stop again to wonder aloud. Solicit statements or questions about the text from the students.
4. Encourage students to wonder beyond the pages of the book and relate the text to their lives and to the world.
5. Record the "I wonder" statements.
6. Explain to the students that the author may answer their questions in the text and that they should listen carefully for the answers.
7. Continue to stop and wonder every few pages.
8. At the end of the book, discuss which statements were answered in the book and return to the book to locate the answers in the text.
9. Help students formulate ideas for finding the answers to statements that were not answered in the book.
10. Once students become familiar with this activity they can be encouraged to create "I wonder" statements when reading independently.

Examples

Wells, Robert E. *Can You Count to a Googol?* 2000. Unp. Morton Grove, Ill.: Albert Whitman. (hc. 0-8075-1060-2; pbk. 0-8075-1061-0).
Grades: 2–3. For students wondering about large numbers, this book satisfies their curiosity. Counting from one to ten to one hundred to one thousand seems easy enough, but the counting continues past one billion, past one trillion, and on to a googol. Fanciful illustrations of children and monkeys balancing bananas, penguins with ice cream cones,

and pennies raining from the sky help students conceptualize the large numbers they are counting. The book concludes with a brief author's note about a googol.

"I Wonder" Statements

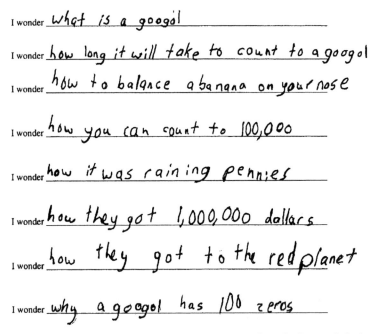

I wonder *What is a googol*

I wonder *how long it will take to count to a googol*

I wonder *how to balance a banana on your nose*

I wonder *how you can count to 100,000*

I wonder *how it was raining pennies*

I wonder *how they got 1,000,000 dollars*

I wonder *how they got to the red planet*

I wonder *why a googol has 100 zeros*

Figure 13.3. These are "I wonder" statements written before and during reading.

Hopkins, Lee Bennett. *Marvelous Math: A Book of Poems.* 1997. 32p. New York: Simon and Schuster Books for Young Readers. (hc. 0-689-80658-2).

Grades: K–8. Silly, humorous, and thought-provoking poems show how math is an integral part of daily living. Sixteen poets contributed their math poems to this collection. The poems encompass a variety of mathematics topics. Vibrant, fanciful artwork fills the pages and sets the tone for this poetic adventure into the world of math. Readers young and old delight in hearing these poems. Many of these poems easily lend themselves to choral reading.

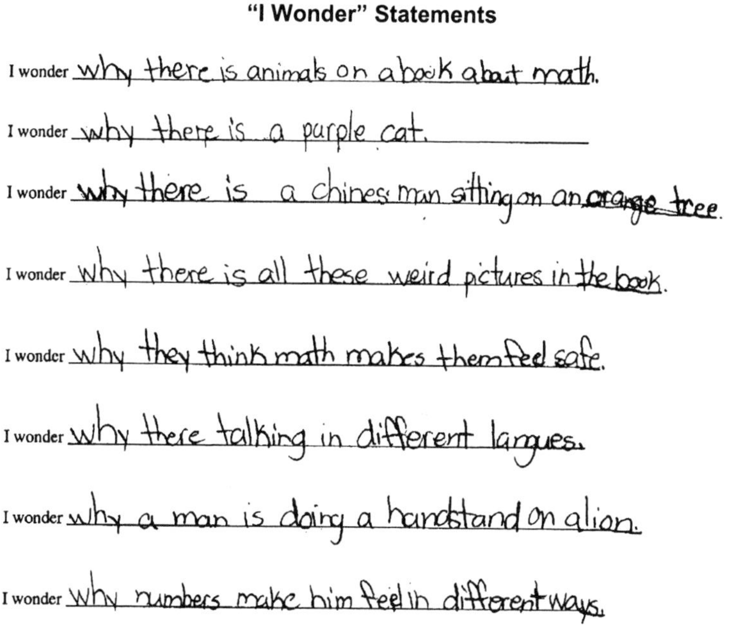

"I Wonder" Statements

I wonder _Why there is animals on a book abut math._

I wonder _why there is a purple cat._

I wonder _why there is a Chinese man sitting on an orange tree._

I wonder _Why there is all these weird pictures in the book._

I wonder _why they think math makes them feel safe._

I wonder _why there talking in different langues._

I wonder _why a man is doing a handstand on a lion._

I wonder _Why numbers make him feel in different ways._

Figure 13.4. Students worked with partners and wrote down "I wonder" statements before and during reading. Since the focus of this activity is on getting students to develop a self-questioning strategy, grammar and spelling errors were not corrected.

Additional Books and Resources

Mannis, Celeste A. *One Leaf Rides the Wind: Counting in a Japanese Garden.* Illustrated by Susan Kathleen Hartung. 2002. Unp. New York: Viking. (hc. 0-670-03525-4).
Grades: P–2. Readers explore a restful Japanese garden and learn a little bit about the Japanese culture in this counting book. The objects in the garden are described in haiku. Lush illustrations fill the pages, which are placed between stunning end papers depicting a koi pond. The book concludes with information about Japanese gardens and haiku.
Leedy, Loreen. *Fraction Action.* 1994. 32p. New York: Holiday House. (hc. 0-8234-1109-5).

Grades: 1–3. Miss Prime's students are ready and eager to learn about fractions. They quickly discover that fractions are everywhere and begin making connections between the class lessons and their own lives. Using manipulatives and drawing diagrams as they read the book helps students understand the concepts. Answers to problems posed throughout the book are found on the last page.

Cato, Sheila. *Multiplication.* Illustrated by Sami Sweeten. 1999. 32p. Minneapolis, Minn.: Carolrhoda Books. (hc. 1-57505-321-7).

Grades: 2–5. Students recognize the familiar everyday events portrayed in this book that show how multiplication is part of daily living. Questions are asked, solutions are given, and then students are challenged to extend the problems before they turn the page. The answers appear in the lower left corner on the next page. Colorful illustrations depict children in a variety of situations and help explain the concepts. A glossary is included. This book is from the A Question of Math series.

Decimals. 2001. 48p. Danbury, Conn.: Grolier Educational. (hc. 0-7172-9300-9).

Grades: 3–5. After introducing decimals, the book explains how to add, subtract, multiply, and divide with them. Readers also learn about changing fractions into decimals and comparing decimals. Clear, succinct text with colorful illustrations and diagrams on two-page spreads provide summaries of the key concepts students learn about decimals. A glossary and a set index conclude the book. This book is volume six of Math Matters.

Schmandt-Besserat, Denise. *The History of Counting.* Illustrated by Michael Hays. 1999. 45p. New York: Morrow Junior Books. (hc. 0-688-14118-8).

Grades: 3–5. This introduction to counting begins with numberless counting systems and then describes how counting systems have developed and changed to fit the needs of the people using them. Students discover that the history of counting is quite fascinating. Muted acrylic on linen illustrations accompany the text. A glossary and an index are included.

Smoothey, Marion. *Ratio and Proportion.* Illustrated by Ann Baum. 1995. 64p. New York: Marshall Cavendish. (hc. 1-85435-776-X).

Grades: 3–5. Everyday objects and events help explain ratio and proportion. Descriptions, colorful illustrations, examples, and problems to solve actively engage young learners. A glossary, answers, and an index conclude the book. This book is from the Let's Investigate series.

How the West Was One + Three χ Four software actively engages students in problem solving as they learn order of operations and negative numbers. This software is appropriate for grades four to eight and is available on CD-ROM for both Macintosh and Windows computers from Sunburst Communications.

Nonfiction Text Features

Nonfiction text contains signposts that alert readers to important information (Harvey, 1998). Students familiar with reading stories have learned that the standard-size text is what is important. Hence, they tend to ignore the large or bold text found in nonfiction texts. Providing students with direct instruction regarding the features of nonfiction text shows them that these features are signposts that provide important clues that help them comprehend what they are reading. These features include fonts and special effects, textual cues, illustrations and photographs, graphics, and text organizers (Harvey, 1998). Fonts and special effects include bold text, italicized text, captions, headings, and subheadings. Textual clues are text structures such as cause–effect, comparison–contrast, problem–solution, question–answer, and sequence. Illustrations and photographs contain additional information that enhances the text and supports comprehension. Graphics include cross sections, diagrams, tables, sidebars, and charts that students may need assistance in learning to read and interpret. Text organizers include the table of contents, index, glossary, and appendix. Students need direct instruction in how to use these organizational features of text. (See figures 13.5 and 13.6.)

Steps

1. Using a word processing program, create a chart for the students to record their observations of nonfiction text features or have the students draw blocks on plain paper and label the blocks with the different features.
2. Gather a stack of nonfiction books for the students to examine.
3. Model how to locate the different features using a nonfiction big book. Demonstrate how to record the information on the charts, making sure that the students understand the different text features listed on the chart.

4. Divide the students into small groups and provide each group with a chart.
5. Let the groups select which books they will examine.
6. Have the students work together to record their observations.
7. As groups finish with one book, have them select another book.
8. Have the students return to a large group and share their discoveries with their classmates.
9. Encourage the students to think about how the nonfiction text features help them understand the material.

Examples

Cato, Sheila. *Division*. Illustrated by Sami Sweeten. 1999. 32p. Minneapolis, Minn.: Carolrhoda Books. (hc. 1-57505-319-5).
Grades: 1–4. Colorful cartoons filled with children in everyday situations introduce the concept of division. Sidebars contain additional information and challenge students to try problems on their own. A glossary concludes the book, which is from the A Question of Math series.

Nonfiction Text Features

Fonts & Special Effects	Textual Cues
_____ headings _____ subheadings _____ bold print _____ color print _____ italic print	_____ problem/solution _____ question/answer
Illustrations & Photographs	Graphics
_____ color _____ black and white	_____ diagrams _____ maps _____ tables _____ graphs
Text Organizers	Other Things I Noticed about the Text
_____ table of contents _____ glossary _____ index _____ sidebars	

Figure 13.5. Students who are not familiar with locating text features can start with simple charts like the one above. They may need assistance as they encounter unfamiliar words in the chart.

Stienecker, David L. *Multiplication.* Illustrated by Richard Maccabe. 1995. 32p. Tarrytown, N.Y.: Marshall Cavendish. (hc. 0-7614-0595-X).

Grades: 4–6. This book is designed for students who already know how to multiply. It contains problems to help them improve their multiplication skills and problems to practice their skills. Diagrams and illustrations provide helpful information along the way. Answers, a glossary, and an index conclude the book. This book is from the Discovering Math series.

Nonfiction Text Features

Fonts & Special Effects	Textual Cues
_____ headings	_____ cause/effect
_____ subheadings	_____ comparison/contrast
_____ bold print	_____ problem/solution
_____ color print	_____ question/answer
_____ italic print	_____ sequence
_____ bullets	
_____ picture captions	
Illustrations & Photographs	**Graphics**
_____ color	_____ diagrams
_____ black and white	_____ cross sections
_____ realistic	_____ maps
_____ cartoon like	_____ tables
	_____ charts
	_____ graphs
Text Organizers	**Other Things I Noticed about the Text**
_____ table of contents	
_____ glossary	
_____ index	
_____ appendix	
_____ timeline	
_____ sidebars	

Figure 13.6. Having students complete charts such as the one above helps them focus on the nonfiction text features that aid in comprehension of the material. Working with a partner or in small groups enables students to help one another as they discuss any unfamiliar terms in the chart, such as *appendix* or *sidebars*.

Additional Books and Resources

Packard, Edward, and Salvatore Murdocca. *Big Numbers: And Pictures that Show Just How Big They Are.* Illustrated by Edward Packard. 2000. Unp. Brookfield, Conn.: The Millbrook Press. (hc. 0-7613-1570-5).
Grades: P–3. This oversized book is just the right size for learning about very big numbers. Bright, colorful cartoon drawings show peas proliferating at an incredible rate as the numbers grow larger and larger. Common objects in familiar contexts are used to describe the numbers, and exponents are introduced as a way to write really big numbers.

Patilla, Peter. *Patterns.* 2000. 32p. Des Plaines, Ill.: Heinemann Library. (hc. 1-57572-967-9).
Grades: K–2. Realistic drawings and photographs show the patterns that are all around us. Patterns in nature, spirals, number patterns, and tessellations are just a few of the ones explored in this mathematical concept book. A glossary, a list of more books to read, answers to questions posed in the text, and an index are included.

Daniels, Terri. *Math Man.* Illustrated by Timothy Bush. 2001. Unp. New York: Scholastic. (hc. 0-439-29308-1).
Grades: K–3. Mrs. Gourd's class takes a field trip to the supermarket to look for math problems. Math Man, a stock boy, dazzles them with his on-the-spot math problem solving and calculations as he helps customers. His real talent shines when the cash registers go on the fritz and he adds up customers' purchases in his head. Humorous watercolor illustrations complement the text.

Fractions. 1999. 48p. Danbury, Conn.: Grolier Educational. (hc. 0-7172-9301-7).
Grades: 3–5. From pizzas to plums to cakes, familiar objects are used to present adding, subtracting, and multiplying fractions. Ratios, proportion, and percent are also explained. Colorful illustrations, bold equations, step-by-step instructions, and definitions tucked into the corners of pages provide the support needed to help students grasp these concepts. A glossary and a set index conclude the book. This book is volume seven of Math Matters.

Ganeri, Anita. *The Story of Numbers and Counting.* 1996. 30p. New York: Oxford University Press. (hc. 0-19-521258-4).
Grades: 3–6. Fascinating facts about numbers, counting, and mathematicians hold readers' attention. This book is a starting point for further

exploration of numbers and counting. Photographs, illustrations, diagrams, and sidebars contain additional information. A timeline, glossary, and an index conclude the book. This book is from the Signs of the Times series.

Smoothey, Marion. *Number Patterns.* Illustrated by Ted Evans. 1993. 64p. New York: Marshall Cavendish. (hc. 1-85435-458-2).
Grades: 4–6. Problems and games are used to introduce students to the patterns all around them. These hands-on explorations are thought-provoking and fun. Helpful hints and problem-solving ideas are included. A glossary, answers, and an index conclude the book. This book is from the Let's Investigate series.

References

Blachowicz, Camille L. Z., and Peter Fisher. "Vocabulary Instruction." In *Handbook of Reading Research Volume III*, edited by Michael L. Kamil, Peter B. Mosenthal, P. David Pearson, and Rebecca Barr, 503–523. Mahwah, N.J.: Lawrence Erlbaum Associates, 2000.

Harvey, Stephanie. "Nonfiction Inquiry: Using Real Reading and Writing to Explore the World." *Language Arts* 80, no. 1 (Sept. 2002): 12–22.

——. *Nonfiction Matters: Reading, Writing, and Research in Grades 3–8.* York, Maine: Stenhouse, 1998.

Harvey, Stephanie, and Anne Goudvis. *Strategies that Work: Teaching Comprehension to Enhance Understanding.* Portland, Maine: Stenhouse, 2000.

McLaughlin, Maureen, and Mary Beth Allen. *Guided Comprehension: A Teaching Model for Grades 3–8.* Newark, Del.: International Reading Association, 2002.

Moyer, Patricia S. "Communicating Mathematically: Children's Literature as a Natural Connection." *The Reading Teacher* 54, no. 3 (Nov. 2000): 246–255.

National Council of Teachers of Mathematics. *Principles and Standards for School Mathematics.* Reston, Va.: National Council of Teachers of Mathematics, 2000. http://standards.nctm.org/ (20 Nov. 2002).

Shaw, Jean M., and Sally S. Blake. *Mathematics for Young Children.* Upper Saddle River, N.J.: Prentice-Hall, 1998.

· 14 ·
Time

The fourth standard of the *Principles and Standards for School Mathematics* (NCTM, 2000) focuses on measurement including concepts such as time, length, distance, temperature, and area. Young children begin learning about measurement by making visual comparisons between objects (Sheffield and Cruikshank, 2000). These comparisons provide the background knowledge they need to learn measurement terms and to manipulate measurement tools. To understand time students need to understand terms such as hours, minutes, seconds, days of the week, months of the year, and seasons of the year. Time is an abstract concept that children come to understand gradually. Books in this chapter provide students with opportunities to learn about time, to experiment with time, and to develop an understanding of the history of time. Questioning the text, creating summary cubes, and playing RIVET, a vocabulary game, are the comprehension strategies described in this chapter to facilitate students' understanding of time.

Questioning the Text

Questioning the text is a prereading strategy that facilitates comprehension by having readers focus on the structure of the text, make connections, and summarize (McLaughlin and Allen, 2002). Prereading questions activate students' background knowledge, help them preview the text, and set purposes for reading (Harris and Sipay, 1990). Additionally, questions propel students to read and study to find answers (Harvey, 2002). Learning to question the text is a skill that develops over time and students need opportunities to practice. Questions such as the ones below provide a starting point for students as they learn to ask questions of the text. The teacher or librarian models this technique by asking and answering a few of these questions before reading a book aloud. Depending on the ages and reading levels of the students, they can work in small groups or with partners to answer some or all of the questions. (See figures 14.1 and 14.2.)

Steps

1. Before reading the text the students answer some of the following questions:

   Is the text structure narrative or expository?

   What questions do I want answered as I read?

   What can I learn from the front cover of the book?

   Do the book flaps contain information that may help me understand the book?

   What does the table of contents tell me?

   What can I determine from the size of the book?

   Am I familiar with the author? What other works by this author have I read?

   What do I already know about the topic of the book? Can I make connections between what I already know and what I think I will learn from this book?

   What can I learn from knowing the genre of the book and examining the writing style of the author?

   Does the book have a summary? What can I learn from the summary?

   Does the back cover provide any additional information?

2. As the students work, the teacher moves between the groups and facilitates as they answer the questions.

3. The groups discuss the answers and summarize the information they have gathered before reading the book.

Examples

Zolotow, Charlotte. *Seasons: A Book of Poems.* Illustrated by Erik Blegvad. 2002. 64p. New York: HarperCollins. (hc. 0-06-026698-8). Grades: P–3. The easy-to-read poems in this book are divided into the seasons of the year. Events throughout the year are seen through the eyes of a child and express the wonder and excitement of simple pleasures. Blegvad's drawings complement the poems and reflect the changes of the seasons. This is from the An I Can Read Book series.

Questioning the Text

What can I learn from the front cover of the book?
    It is about poems and seasons.
    Children are riding a horse.
    There is a dog in the book.
What does the table of contents tell me?
    There are four parts to the book.
    Each part has poems about different seasons.
What can I determine from the size of the book?
    It is small.
    It is easy to hold.
What do I already know about the topic of the book? Can I make connections between what I already know and what I think I will learn from this book?
    I know there are four seasons.
    It snows in winter.
    Christmas is in winter.
    No school in summer.
    I swim in the summer.
Does the back cover provide any additional information?
    The child is walking in the snow.
    The sun is out.

Figure 14.1. Teachers and librarians can model this prereading strategy by thinking aloud as they answer the questions and elicit responses from the students.

Zubrowski, Bernie. *Clocks.* Illustrated by Roy Doty. 1988. 112p. New York: Morrow Junior Books. (hc. 0-688-06926-6; pbk. 0-688-08925-8).

Grades: 3–6. Students learn the history of time, discover how to make a variety of clocks, and then conduct experiments with the clocks they make. Detailed black-and-white line drawings show how to make the clocks described in the book. This book encourages students to become actively involved in learning about clocks as they construct the clocks using the directions in the book and then record observations as they complete the experiments in the book. At the end of the book, the author challenges readers to become clock makers by designing and

building their own clock. This is a Boston Children's Museum Activity
Book.

Questioning the Text

Is the text structure narrative or expository?

expository

What can I learn from the front cover of the book?

how to build our own clocks

Do the book flaps contain information that may help me understand the book?

Yes

What does the table of contents tell me?

*Chapters   What page subjects are on
Introduction*

Does the book have a summary? What can I learn from the summary?

No

Does the back cover provide any additional information?

No

Figure 14.2. Although the two boys who answered these questions only
made brief written responses, they engaged in a lively discussion about
the contents of the book before reading.

Additional Books and Resources

Dragonwagon, Crescent. *Alligators and Others All Year Long: A
   Book of Months.* Illustrated by Jose Aruego and Ariane Dewey.
   1993. Unp. New York: Macmillan Publishing. (hc. 0-02-733091-5).

Grades: P–2. As young readers learn the months of the year, they have fanciful, colorful illustrations of familiar objects and lyrical verses to help them remember the events associated with each month.

Older, Jules. *Telling Time.* Illustrated by Megan Halsey. 2000. Unp. Watertown, Mass.: Charlesbridge Publishing. (hc. 0-88106-396-7; pbk. 0-88106-397-5).

Grades: K–3. From seconds to hours, from days to weeks, and from months to years, readers learn that time comes in chunks. Readers also learn how to tell time using both digital and analog clocks. And just in case students encounter a clock with Roman numerals, there is a chart that explains what they mean. Clean, concise text and clever drawings make learning to tell time fun. Internet resources for learning more about time conclude the book.

Chapman, Gillian, and Pam Robson. *Exploring Time.* 1995. 32p. Brookfield, Conn.: The Millbrook Press. (hc. 1-56294-683-8; pbk. 1-56294-683-8).

Grades: 3–5. Color photographs, diagrams, drawings, and succinct text provide students with a wealth of information on this abstract concept. Some chapters discuss change over time, geological time, solar time, lunar time, measuring time, and traveling time. The book contains activities and projects for hands-on explorations, a glossary, and an index.

Skurzynski, Gloria. *On Time: From Seasons to Split Seconds.* 2000. 41p. Washington, D.C.: National Geographic Society. (hc. 0-7922-7503-9).

Grades: 4–8. Throughout history civilizations have measured time first by observing natural phenomena and then by using clocks and watches. Photographs, illustrations, and informative text explain the history of time and detailed facts about time. Also included are fascinating anecdotes about Columbus, Galileo, Einstein, and others. An index concludes the book.

Duffy, Trent. *The Clock.* Illustrated by Toby Welles. 2000. 79p. New York: Atheneum Books for Young Readers. (hc. 0-689-82814-4).

Grades: 4 and up. From Stonehenge to atomic clocks over the course of history, humans have measured time. A foldout illustration includes details on the inner working of clocks. Lively text and photographs tell the history of clocks and the men who invented and perfected them. Books for further reading and an index conclude the book. This book is from the Turning Point Inventions series.

Hours, Days, and Years. Color illustrations by Carol J. Stott. 1991. 48p. Mankato, Minn.: Capstone Press. (hc. 1-56065-065-6).

Grades: 5–6. An introduction explains how Robert L. Ripley began his
collection of curiosities. Contained within the pages of this slim volume are odd and interesting bits of information about time, clocks, and
calendars. This book is from the Ripley's Believe It or Not! Mind
Teasers series.

Smoothey, Marion. *Time, Distance, and Speed.* Illustrated by Ted
  Evans. 1993. 64p. New York: Marshall Cavendish. (hc. 1-85435-
  467-1).

Grades: 6 and up. Basic facts about time, distance, and speed are presented. Then, students become involved in activities and solve problems to fully explore the concepts. Drawings and diagrams illustrate the
problems and provide information students need to solve them. A glossary, answers to the problems posed in the book, and an index are included. This book is from the Let's Investigate series.

Cave of the Blue Falls software, which is part of the Fizz and Ma-
rina's Math Adventures series, has students exploring the caves below
Blue Falls. As they explore, students develop their addition and subtraction skills and they learn about units of measurement, money, and
time. This software is appropriate for grades two and three and is available on CD-ROM for both Macintosh and Windows computers. The
software is available from Tom Snyder Productions.

Math for the Real World software places math skills such as telling
time and counting money in real-life situations. Students develop their
math skills as they use their critical thinking skills to solve the problems. This software is appropriate for grades four and up and is available on CD-ROM for both Macintosh and Windows computers. The
software is available from Sunburst Communications.

The Clocks and Time web site contains a link to the official U.S.
Time at the U.S. Naval Observatory. There are also links to clock
making and watchmaking, the history of timekeeping, sundials, and a
link for educational resources. If you want to set a clock, simply learn
more about time, or find out how clocks work, this is the web site to
access at http://www.ubr.com/clocks/index.html.

Summary Cubes

Summary cubes provide students with a format for succinctly reiterat-
ing the key points of expository or narrative text (McLaughlin and Al-

len, 2002). Summarizing requires readers to briefly tell about the main points without including too much information (Harvey, 1998). Summarizing can be a difficult skill for students to learn, as they want to include every detail without concern for the importance of the details. This skill takes time to develop and working with partners or in small groups provides students support as they learn to summarize. As students work with partners or in small groups they verbalize and this makes them aware of their misunderstandings (Temple and Gillet, 1996). Talking to their peers as they read and respond to literature provides opportunities for rich learning as students work together to construct meaning from the text (Guice, 1995). Students enjoy creating summary cubes either working in large group settings with the teacher or working with a partner. They enthusiastically add illustrations and when they finish, they cut and tape their cubes together, eager to share them with their classmates. The information on the sides of the cube can be changed to suit expository and narrative text and to meet the librarian's or teacher's objectives for the lesson. (See figures 14.3 and 14.4.)

Steps

1. Create a summary cube template.
2. Distribute the cube templates to the students and discuss the information they are to write on each side of the cube.
3. Model how to locate information in the text to complete the cube.
4. Demonstrate how to cut out the cube and tape it together.
5. Have the students read the text and create their cubes.
6. Once students have completed their cubes, they can share them with their classmates and display them in the classroom.

Examples

Banks, Sara Harrell. *A Net to Catch Time.* Illustrated by Scott Cook. 1997. Unp. New York: Alfred A. Knopf. (hc. 0-679-86673-6).
Grades: K–3. The Gullah have a term for each part of the day from early in the morning until late at night. Readers learn the terms as they spend the day with a young boy named Cuffy while he catches crabs, helps his grandmother make deviled crabs, and then sells them to the people on the ferry. This is a heartwarming story that records in words and pastel pictures the disappearing Gullah culture. A glossary of Gul-

lah terms begins the book and an author's note on the Gullah culture
concludes the book.

Summary Cube

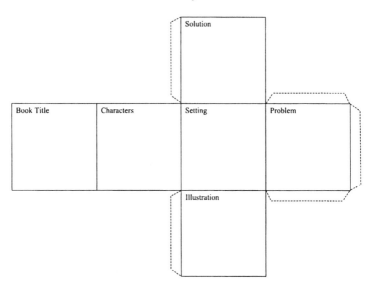

Figure 14.3. The drawing tools in a word processing program were
used to create this summary cube template for use with narrative text.
Creating and saving the summary cube as a template enables teachers
and librarians to easily change the information required to complete the
cube. The information required to complete the cube can be adapted to
different books and to students at various grade levels.

Dolan, Graham. *The Greenwich Guide to Time and the Millennium.*
   Illustrated by Jeff Edwards. 1999. 48p. Des Plaines, Ill.: Heinemann Library. (hc. 1-57572-802-8).
Grades: 4–7. Sundials, Greenwich Mean Time, longitude, time zones,
and calendars are just some of the topics presented in this informative,
fun-to-read text. The book contains a great deal of information that may
not be presented in the students' textbooks. Photographs, labeled diagrams, illustrations, and brief paragraphs with key words in bold text
explain the time concepts to readers. A glossary, a bibliography, and an
index are included.

Summary Cube

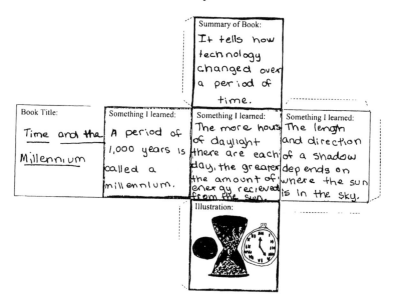

Figure 14.4. This summary cube was created by an eighth-grade student. She and her partner read the book together and discussed what they read. Then, each created a summary cube.

Additional Books and Resources

McMillan, Bruce. *Time To . . . .* 1989. Unp. New York: Lothrop, Lee & Shepard Books. (hc. 0-688-08855-4).
Grades: P–1. Readers spend the day with a young boy and follow his daily routine as the hours tick away. Young readers learn that sequenced activities mark the passage of time just as the rotating hands on the clock show the passage of time. Clocks mark the passage of time in both analog and digital formats. Color photographs of a young boy, his family, and his school friends illustrate the book.

Harper, Dan. *Telling Time with Big Mama Cat.* Illustrated by Cara Moser and Barry Moser. 1998. Unp. San Diego, Calif.: Harcourt Brace. (hc. 0-152-01738-0).
Grades: P–3. Readers follow Big Mama Cat as she moves through her busy day always mindful of the time. For example, she knows that at

11:00 the sun will be warming the big stuffed chair and that she needs to be there sleeping. However, at 11:05 she is removed from the forbidden chair. A foldout clock with moveable hands is included so that readers can practice telling time with Big Mama Cat as she moves through her day.

Appelt, Kathi. *Bats around the Clock.* Illustrated by Melissa Sweet. 2001. Unp. New York: William Morrow. (hc. 0-688-16470-6).

Grades: K–2. Bats dance around the clock at American Batstand hosted by Click Dark. Every hour on the hour the dancers move to a new dance step such as the Twist, the Swim, and the Jitterbug. The lively rhyming text holds the attention of young readers, and older readers enjoy revisiting their youth. A mouse and a clock are stationed on each page to mark the passage of time.

Hopkins, Lee Bennett, editor. *It's About Time!* Illustrated by Matt Novak. 1993. 36p. New York: Simon and Schuster Books for Young Readers. (hc. 0-671-78512-5).

Grades: K–3. As the day ticks away on the clock in the corner of the page, this collection of poems about time marks its passing with familiar daily activities. Colorful illustrations draw young readers into the pages as they listen to the words of the poems.

Branley, Franklyn M. *Keeping Time.* Illustrated by Jill Weber. 1993. 105p. Boston, Mass.: Houghton Mifflin. (hc. 0-395-47777-8).

Grades: 3–6. Science, folklore, and hands-on activities entice readers to learn about and explore the concept of time. The book is filled with fascinating facts and interesting anecdotes that motivate students to read and learn. Black-and-white line drawings and diagrams complement the text. A bibliography and an index conclude the book.

The Local Times around the World web site shows the time for regions and countries around the globe. Simply click on a region or a country and the local time appears on the screen. This fun-to-use web site is accessed at http://times.clari.net.au/index.html.

RIVET

RIVET is a prereading strategy developed to introduce vocabulary words, to activate students' prior knowledge, and to encourage students to make predictions about the text before reading (Cunningham, 2000). In this activity, students guess the vocabulary words as the teacher slowly writes them on the board letter by letter. RIVET is so named because, according to Cunningham, students are riveted to the board as they attempt to guess the words appearing before their eyes. (See figures 14.5 and 14.6.) Once the words are written on the board, students discuss the definitions and then make predictions about the story based on the words. Making predictions requires the students to activate their prior knowledge, which makes it available to help them understand the text (Cunningham, 2000). This activity works with either narrative or expository text.

Steps

1. Preview the reading selection and select key vocabulary words. The number of words selected depends on the age and reading levels of the students.
2. Write numbers in a column on the board to correspond to the number of words selected. For example, if you have decided on seven vocabulary words, write the numbers one to seven on the board in a column.
3. Next to the numbers, draw lines equal to the number of letters in each word.
4. Students can create their own game board by copying what you have written on the board on their own paper.
5. Begin by filling in the letters to the first word on the board and continue writing down letters until a student correctly guesses the word. Encourage students to call out the answer as you write down the letters and to write the letters down on their own paper.
6. Ask the child who guesses the word correctly to help finish spelling the word.
7. Continue writing letters until all of the words have been spelled out.
8. Invite the students to discuss the meanings of the words.
9. Have the students use the list of words to predict events in the story.
10. Encourage the students to suggest a variety of different possibilities for the events in the story.
11. Read the book aloud to the students or have them read it silently.
12. After reading the story, have students discuss their predictions and what actually happened in the book.

Examples

Mandell, Muriel. *Simple Experiments in Time with Everyday Materials.* Illustrated by Frances Zweifel. 1997. 96p. New York: Sterling Publishing. (hc. 0-8069-3803-X).
Grades: 2–4. The book describes how to tell time using the moon, the sun, and the stars. There are experiments in the book that actively engage students in learning a variety of terms and in developing a deeper understanding of the concept. A glossary and an index conclude the book.

RIVET

1._ _ _ _ _ _ _ _ _ _ _ _	(constellation)
2._ _ _ _ _ _ _ _ _ _	(horologist)
3._ _ _ _ _ _ _ _	(latitude)
4._ _ _ _ _ _ _ _ _	(longitude)
5._ _ _ _ _ _ _ _	(meridian)

Figure 14.5. When selecting words, consider words such as "horologist" which are just plain fun to learn. A horologist is a clock maker.

Glover, David. *Time.* Photographs by Jon Barnes. 1996. 48p. Chicago, Ill.: World Book. (hc. 0-7166-1729-3).
Grades: 4–6. Hands-on explorations of time fill the pages of this marvelous book. Readers follow the illustrated directions to create a variety of clocks and a time capsule. The book concludes with a glossary and an index. From the Make It Work! series.

RIVET

1.a r c h a e o l o g i s t	(archaeologist)
2.c a l i b r a t e	(calibrate)
3.c e l _ _ _ _ _ _	(celestial)
4._ _ _ _ _ _ _ _ _	(geological)
5._ _ _ _ _ _ _ _ _	(hemisphere)
6._ _ _ _ _ _ _ _ _	(memorabilia)
7._ _ _ _ _ _ _ _ _	(planisphere)
8._ _ _ _ _ _ _ _ _ _ _ _	(quartz crystal)

Figure 14.6. In this example, the students have guessed the first two words and are working on the third word.

Additional Books and Resources

Nelson, Robin. *A Week.* 2002. 23p. Minneapolis, Minn.: Lerner Publications. (hc. 0-8225-0178-3).
Grades: P–1. Color photographs of children at home, at school, and at play mark the passage of a week. Large print with few words on the page makes this a book young readers can read on their own. Bold text highlights the key words. Fun week facts, a glossary, and an index conclude the book. This book is from the First Step Nonfiction series.
Shields, Carol Diggory. *Day by Day a Week Goes Round.* Illustrated by True Kelley. 1998. Unp. New York: Dutton Children's Books. (hc. 0-525-45457-8).
Grades: P–2. Lively verse and bright, colorful illustrations tell the story of the days of the week. Children romp through the pages of the book as the week spins around and starts again. Young children relate to the families and familiar activities depicted throughout the book.
Updike, John. *A Child's Calendar.* Illustrated by Trina Schart Hyman. 1999. Unp. New York: Holiday House. (hc. 0-8234-1445-0).
Grades: P–2. Readers follow along as two families move through the months of the year delighting in the small pleasures that come with each month. Each month has a detailed watercolor illustration and melodic verse to savor. Readers relate to the families, day-to-day lives and activities. This is a book to read again and again.
Axelrod, Amy. *Pigs on the Move: Fun with Math and Travel.* Illustrated by Sharon McGinley-Nally. 1999. Unp. New York: Simon and Schuster Books for Young Readers. (hc. 0-689-81070-9).
Grades: P–3. The pig family misses their plane on their way to Bean Town to spend Christmas with the cousins. After four different airplane flights they land in Bean Town where Santa has come and gone and the cousins are all asleep. As readers track the pig trek they learn about time, time zones, and distance. Bright, colorful pictures and rollicking narrative maintain the interest of young readers as they discover that math and time are everywhere. Information on time zones, questions for extending the story, and information on the pigs' route conclude the book.
Murphy, Stuart J. *Game Time!* Illustrated by Cynthia Jabar. 2000. 33p. New York: HarperCollins. (hc. 0-06-028024-7; pbk. 0-06-446732-5).
Grades: 2–4. The soccer championship is at stake and the teams are ready to play. Time is of the essence as the game begins. As readers

cheer for the Huskies they also learn about time. Lively, color illustrations capture the excitement of the game. On the last two pages are
activities for extending the book.

Harrison, Michael, and Christopher Stuart Clark, eds. *The Oxford
Treasury of Time Poems.* 1998. 155p. New York: Oxford University Press. (hc. 0-19-276175-7).
Grades: 6 and up. Silly, serious, thought-provoking poems are all included in this anthology that explores the nuances of time. The illustrations accompanying the poems are as varied as the poems. An index of
titles and first lines and an index of authors conclude the book.

A Walk through Time depicts the evolution of the measurement of
time including information on ancient calendars, early clocks, mechanical clocks, atomic clocks, and time zones. This site is maintained
by the National Institute of Standards and Technology Physics Labo-
ratory and can be accessed at http://physics.nist/gov/time.

References

Cunningham, Patricia M. *Phonics They Use: Words for Reading and
Writing.* New York: Longman, 2000.
Guice, Sherry L. "Creating Communities of Readers: A Study of Chil-
dren's Information Networks as Multiple Contexts for Responding
to Texts." *Journal of Reading Behavior* 27, no. 3 (Sept. 1995):
379–397.
Harris, Albert J., and Edward R. Sipay. *How to Increase Reading Abil-
ity: A Guide to Developmental and Remedial Methods,* 9th ed.
White Plains, N.Y.: Longman, 1990.
Harvey, Stephanie. "Nonfiction Inquiry: Using Real Reading and
Writing to Explore the World." *Language Arts* 80, no. 1 (Sept.
2002): 12–22.
——. *Nonfiction Matters: Reading, Writing, and Research in Grades
3–8.* York, Maine: Stenhouse, 1998.
McLaughlin, Maureen, and Mary Beth Allen. *Guided Comprehension:
A Teaching Model for Grades 3–8.* Newark, Del.: International
Reading Association, 2002.
National Council of Teachers of Mathematics. *Principles and Stan-
dards for School Mathematics.* Reston, Va.: National Council of

Teachers of Mathematics, 2000. http://standards.nctm.org/ (20 Nov. 2002).

Sheffield, Linda Jensen, and Douglas E. Cruikshank. *Teaching and Learning Elementary and Middle School Mathematics*, 4th ed. New York: John Wiley, 2000.

Temple, Charles, and Jean Gillet. *Language and Literacy: A Lively Approach*. New York: HarperCollins, 1996.

· 15 ·
Money

Students' background knowledge and previous experiences provide a foundation for learning about money. They know it costs money to buy the toys and games they see advertised on television. Classroom learning that builds on these experiences and provides connections between them facilitates students' deeper understanding of money. Nonfiction books about money provide students with the knowledge they need to spend and save money (Whitin and Wilde, 1992). Additionally, nonfiction books introduce them to economics concepts. Fiction books give students stories with familiar settings and events that provide them with a variety of contexts for learning about money. The *Principles and Standards for School Mathematics* (NCTM, 2000) first standard is numbers and operations. As students learn to count money, they are developing their number sense and practicing operations they have previously learned. As with other mathematics concepts an understanding of money develops gradually and requires that students have opportunities to manipulate concrete objects. Preview–predict–confirm charts, book boxes, and coding the text are strategies that help students make sense of the material prior to and during reading.

Preview–Predict–Confirm

Preview–predict–confirm charts require students to quickly preview a book and then make predictions about words they think they will encounter in the text (Yopp and Yopp, 2001). Making predictions before reading activates students' prior knowledge of the topic and sets the stage for learning. Predicting which words will appear in the text arouses their imaginations. Students eagerly read the text in order to confirm their predictions. (See figures 15.1 and 15.2.)

Steps

1. Each student needs a copy of the book to quickly examine for a few minutes.
2. Students close the book and brainstorm a list of words they think will appear in the text. The teacher writes the words on the board for all of the students to see.
3. As students contribute words to the list, they give brief explanations as to why they think the words will appear in the text.
4. Students read the book or follow along as the book is read aloud.
5. After reading the book, the students return to their list of words and revisit the text to confirm which words appeared in the story.

Examples

Brisson, Pat. *Benny's Pennies.* Illustrated by Bob Barner. 1993. Unp. New York: Random House. (pbk. 0-440-41016-9).
Grades: P–2. With five shiny new pennies and requests from his family, Benny sets out to spend his pennies. He returns home without his pennies, but his arms are filled with gifts for his family. A cumulative refrain and colorful collage illustrations assure that this is a book that students want to read again and again.

Preview–Predict–Confirm Chart

Words	Appeared in Text	
	Yes	No
pennies		
flowers		
paper hat		
dog		
cat		
fish		

Figure 15.1. This is what a list of predicted words might look like for this book.

Maestro, Betsy. *The Story of Money.* Illustrated by Giulio Maestro. 1993. 48p. New York: Clarion Books. (hc. 0-395-56242-2).
Grades: 3–6. Beginning with bartering, this is the story of money from past to present. Beautiful, detailed illustrations depict money from all around the globe and show the history and development of money and monetary systems. The book concludes with additional information about money.

Preview–Predict–Confirm Chart

Words	Appeared in Text	
	Yes	No
market		
village		
ships		
money		
coins		
map		
river		
mountains		
horses		
carts		
buying		
selling		

Figure 15.2. Charts such as this one for older students contain more words.

Additional Books and Resources

Williams, Rozanne Lanczak. *The Coin Counting Book.* 2001. Unp. Watertown, Mass.: Charlesbridge Publishing. (hc. 0-88106-325-8; pbk. 0-88106-326-6).
Grades: K–2. Photographs of real money and rhyming verse make learning to count money fun and easy. The number of pennies in a nickel, the number of nickels in a quarter, and the number of quarters in a dollar are just a few of the coin combinations illustrated in the book. Number sentences below the pictures of actual coins provide additional help as students learn to count money.

Simarco, Elizabeth. *At the Bank.* Photographs by David M. Budd. 2000. 32p. Chanhassen, Minn.: The Child's World. (hc. 1-56766-572-1).

Grades: K–2. Most young students have been to a bank with their parents; however, few understand exactly what happens in a bank. Using the familiar context of a trip to the bank, this book explains in easy-to-understand text and photographs exactly what happens in a bank. Color photographs and large-print text with glossary words in bold make this a book young students can read on their own. A glossary and an index are included.

Leedy, Loreen. *The Monster Money Book.* 1992. Unp. New York: Holiday House. (hc. 0-8234-0922-8).

Grades: K–3. With fifty-four dollars in their treasury the Monster Club has tough decisions to make as they look for ways to spend their money. Should they spend the money, invest the money, or donate the money? Friendly monsters introduce students to money in a practical easy-to-understand manner. A glossary concludes the book.

Adams, Barbara Johnson. *The Go-Around Dollar.* Illustrated by Joyce Audy Zarins. 1992. Unp. New York: Four Winds Press. (hc. 0-02-700031-1).

Grades: 1–3. Readers follow along as a dollar bill changes hands. It all starts when two boys find a dollar on their way home from school and the dollar eventually ends up in a frame as the first dollar Carlos gets when he opens his new ice cream store. Sidebars throughout the book contain fascinating facts about dollars.

Abeyta, Jennifer. *Coins.* 2000. 48p. New York: Children's Press. (hc. 0-516-23329-7; pbk. 0-516-23529-X).

Grades: 2–4. This informative book about coins and coin collecting motivates students to begin checking the coins in their pockets. The last chapter in the book contains instructions on starting a coin collection. A glossary, books and magazines for further reading, resources, and an index conclude the book.

Godfrey, Neale S. *Neale S. Godfrey's Ultimate Kids' Money Book.* Illustrated by Randy Verougstraete. 2002. 122p. New York: Simon and Schuster Books for Young Readers. (hc. 0-689-81717-7; pbk. 0-689-81489-5).

Grades: 3–6. The history of money, earning money, saving money, budgeting, banking, and obtaining credit are just some of the topics covered in this book. Bright, attractive illustrations, charts, and diagrams provide additional information to help readers comprehend the text. A glossary and an index conclude the book.

The United States Mint web pages for children are available at www.usmint.gov/kids. This site has links to games, cartoons, a time machine, coin news, coin camp, and resources for teachers. Students travel through time to learn about the printing of coins.

Book Boxes

Book boxes contain a collection of objects related to a particular book. They stimulate children's interest in books and motivate them to actively read the books (Yopp and Yopp, 2001). Before reading, students examine the objects and make predictions about how the objects are related to the text. Children make predictions based on their prior knowledge and experiences (Routman, 1994). As they make predictions students are activating their prior knowledge and making connections between their experiences and what they think will happen in the book. In order to learn from text students not only need skills and strategies, they need a desire to examine the text to gain understanding (Jetton and Alexander, 2001). Making predictions before reading helps students gain meaning from text. (See figures 15.3 and 15.4.)

Steps

1. Select several objects in some way related to the book and place them in a box.
2. Tell the students that the box contains objects related to the content of the book they are going to read.
3. Have the students take turns drawing objects out of the box. As each object is taken from the box, have the students identify it.
4. Ask students to predict how the object is related to the book. Allow ample time for discussion of each object.
5. After discussing the objects, have the students read the book.
6. After reading, have the students examine the objects again and determine how their predictions matched the content of the book.

Examples

Wells, Rosemary. *Bunny Money.* 1997. Unp. New York: Dial Books for Young Readers. (hc. 0-8037-2146-3).

Chapter 15

Grades: P–2. Ruby grabs her wallet and Max locates his lucky quarter
and the two are ready for a shopping excursion to buy Grandma's
birthday present. In a day filled with misadventures Ruby patiently
takes care of her younger brother and in the end they find presents that
they consider perfect for Grandma.

Book Box

Items	Connections to Book Content
vampire teeth	Max's gift to Grandma
small bag of laundry detergent	Ruby had to wash Max's clothes
peanut butter & jelly sandwich	Max's lunch
wrapping paper	Grandma's earrings were wrapped
quarter	Used to call Grandma to come and pick them up

Figure 15.3. Items in the book box should stimulate children's thinking
about the content of the book. This is a collection of possible items for
Bunny Money.

Otfinoski, Steve. *The Kid's Guide to Money: Earning It, Saving It,
Spending It, Growing It, Sharing It.* 1996. 128p. New York:
Scholastic. (pbk. 0-590-53853-5).
Grades: 4–8. Students discover ways to earn money. Then they learn
about spending it, saving it, donating it, borrowing it, and investing it.
Appendices contain lists of organizations, information on how to read
stock tables, a list of books for further reading, a glossary, and an in-
dex.

Book Box

Items	Connections to Book Content
restaurant receipt	how to figure a tip
magazine advertisement	becoming a wise consumer
bank deposit slip	importance of saving money
returned check	how to write and endorse a check
pamphlet on a local charity	donating money
newspaper business section	stock charts

Figure 15.4. Items in this box can easily be collected from around the
house.

Additional Books and Resources

Leedy, Loreen. *Follow the Money.* 2002. Unp. New York: Holiday House. (hc. 0-8234-1587-2).

Grades: P–3. Students spend the day with a brand new quarter, George, as he travels from the Federal Reserve to a variety of locations around town including a drink machine, a pet store, a washing machine, and a garage sale. Bright, colorful cartoon illustrations sprinkled with humor and fun assure that young readers will follow along as George travels through the city. Additional information about money and a glossary conclude the book.

Trapani, Iza. *How Much Is That Doggie in the Window?* 1997. Unp. Boston: Whispering Coyote. (hc. 1-58089-031-8).

Grades: P–3. This adaptation of a beloved childhood song has a young boy spending the money he has saved to buy a dog. He spends the money caring for his family. His sister gets frozen yogurt after a fall, his mother gets chocolates after a bee sting, and his father gets a box of tissues after he sneezes. By the end of this heartwarming tale, the boy has a dog.

Axelrod, Amy. *Pigs Will Be Pigs: Fun with Math and Money.* Illustrated by Sharon McGinley-Nally. 1994. Unp. New York: Four Winds Press. (hc. 0-02-765415-X).

Grades: K–3. With empty stomachs, an empty refrigerator, and empty wallets, the pig family goes on a mad search through the house to find enough money to go out for dinner. They locate $34.67 and set off for dinner. When they return home to relax, they discover a house turned upside down from their money hunt. Readers young and old relate to this story. The book concludes with a restaurant menu and ideas for extending the story.

McBrier, Page. *Beatrice's Goat.* Illustrated by Lori Lohstoeter. 2001. Unp. New York: Atheneum Books for Young Readers. (hc. 0-689-82460-2).

Grades: K–3. Based on a true story, this book tells how the life of a family in Uganda is dramatically altered when they receive a goat from the Heifer Project International. Money the family makes by selling milk and cheese from the goat is used to buy uniforms and books so that Beatrice is able to attend school. Heifer Project International provides poor families around the world with farm animals donated by churches, schools, and individuals.

Nolan, Amy. *The Kid's Allowance Book.* Illustrated by Debbie Palen.
    1998. 86p. New York: Walker and Company. (hc. 0-8027-8651-0;
    pbk. 0-8027-7532-2).
Grades: 3–6. Some of the information in this useful, practical guide to
allowances came from questionnaires completed by students between
the ages of nine and fourteen and their parents. Sidebars containing
quotes and tips from students and cartoon illustrations add to the appeal
of the book. A troubleshooting guide for dealing with allowance problems and a collection of resources for learning more conclude the book.
Dolan, Edward F. *In Sports Money Talks.* 1996. 144p. New York:
    Twenty-First Century Books. (hc. 0-8050-4569-4).
Grades: 6–8. As more and more money flows into sports, it changes the
games and causes problems. Dolan explores these changes and problems. At the end of the book he has a fans' wish list of positive
changes. An extensive bibliography and an index are included.

Hot Dog Stand: The Works software is a simulation that gives students the chance to operate a hot dog stand at a sports arena. They learn
to order supplies, keep records, determine prices, and market their
products. Along the way, they encounter challenges that require them
to rethink their prices and strategies. This software is appropriate for
grades three and up and is available on CD-ROM for both Macintosh
and Windows computers from Sunburst Communications.

The Math in Daily Life web site involves students in hands-on activities as they use math in common, everyday situations. Students explore the use of numbers in cooking, buying a new car, and saving for
retirement. This site is sponsored by Annenberg/CPB and is located at
http://www.learner.org/exhibits/dailymath.

Coding the Text

Coding the text actively involves students in their reading by having
them make connections between their prior knowledge and the text
(Harvey and Goudvis, 2000). Connections can be text-self, text-text,
and text-world. Text-self connections occur when the reader makes a
personal connection to the information in the text. Text-text connections are those between the text currently being read and text read previously. Text-world connections are those between the text and world
events. Students enjoy writing their connections on sticky notes and

placing them inside the book. Reading through the sticky notes in the book provides teachers with insights into their students' lives and their prior experiences.

As students read, they discover relationships between content areas and transfer the information between the content areas (Goforth, 1998). Coding the text encourages students to look for these relationships and make connections between the content areas. Gathering meaning from text involves a transaction between reader and text (Goforth, 1998). Readers form their own unique connections to text, whether they are reading alone or with a group. (See figures 15.5 and 15.6.)

Steps

1. Model this strategy when reading aloud a text selection. When a connection can be made, explain the connection aloud to the students and record the connection on a sticky note that is placed in the book near the text.
2. This strategy is first practiced in small groups, then with a partner, and eventually students use the strategy when reading independently.
3. Students read the selected text looking for connections as they read.
4. Students record the type of connection on their sticky notes. The connections can be text-self, text-text, and text-world.
5. Students write one or two brief comments about the connection on the sticky note.
6. When they finish reading, students discuss the connections they recorded in the text in either small or large group discussions.
7. When they are finished with the text students may want to save the sticky notes in a reading or writing notebook. These may be later used as ideas for further research or writing prompts.

Examples

Zimelman, Nathan. *How the Second Grade Got $8,205.50 to Visit the Statue of Liberty.* 1992. Unp. Morton Grove, Ill.: Albert Whitman. (hc. 0-8075-3431-5).
Grades: K–3. When the second grade set out to raise money for a trip to the Statue of Liberty, little did they realize that every fund-raising

venture would come with its own set of unique expenses. This is an absolutely delightful tale that readers young and old enjoy.

Coding the Text

Text-Self	Text-Text	Text-World
We have a paper drive at our school.	We learned about counting money in *The Coin Counting Book.*	People in other countries drive cars.

Figure 15.5. These sticky notes are examples of ones created as a teacher read aloud the book to a small group of students.

Schwartz, David M. *If You Made a Million.* Illustrated by Steven Kellogg. 1989. Unp. New York: Lothrop, Lee & Shepard Books. (hc. 0-688-07018-3; pbk. 0-688-07017-5).
Grades: 1–5. Marvelosissimo the Mathematical Magician explains about earning and investing money, accruing dividends and interest, and paying off loans. Lively, animated illustrations help him show readers how to make a million dollars. A lengthy note at the end of the book explains the information in the book in more detail.

Coding the Text

Text-Self	Text-Text	Text-World
I feed my fish every night.	The castle reminds us of Hogwarts in Harry Potter.	Rhinoceroses live in different parts of the world.

Figure 15.6. These are some of the sticky notes written by a small group of students while they were reading. Note that they individually and collectively made connections to the text.

Additional Books and Resources

Parker, Nancy Winslow. *Money, Money, Money: The Meaning of the Art and Symbols on United States Paper Currency.* 1995. 32p. New York: HarperCollins. (hc. 0-06-023411-3).
Grades: 2–7. The history of the people, the symbols, and the buildings found on paper money makes fascinating reading. Students enjoy the intriguing and amusing details included in the text. Labeled illustrations provide additional information and an index concludes the book.

Manes, Stephen. *Make Four Million Dollars by Next Thursday!* Illustrated by George Ulrich. 1997. 87p. New York: Dell Publishing. (pbk. 0-440-41370-2).
Grades: 3–6. Jason stumbles upon Dr. K. Pinkerton Silverfish's guide to making money and faithfully sets out to follow his step-by-step instructions to wealth. Students chuckle as Jason carries out the increasingly bizarre schemes and in the end learns that there are more important things than trying to get rich quick.

Wilkinson, Elizabeth. *Making Cents: Every Kid's Guide to Money.* Illustrated by Martha Weston. 1991. 128p. New York: Little, Brown. (hc. 0-316-94101-8; pbk. 0-316-94102-6).
Grades: 3–7. Readers looking for ways to earn money find a variety of ideas in the chapters in this book. Illustrations, photographs, and stories about real children and how they earn money enhance this useful text. The last chapter contains information on the economics of making money.

Wyler, Rose, and Mary Elting. *Math Fun with Money Puzzlers.* Illustrated by Patrick Girouard. 1992. 64p. New York: Simon and Schuster. (hc. 0-671-74313-9; pbk. 0-671-74314-7).
Grades: 4–8. Interesting facts about money introduce readers to a collection of puzzles, problems, games, and jokes that require them to use their math skills, critical thinking skills, and problem-solving skills. The answers are found on the next page in the book. Black-and-white line drawings and diagrams provide clues to help solve the problems. An index is included.

Barkin, Carol, and Elizabeth James. *Jobs for Kids: The Guide to Having Fun and Making Money.* Illustrated by Roy Doty. 1990. 113p. New York: Lothrop, Lee & Shepard Books. (hc. 0-688-09234-8).
Grades: 5–8. Job seekers should first consider their interests before they begin job hunting. This is only one of the many practical tips included

in this book. There is practical advice about finding jobs, staying safe while working, selling things they make, and working in their parents' business. Many of the usual jobs for kids such as babysitting, pet sitting, yard work, and tutoring are included.

Mayr, Diane. *The Everything Kids' Money Book.* 1999. 131p. Avon, Mass.: Adams Media Corporation. (pbk. 1-58062-685-8).
Grades: 4–8. Readers learn everything from the history of money to the intricacies of the stock market. Sidebars containing fun facts and word definitions enhance the informative text as do the clever illustrations and the detailed diagrams. The book concludes with resources for learning more and an index. This is An Everything series book.

Ice Cream Truck software is a simulation that gives students the chance to own an ice cream truck. Of course, with ownership comes opportunities for problem solving and strategic planning as they ponder the relationships between costs, prices, and profits. This software is appropriate for grades two through six and is available on CD-ROM for both Macintosh and Windows computers from Sunburst Communications.

Consumer Reports.org 4 Kids maintained by Consumer Union, publishers of *Consumer Reports,* contains information on product tests, toy tests, advertising tricks, getting the most for your money, and teacher resources. This site is available at http://www.zillions.org.

References

Goforth, Frances S. *Literature and the Learner.* Belmont, Calif.: Wadsworth, 1998.

Harvey, Stephanie, and Anne Goudvis. *Strategies that Work: Teaching Comprehension to Enhance Understanding.* Portland, Maine: Stenhouse, 2000.

Jetton, Tamara L., and Patricia A. Alexander. "Learning from Text: A Multidimensional and Developmental Perspective." *Reading Online.* http://www.readingonline.org/articles/handbook/jetton/index.html (12 July 2001).

National Council of Teachers of Mathematics. *Principles and Standards for School Mathematics.* Reston, Va.: National Council of Teachers of Mathematics, 2000. http://standards.nctm.org/ (20 Nov. 2002).

Routman, Regie. *Invitations: Changing as Teachers and Learners, K–12*. Portsmouth, N.H.: Heinemann Library, 1994.

Whitin, David J., and Sandra Wilde. *Read Any Good Math Lately?: Children's Books for Mathematical Learning, K–6*. Portsmouth, N.H.: Heinemann Library, 1992.

Yopp, Ruth Helen, and Hallie Kay Yopp. *Literature-Based Reading Activities*, 3rd ed. Boston, Mass.: Allyn and Bacon, 2001.

· 16 ·
Problem Solving

Problem solving is a skill that students use daily in a variety of situations. Practice solving authentic, meaningful problems helps students realize that this is a vital skill to learn. Problem solving is one of the mathematics process standards from the *Principles and Standards for School Mathematics* (NCTM, 2000). Solving problems requires students to think critically, combining what they already know with the information presented in the problems. Opportunities to reason and discuss the problems with classmates promote understanding. Students first examine the problems and determine what information is needed to solve them and what information is extraneous. Then, they determine what procedures and operations they will use to solve the problems and develop an understanding of what the correct answer should be. Discussion webs, word problem reading guides, and establishing a perspective are strategies that assist students as they learn to examine problems and as they learn to solve them. Using strategies such as these enables students to develop an understanding of when and why certain processes and operations are used. Further, these strategies provide students opportunities to work collaboratively with their classmates and to reflect on their work.

Discussion Webs

Discussion webs enable students to think aloud and talk with their classmates as they examine word problems (Vacca and Vacca, 2002).

Completing discussion webs focuses students' attention on each part of the problem. As students discuss word problems, they help one another make sense of the problems and they develop shared understandings. Talking about the problems with other students encourages them to reflect on the processes used to solve problems. Students may need to be reminded to be accepting of everyone's comments and to be open to different interpretations. As students solve problems they learn that there may be more than one way to solve them. When completing discussion webs, younger students may work in a large group or small groups with teacher direction. For older students, working on discussion webs in small groups or with partners provides them with assistance as they work to solve the problems without direct guidance from the teacher. (See figures 16.1 and 16.2.)

Steps

1. Activate students' prior knowledge to help them understand the problem.
2. Have the students read the problem and discuss the relevant and the irrelevant information contained in the problem with their partners.
3. As they work students write the relevant information in the "yes" column and the irrelevant information in the "no" column.
4. Have the partners join another pair of partners to discuss the information they placed in each column.
5. Tell the students that they have three minutes to reach consensus on the information in the columns and to determine the group spokesperson.
6. The group spokespersons report their decisions to the class. The teacher records the decisions on a large chart to share with the class.
7. Students then work together to solve the problem and write the solution at the bottom of the chart.

Examples

Lewis, J. Patrick. *Arithme-Tickle: An Even Number of Odd Riddle-Rhymes.* Illustrated by Frank Remkiewicz. 2002. 32p. San Diego, Calif.: Silver Whistle. (hc. 0-15-216418-9).

Grades: K–3. Bright, colorful pictures grab students' attention and the rhyming, quizzical riddles hold their attention as they read, calculate, and solve these math word problems. The answers are written backwards at the end of the riddle.

One of the riddles involves Jennifer Hennessy getting on the scale and weighing herself and then picking up her dog and weighing them both. How can she determine how much the dog weighs? What information in the riddle is needed to solve the problem and what information is not needed? The discussion web for this problem might look something like this.

Discussion Web

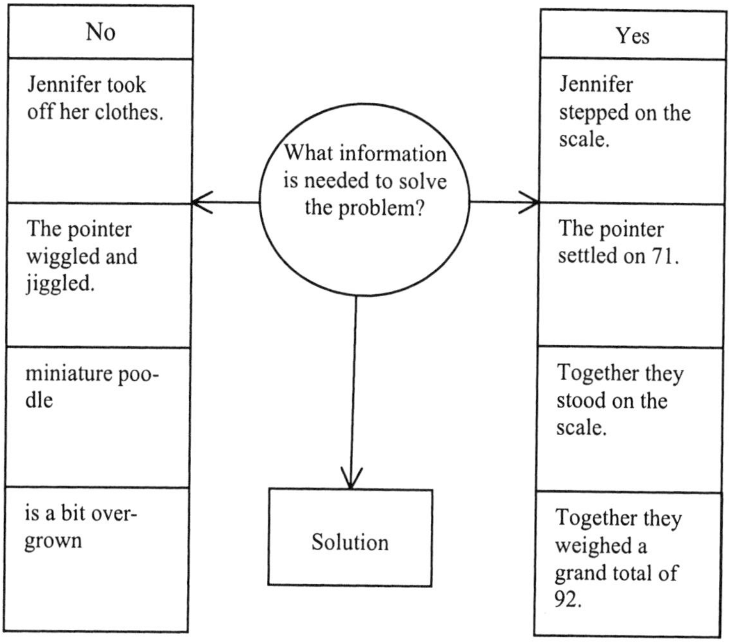

No		Yes
Jennifer took off her clothes.	What information is needed to solve the problem?	Jennifer stepped on the scale.
The pointer wiggled and jiggled.		The pointer settled on 71.
miniature poodle		Together they stood on the scale.
is a bit overgrown	Solution	Together they weighed a grand total of 92.

92 pounds – 71 pounds = 21 pounds
Jennifer's dog weighs 21 pounds.

Figure 16.1. A completed discussion web for this problem might look like this.

Wise, Bill. *Whodunit Math Puzzles.* Illustrated by Lucy Corvino. 2001. 96p. New York: Sterling Publishing. (hc. 0-8069-5986-0). Grades: 4–8. Rather than ordinary word problems, these are mysteries to be solved. Math sleuths enjoy reading the entertaining puzzles and then solving the mysteries. The answers to the puzzles and an index are included. For example, one of the puzzles involves a football team whose players are getting robbed. The burglar has challenged them to figure out which two players are next.

Discussion Web

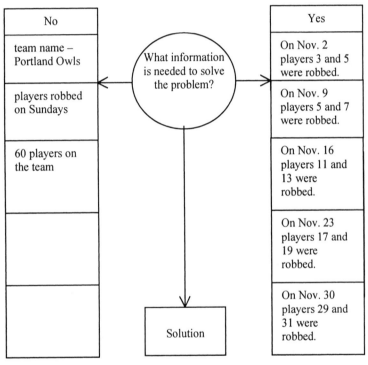

Next Sunday, players 41 and 43 will be robbed, as they are the next pair of twin prime numbers.

Figure 16.2. The important information needed to solve this problem was the players' jersey numbers. The police chief's sidekick, Cal, examined the numbers and discovered a pattern.

Additional Books and Resources

Pinczes, Elinor J. *One Hundred Hungry Ants.* Illustrated by Bonnie
MacKain. 1993. Unp. New York: Scholastic. (hc. 0-590-67298-3).
Grades: K–2. Problem solve with one hundred hungry ants as they try
to figure out which marching formation will get them to the picnic
spread the fastest. As the frantic ants scurry to their destination, other
animals are heading away from the picnic, their arms laden with
bounty.

Tang, Greg. *Math for All Seasons: Mind-Stretching Math Riddles.*
Illustrated by Harry Briggs. 2002. Unp. New York: Scholastic. (hc.
0-439-21042-9).
Grades: K–3. Vivid, uncluttered illustrations are used to teach students
to solve riddles using grouping and adding rather than counting. Each
of the riddles contains hints on how to group the objects. Instructions
for quickly solving the riddles are found at the end of the book.

Murphy, Stuart J. *Probability: Probably Pistachio.* Illustrated by
Marsha Winborn. 2001. 33p. New York: HarperCollins. (hc. 0-06-
028028-X; pbk. 0-06-446734-1).
Grades: 1–3. Students relate to Jack as he encounters probability in his
daily life from the lunchroom to the practice field. Activities for extending the text are included. This book is from the MathStart series.

Pappas, Theoni. *The Adventures of Penrose the Mathematical Cat.*
1997. 114p. San Carlos, Calif.: Wide World Publishing/Tetra.
(pbk. 1-884550-14-2).
Grades: 2–6. Penrose leads the way on a mathematical romp of discovery. Students explore fractals, infinity, golden rectangles, and other
mathematical concepts through amusing stories and hands-on activities.

Tang, Greg. *The Grapes of Math: Mind-Stretching Math Riddles.* Illustrated by Harry Briggs. 2001. Unp. New York: Scholastic. (hc.
0-439-21033-X).
Grades: 2–6. Colorful, vibrant drawings visually depict these math riddles that can easily be solved using some simple problem-solving techniques. These techniques are fun to learn and with some encourage-
ment, students learn to use them to solve other math problems.

Markle, Sandra. *Discovering Graph Secrets: Experiments, Puzzles,
and Games Exploring Graphs.* 1997. 36p. New York: Atheneum
Books for Young Readers. (hc. 0-689-31942-8).
Grades 3–6. Bar graphs, line graphs, pictographs, and circle graphs are
explored through hands-on activities that have students solving prob-

lems as they learn to use graphs. Colorful text and graphics catch the
readers' attention and motivate them to explore this book that makes
learning about graphs fun. Solutions and an index are included.

Word Problem Reading Guides

Word problem reading guides contain statements related to the three
levels of reading comprehension: literal, interpretative, and inferential.
While all of these levels are intertwined, it is beneficial for students to
be aware of the three levels. Reading guides facilitate students' active
comprehension of the problems (Vacca and Vacca, 2002). These guides
are to help focus students' attention and are not used all the time. With
practice, students should be able to internally carry on these processes
when confronted with problems to solve. Careful, systematic examination of the problems enables students to develop patterns for solving
problems. (See figures 16.3 and 16.4.)

Steps

1. Read the problem and write down statements reflective of the interpretative level of comprehension. These go on level two of the
   chart, Math Ideas.
2. Look at the level two statements and return to the problem to find
   factual information to support the statements in Math Ideas. Write
   the factual information in level one, Facts of the Problem.
3. On the third level, Numbers, write statements that will help students make connections between their prior knowledge and the information in the problem that will help them solve the problem.
4. Older students will be able to work on their own or in cooperative
   groups. For younger students this will be a more teacher-directed
   activity with shorter, easier problems.

Examples

Schwartz, David M. *If You Hopped Like a Frog.* Illustrated by James
    Warhola. 1999. Unp. New York: Scholastic. (hc. 0-590-09857-8).
Grades: 3–5. This is a wonderful book filled with "What ifs." For example, What if you had a tongue like a chameleon? How long would

your tongue be? Bright, colorful illustrations depict all of the silly "What ifs" suggested in the book. At the end of the book are instructions for figuring out all of the silly ideas.

Word Problem Reading Guide

Problem: A chameleon's tongue is half the length of its body. If the chameleon is 1 foot long his tongue is approximately 6 inches long. If you had a tongue like a chameleon, how long would your tongue be? Could you sit at the table and eat the food off your plate with your tongue?

1. Facts of the Problem
   Directions: Read the word problem and check those statements that are facts or that you think will help you solve the problem.

   Facts   Will Help

   _____   _____   The chameleon's tongue is half the length of its body.

   _____   _____   A chameleon can change colors.

   _____   _____   If a chameleon is 3 inches long, its tongue will be about 1.5 inches long.

   _____   _____   If you were 4 feet tall and had a tongue like a chameleon, your tongue would be about 2 feet long.

2. Math Ideas
   Directions: Read the math statements below. Check those that you think pertain to this problem. You may want to look back at part 1.

   _____   Subtraction answers can be checked by addition.

   _____   Subtraction means to take away.

   _____   A fraction represents the division of 2 numbers.

   _____   Division tells us how many times a number fits into another number.

   _____   Division can be checked by multiplication.

3. Numbers
   Directions: Look at the possible solutions listed below. Check those that will help you solve this problem. You can look back at parts 1 and 2.

   _____   Divide your height by 1/2.

   _____   Multiply your height by 2.

   _____   Multiply your height by 0.5.

   _____   Subtract 2 feet from your height.

Once you complete the word problem guide, solve the problem.

Figure 16.3. The word problem in this chart has students comparing the length of their tongue to the length of a chameleon's tongue.

Salvadori, Mario, and Joseph P. Wright. *Math Games for Middle School: Challenges and Skill-Builders for Students at Every Level.* 1998. 168p. Chicago, Ill.: Chicago Review Press. (pbk. 1-55652-288-6).

Grades: 6–8. The goal of this book is to show students that math is fun and enjoyable. Clear, detailed introductions with labeled diagrams explain the essential concepts. These are followed by problems to solve and the answers are found at the end of the book.

Word Problem Reading Guide

Problem: A shoe store owner buys 1,000 pairs of shoes at $30 a pair. She sells 750 pairs for $50 a pair. When the rest of the shoes do not sell she puts them on sale for $25 a pair. What is the average amount of money she made or lost on the shoes?

1. Facts of the Problem
   Directions: Read the word problem and check those statements that are facts or that you think will help you solve the problem.

   Facts   Will Help

   _____   _____   1,000 pairs of shoes were bought.
   _____   _____   Each pair of shoes cost the store owner $30.
   _____   _____   There were 735 pairs of tennis shoes.
   _____   _____   540 pairs of shoes sold for $50 a pair.
   _____   _____   The shoes that did not sell for $50 a pair sold for $25 a pair.

2. Math Ideas
   Directions: Read the math statements below. Check those that you think pertain to this problem. You may want to look back at part 1.

   _____   To figure the average you need to divide.
   _____   Multiplication is repeated addition.
   _____   Multiplication is commutative.
   _____   Repeated subtraction is called division.

3. Numbers
   Directions: Look at the possible solutions listed below. Check those that will help you solve this problem. You can look back at parts 1 and 2.

   _____   1,000 χ $30
   _____   1,000 – 750
   _____   750 χ $50
   _____   250 χ $25
   _____   750 χ $25
   _____ $13,750/1,000

Figure 16.4. Word problem reading guides provide a structured format for students to follow as they solve problems.

Additional Books and Resources

Chorao, Kay. *Number One Number Fun.* 1995. Unp. New York: Holiday House. (hc. 0-8234-1142-7).
Grades: P–2. These are simple word problems for the youngest students. There are pages filled with prancing, cavorting animals to add and subtract. The number sentences that match the word problems and the answers are included on the pages. While the problems may not be complex enough to create a word problem reading guide, they do lend themselves to introducing the format of the guide to students as they read the book and solve the problems.

Schwartz, David M. *How Much Is a Million?* Illustrated by Steven Kellogg. 1985. Unp. New York: Lothrop, Lee & Shepard. (hc. 0-590-43614-7).
Grades: 1–5. Take a fanciful journey with Marvelossissimo the Mathematical Magician as he explains how much a million really is. Students enjoy learning about large numbers and this book enables them to use their imaginations as they determine what it takes to have a million. The calculations used to answer the question are located at the end of the book.

Adler, David. *Easy Math Puzzles.* Illustrated by Cynthia Fisher. 1997. Unp. New York: Holiday House. (hc. 0-8234-1283-0).
Grades: 2–5. These are fun and silly stumpers that require students to stop and think to solve the puzzles. Students enjoy working these with a friend as sometimes the puzzles take a bit of thinking and figuring. Zany illustrations provide hints to the answers located at the end of the book.

Neuschwander, Cindy. *Sir Cumference and the Great Knight of Angleland: A Math Adventure.* Illustrated by Wayne Geehan. 2001. 32p. Watertown, Mass.: Charlesbridge Publishing. (hc. 1-57091-170-3; pbk. 1-57091-169-X).
Grades: 3–6. Young Radius must set out alone on a quest in order to become a knight. Armed with a family heirloom, a round golden medallion, he sets off for adventure. The book is filled with word play and math problems. Companion books by the same author are *Sir Cumference and the First Round Table* and *Sir Cumference and the Dragon of Pi.*

Müller, Robert. *The Great Book of Math Teasers.* 1989. 96p. New York: Sterling Publishing. (pbk. 0-8069-6953-9).
Grades: 4–8. From candles to candies, from gardeners to soap, everyday people, events, and objects are woven into these thought-provoking

math problems. Black-and-white line drawings illustrate many of the problems and aid students as they work on the problems. The back cover of the book warns students that once they do one, they will get hooked on doing more. The answers to the problems and an index are located at the back of the book.

Lobosco, Michael L. *Mental Math Challenges.* 1999. 80p. New York: Sterling Publishing. (hc. 1-895569-50-8).

Grades: 5–7. Bright, colorful pages filled with step-by-step instructions and detailed diagrams assure that students can successfully solve these challenges. Challenges include learning how to solve algebra problems with a geometry card and finding the value of pi with the Buffon tooth-pick experiment. These challenges make learning fun and are great activities for small groups. Each challenge includes a list of materials students need to complete the activity.

Smoothey, Marion. *Let's Investigate Number Patterns.* Illustrated by Ted Evans. 1993. 64p. New York: Marshall Cavendish. (hc. 1-85435-458-2).

Grades: 5–7. Word problems and games engage students in intriguing investigations that help them discover and understand number patterns including the Fibonacci Sequence and Pascal's Triangle. These are fun hands-on activities that students enjoy completing with their class-mates. The answers to the problems, a glossary, and an index are in-cluded.

Puzzle Tanks uses logic puzzles to develop students' problem-solving skills. Students transfer liquids between storage tanks as they work to reach target amounts. This is a great activity for small groups of students as the puzzles can be quite challenging. The software is appropriate for grades three through eight and is available for both Macintosh and Windows computers from Sunburst Communications.

Math in Daily Life demonstrates to upper elementary students how mathematics is used in common situations every day, such as deciding to buy or lease a car, figuring the area of a house to buy carpet, and converting recipes. While much of the site is text, there are interactive charts and calculators. The site also contains a link to a wealth of on-line resources for both teachers and students. Annenberg/CPB, a part-nership between The Annenberg Foundation and the Corporation for Public Broadcasting, sponsors this web site, which is located at http://www.learner.org/exhibits.dailymath/.

Perspective

Helping students examine problems from a set perspective enables them to activate their prior knowledge and use that knowledge to solve problems (Vacca and Vacca, 2002). Establishing a role for them to play as they work to solve the problems helps them activate and use any prior experiences they may have that can be used to solve the problems. Students can be encouraged to use their imaginations to visualize themselves in their assigned roles and to help them develop perspectives for examining the problems. This activity enables students to become actively involved in solving real-life problems and helps them make connections between classroom learning and their everyday lives. (See figures 16.5 and 16.6.)

Steps

1. Decide on a problem or story that lends itself to examination from a set perspective.
2. Assign each student a role and tell them to use their imaginations to help them visualize themselves in the role.
3. Tell them that as you read the problem or story aloud they are to listen and think about how their character will respond.
4. After reading have the students discuss the problem or story from the perspective of the role they have assumed.

Examples

Murphy, Stuart J. *Safari Park*. Illustrated by Steve Bjorkman. 2002. 33p. New York: HarperCollins. (hc. 0-06-028914-7; pbk. 0-06-446245-5).
Grades: 2–3. Grandpa collected 100 tickets to Safari Park and he took his five grandchildren to enjoy the amusement rides. His grandchildren, Paul, Abby, Chad, Alicia, and Patrick, each received twenty tickets. Before Paul could spend any of his tickets, he lost them. So, Grandpa tells the other children that they will each have to take Paul on one ride. The children have to problem solve to figure out how to spend their tickets and to include Paul on one of their rides. This book is from the MathStart series.

Perspective

Grandfather has given Paul, Abby, Chad, Alicia, and Patrick each twenty tickets to spend at Safari Park on amusement rides and food. Since Paul has lost his tickets, Grandpa says Abby, Chad, Alicia, and Patrick each have to take Paul along on one of the rides. Decide if you will be Abby, Chad, Alicia, or Patrick. Consult the chart on pages six and seven in the book to find out how much the different rides and food cost. There are several different ways for you to spend your tickets. Which amusement rides do you want to ride? How many rides can you afford? On which ride will you take Paul? Do you have enough tickets to buy food? Record your responses below. Remember that there is no one correct response, but you do have to include Paul.

Name of Character _____

    Tickets Needed   Rides and Food

    _____   _____

    _____   _____

    _____   _____

Figure 16.5. After the students have decided which rides and food they will spend their tickets on, have them record their answers in a chart like the one above. Then, read the story aloud and have them listen to determine how their character spent the twenty tickets and how they included Paul in their spending.

Guthrie, Donna, and Jan Stiles. *Real World Math: Money & Other Numbers in Your Life.* Illustrated by Robyn Kline. 1998. 128p. Brookfield, Conn.: The Millbrook Press. (hc. 0-7613-0251-4).
Grades: 6–8. Problem solving is fun when applied to real-life situations. Students see a purpose for solving the problems presented in this book as they realize that these are problems they will face as they grow up and want to own a car and rent an apartment. The book is filled with practical, useful tips about money. Students learn how to keep a checkbook, why social security numbers are needed, the pitfalls of credit cards, and other things they need to know to be wise consumers. Black-and-white line drawings, charts, and sidebars contain additional information. Resources, references, and an index are included.

Perspective

Sarah and Jane want to rent an apartment that is near the bus line. They found one that rents for $600 a month. They will have to pay the first month's rent and a security deposit of two-thirds of the monthly rent. The phone company charges a $40 installation fee. The utility company charges $45 to turn on the electricity. Since Sarah makes more money than Jane she has agreed to pay five-eighths of the rent each month. How much will each girl have to pay to rent the apartment and turn on the phone service and the electricity? What other expenses might they encounter?

Sarah	Jane	Procedure for Figuring Expenses	Expenses
___	___	_____	___
___	___	_____	___
___	___	_____	___
___	___	Total Expenses	___

Figure 16.6. In this example, students take on the role of either Sarah or Jane as they figure out how much it is going to cost them to rent an apartment.

Additional Books and Resources

Hamm, Diane Johnston. *How Many Feet in the Bed?* Illustrated by Kate Salley Palmer. 1991. Unp. New York: Simon and Schuster Books for Young Readers. (hc. 0-671-72638-2).
Grades: P–2. On Sunday morning Dad plans on sleeping late, but his plans are disrupted as one by one the three children and Mom join him in bed. As family members clamber into bed, the number of feet in the bed increases. Students can be assigned a role as one of the family members as they keep track of how many feet are in the bed each time a family member climbs in or out of bed.

Pinczes, Elinor J. *A Remainder of One.* Illustrated by Bonnie MacKain. 1995. Unp. New York: Scholastic. (pbk. 0-590-76971-5).
Grades: P–2. Poor Private Joe. It seems that no matter which marching formation the twenty-five bug-soldiers use, Joe has to sit on the sidelines so the troops' lines will be evenly matched. Students can look at the problem from Joe's perspective and use counting manipulatives to help Joe figure out which formation will let him join the marching troop.

Merriam, Eve. *12 Ways to Get to 11.* Illustrated by Bernie Karlin. 1996. Unp. New York: Simon and Schuster. (hc. 0-671-75544-7).
Grades: P–3. Young readers learn that there are twelve different fact families that total eleven. Houses, chimneys, cars, rabbits, peanuts, and bites from an apple are just some of the things readers count as they discover combinations that add up to eleven.

Scieszka, Jon, and Lane Smith. *Math Curse.* Illustrated by Lane Smith. 1995. Unp. New York: Viking. (hc. 0-670-86194-4).
Grades: 1–4. Victims of the math curse are doomed to spend their days imagining that they are surrounded by math problems. Everything they do and everything they see are math problems to be solved. Readers follow along as a hapless victim tries to solve all the math problems she encounters in the course of a day.

Demi. *One Grain of Rice: A Mathematical Folktale.* 1997. Unp. New York: Scholastic. (pbk. 0-590-93999-8).
Grades: 2–5. A clever young girl tricks the raja out of enough rice to feed all the hungry people in the land by simply asking the raja to give her one grain of rice and then to double the amount of rice she is given every day for thirty days. Sixteenth- and seventeenth-century Indian miniature paintings were the inspiration for the delicate illustrations that accompany this folktale. A table at the end of the book shows the amount of rice she received each day.

Anno, Mitsumasa. *Anno's Magic Seeds.* 1992. Unp. New York: Philomel. (hc. 0-399-22538-2).
Grades: 3–8. A wizard gives Jack two magic seeds and so begins this multilayered math story. As Jack's seeds begin to multiply students embark on a journey of discovery using simple addition and subtraction skills to solve the math problems woven into the story and illustrations. This is more than a math problem as there is also a lesson to learn from the story.

Math Mysteries: Whole Numbers software focuses on developing students' problem-solving skills. The software is appropriate for fourth through seventh grades and is available for both Macintosh and Windows computers from Tom Snyder Productions.

References

National Council of Teachers of Mathematics. *Principles and Standards for School Mathematics.* 2000. Reston, Va.: National Council of Teachers of Mathematics. http://standards.nctm.org/ (20 Nov. 2002).

Vacca, Richard T., and Jo Anne L. Vacca. *Content Area Reading: Literacy and Learning across the Curriculum*, 7th ed. Boston, Mass.: Allyn and Bacon, 2002.

Author Index

Title Index

Subject Index

About the Authors

Kathryn I. Matthew received undergraduate and graduate degrees from the University of New Orleans. She received an Ed.D. in curriculum and instruction from the University of Houston. She has worked in elementary schools in Texas and Louisiana as a classroom teacher, English as a second language specialist, and technology specialist. At the university level she has taught children's literature, reading, language arts, technology, and research classes. Kathryn co-authored *Colonial America in Literature for Youth: A Guide and Resource Book*, the *Neal-Schuman Guide to Recommended Children's Books and Media for Use with Every Elementary Subject,* and *Technology, Reading and Language Arts*. She and her husband, Chip, live in Sugar Land, Texas.

Kimberly Kimbell-Lopez received undergraduate and graduate degrees from the Northeast Louisiana University, Monroe, Louisiana. She received an Ed.D. in curriculum and instruction from the University of Houston. She has worked in elementary schools in Texas and Louisiana as a classroom teacher, grade level specialist, and language arts/social studies specialist. At the university level she has taught children's literature, reading, language arts, and technology classes. Kimberly wrote *Connecting with Traditional Literature: Using Folktales, Fables and Legends to Strengthen Students' Reading and Writing*. She and her husband, Paul, live in Ruston, Louisiana, with their two daughters.